PRAISE FOR TRAVIS J. BOOKOUT

In his new book, *God with Us: 52 Reflections on the Gospel of Matthew*, Travis Bookout offers to be our guide and traveling partner as we seek a deeper and more practical understanding of the first gospel. At the very outset, he writes, "This book is best read with an open Bible." Travis writes clearly and simply while, at the same time, demonstrating a broad background in biblical scholarship. He integrates his textual study with a mature awareness of everyday human struggles and church challenges. I highly recommend this book. You will be blessed by the journey!

— BRUCE D. MCLARTY, MINISTER IN RESIDENCE AT FREED HARDEMAN UNIVERSITY

Preachers, Bible class teachers, and small group leaders alike will greatly benefit from Travis Bookout's fifty-two reflections on the Gospel of Matthew. In each chapter/reflection Bookout helpfully lays out the big ideas of the text at hand but doesn't shy away from the minutiae when relevant. A hallmark of a good teacher is the ability to ask good questions, and the reflection questions at the close of each chapter provide great discussion starters for small groups.

— DR. KEVIN BURR, MINISTER, AUTHOR, PROFESSOR, AND HOST OF *FAITH IN THE FOLDS* PODCAST

The gospel of Matthew is far more than just a historical recitation of Jesus's life. Matthew, as well as Mark, Luke, and John, is beautifully written with themes and movements giving it life. Travis helps readers see these themes in a way that is informed and practical. My prayer is that this work helps Christians read the gospels more intentionally, and more faithful to the way the spirit intended it to be read.

— DR. JEREMIE BELLER, DEAN OF OKLAHOMA CHRISTIAN UNIVERSITY'S COLLEGE OF BIBLE

Travis Bookout underpromises and over-delivers. He warns his readers that these are devotional thoughts, but throughout the book, each thought is a rich insight that is deeply informed by the text. He blends together the practical and the theological into an amazing journey for the reader through the gospel of Matthew. His book *God With Us* is correctly titled because you feel that God is there with you in each of his reflections. Be prepared for the satisfying feeling of numerous "ah ha" moments throughout the book.

— MATTHEW MORINE, MINISTER OF THE CASTLE ROCK CHURCH OF CHRIST, AUTHOR OF *WILD TRANSFORMATION* AND *NATURAL EVANGELISM*

GOD WITH US

52 REFLECTIONS ON THE GOSPEL OF MATTHEW

TRAVIS J. BOOKOUT

Manufactured in the United States
Cataloging-in-Publication Data
Bookout, Travis J.
God with us: 52 reflections on the gospel of Matthew / by Travis J. Bookout
p. cm.
Includes Scripture index.
ISBN: 978-1-956811-65-0 (pbk.); 978-1-956811-66-7 (ebook)
1. Bible. Matthew—Criticism, interpretation, etc. I. Author. II. Title.
226.206—dc20
Library of Congress Control Number: 2024945853

Cover image Nativity Scene, Adoration of the Magi altarpiece by Girolamo Macchietti in the Basilica di San Lorenzo in Florence, Italy © Zatletic / Adobe Stock

Cover design by Brad McKinnon and Brittany Vander Maas.

For information:

Cypress Publications
3625 Helton Drive, PO Box HCU
Florence, AL 35630

www.hcu.edu

CONTENTS

To my sons Oliver and Levi,
to whom belongs the kingdom of heaven
(Matthew 19:14)

ACKNOWLEDGMENTS

I am deeply appreciative of the many who played a significant role in bringing about this book. I am thankful most of all to my wife, Lauren, and my two sons, Oliver and Levi. Their encouragement and love have meant the world to me, and I could not have written this book without their support.

I also want to thank the Maryville Church of Christ, who supported and encouraged me as I studied, taught, wrote, and preached many times on topics and passages within this book. The eldership has been a constant source of encouragement to me in my writing. Thank you to Herb Byrd, David Dudley, David Holloman, Tom Langley, Ron Matthews, David Pittman, Randy Puryear, Rob Stevenson, Jim Taylor, Randy Winstead, and Artan Xhaferaj. Your leadership and example have been a tremendous blessing in my life and ministry.

A special thank you to Wes McAdams, Dr. Matthew Morine, Dr. Jeremy Beller, Dr. Bruce McLarty, and Dr. Kevin Burr for reading and endorsing this book. Also, a huge thank you to my friend Kyle Savage, who read, proofread, and offered helpful comments and thoughts on every reflection. You improved this book drastically. I am thankful for Tom Langley and the World English Institute (WEI), who have not only encouraged me to write but also use this series of books in their curriculum. I encourage everyone to get involved with the good work taking place at WEI.

I also want to acknowledge my appreciation for the many who have read and helped advertise and share my writings with others. I'm thinking of wonderful people like Bledi Valca, Steve and Karen Bookout (mom and dad), Troy Rogers, Garrett Bookout, David Pharr, Brandon Watson, and many others.

Finally, I want to thank the entire team at Cypress Publications: Brad McKinnon, Bill Bagents, Brittany Vander Maas, and everyone else whose tireless efforts and dedication made it possible for you to hold this book in your hands. Cypress Publications is a pleasure to work with.

FOREWORD

WES MCADAMS

So many of us want Jesus to be our Savior, but far too few of us want to obey Him completely as our King. According to Matthew's gospel account, Jesus is king and the long-anticipated kingdom of heaven has arrived on earth through Him. Which leads us to ask important questions like: What is the nature of Jesus's kingdom? How does Jesus "fulfill" the Law and the prophets? What does it look like to be a citizen of the kingdom of heaven and live in obedience to King Jesus? Travis Bookout does an incredible job drawing out practical and straightforward answers to these questions from Matthew's gospel account.

I suspect we have all had the experience of reading a book and thinking, "I have always wanted to say something like that, but have never had the words." As I read Travis Bookout's, *God With Us,* I had that thought over and over again. He was able to masterfully articulate so many important truths about Jesus that I have never been able to express. More than that, he helped me understand and appreciate Jesus in whole new ways. I am grateful for this work and humbled to lend my voice in order to recommend it to others.

I have an incredible respect for authors like Bookout, who

are cautious in drawing conclusions and making applications. He respects the text and goes no further than is warranted. He is not interested in wild speculations but anchors everything he says to the text.

That said, he is also incredibly bold in what he writes. This book will encourage you, but will also challenge you. It will challenge you to give your allegiance completely to King Jesus. This is especially true in the chapters that cover the Sermon on the Mount. He challenges us to take Jesus seriously and build our lives on the rock of Jesus's words. What would it look like if we actually lived according to the Sermon on the Mount?

The answer to that question might surprise you. Contrary to what some may teach, following the teachings of Jesus is not an avenue to health and wealth. In fact, if we lived according to the Sermon on the Mount, we would often experience exactly what Jesus said we would experience. We would be reviled, persecuted, and have all kinds of evil uttered against us falsely on His account (Matthew 5:11). People would slap us on one cheek and laugh when we turned to them the other also (Matthew 5:39). They would take advantage of our generosity and ridicule our compliance to their unfair demands (Matthew 5:40–42).

However, if we truly took Jesus at His word, we would consider this life of persecution and ridicule to be the "blessed" life. We wouldn't be surprised, think something had gone terribly wrong, or take up arms to retaliate. If we were obeying Jesus, we would rejoice that we were counted worthy of suffering the way the prophets suffered (Matthew 5:11–12). This life of obedience, regardless of the consequences, is the way of the cross and is the path that leads to life.

Bookout does a fantastic job encouraging us to take up our cross and follow Jesus in this way. However, he is also quick to remind us that we are not saved by our works. We are not saved by how well we obey the commands of Jesus. We are saved by the grace and mercy of God, through the sacrifice of Jesus. It is the obedience and faithfulness of Jesus—not our own obedience and faithfulness—that saves. We obey Jesus out of grateful loyalty, because of what He did for us. We do not obey in an effort to save ourselves or earn salvation.

As you read *God With Us,* you can be sure you are reading the work of someone who is well-read and steeped in a scholarly understanding of the biblical text. However, Bookout skillfully expresses that academic understanding in a simple and easy-to-understand style. The book is as well-researched as any commentary I have read—but is approachable and enjoyable as a devotional guide. This is a book you will want to read weekly, as it is designed to be read, but also a book you will want to come back to over and over again as a reference book.

Finally, I must say the true test of whether or not a Bible study resource is commendable is how it impacts the reader's relationship to Jesus. I can honestly say this book passes that test with flying colors. I am confident that, when you finish studying Matthew with Travis Bookout's guide, you will be more in love with Christ and more committed to living in obedience to Him.

INTRODUCTION

This book is the third in a series of studies going through the four gospels. The first is *King of Glory: 52 Reflections on the Gospel of John,* and the second is *Cruciform Christ: 52 Reflections on the Gospel of Mark.* This third study offers 52 reflections on the Gospel of Matthew that seek to draw the reader into closer fellowship with God, more faithful obedience to Christ, greater appreciation for the Scriptures (both Old and New), and hopefully to stimulate a desire for further study and reflection.

I always want to be clear that I'm offering "reflections" on the text. My prayer is that those reflections are faithful to the intentions of the author and honor God, but I'm not offering a strictly historical or exegetical commentary on the text. There is exegesis, history, theology, and commentary in this book, but there are also personal meditations that arise in my mind as I study. I cannot say that everything I contemplated or recorded is exactly what Matthew had in mind, but that often happens with great literature. It stimulates the mind to consider much more than was just written. Matthew, the great writer, has been stimulating minds for two thousand years, and this book is the fruit of the time I spent learning from him.

Many texts in Matthew are not covered simply due to the

length and purpose of this book. There is no way to discuss every verse in 52 short reflections. Plus, this book also comes after I have already written on the Gospel of Mark. Bible students have long noted that the vast majority of Mark's text is found within Matthew. Matthew has a good bit of his own unique material and his own twist on the material shared with Mark. For the most part, in this book, I focus on the material unique to Matthew or on ways Matthew diverges from Mark. If the story is included in both Mark and Matthew, I'm more likely to have addressed it in *Cruciform Christ*.

In this book, the majority of the reflections are on major themes central to Matthew (the first several reflections discuss these themes, but they are traced and developed throughout), the birth narrative in Matthew (which is not in Mark or John and is quite different from Luke), and the major speeches of Jesus throughout Matthew (especially the Sermon on the Mount which I spend more pages on than anything else). There are still some reflections that deal with shared material between Matthew and Mark, but I attempt to show Matthew's unique style and interpretation of those events as we reflect on those stories together.

I also know that my personal reflections are hardly my own anymore. I've had too many conversations and classes, listened to too many lectures and podcasts, and read too many books to approach Matthew without a great deal of influence from others. Please pay attention to the footnotes as you read through. I did not begin this book as a research project, and I didn't want to have pages of footnotes. However, I've tried to be aware of when my observations were influenced by others. It's hard to offer completely unique reflections when my approach to the text has been shaped by those I have read. I am indebted to many scholars, teachers, and Christian thinkers whose labor has benefited my Bible study and ministry. I hope the footnotes and citations will encourage you to read those authors also.

This book is best read with an open Bible. Most of the reflections begin with a suggested reading from the Bible. The reflections are then written on the assumption that you have done that reading and are familiar with the content. There will also be a lot of time spent in the Old Testament (Matthew does that). As we reference Old Testament passages, it will be worth your time to go back and read them. Much of what Matthew writes is best grasped against the backdrop of Israel's Scriptures. We need to be invested in them.

Our study will not answer every question you have about the text, and it may raise a few questions not previously considered. But those unanswered questions are where meditation, reflection, and conversation often occur. I tend to think the Bible intentionally leaves us with ambiguity for the purpose of facilitating community and contemplation. I like to let that happen and not force my answers onto the text. I have ended each reflection with a series of questions to help you begin your own reflections on the text. I encourage you to read, meditate, and discuss those questions with others.

The Gospel of Matthew heads our New Testament, and its influence has dominated Christian history. If you count the ancient commentaries, homilies, and manuscripts, you'll find that Matthew holds a special status among the gospels. Its influence is far-reaching and has not died out in two thousand years. Matthew tells the story of God's presence reuniting with Israel in the person of Jesus to bring about the reign of heaven on earth in the least expected ways possible.

This story is called the gospel and can transform you like no other. Buckle up and join us on a journey as we grapple with what it means to see Jesus as "God With Us."

REFLECTION 1
FULFILLING SCRIPTURE

The Long-Awaited Messiah

THE ARRIVAL of Jesus the Messiah, the son of David, the son of Abraham, was no accident (Matt 1:1). Matthew wants you to know this has long been God's plan. Do not be misled by your first instincts or natural intuition. Gut feelings are a poor guide. Admittedly, the arc of Jesus's life does not follow the template of any ordinary Messiah, but Jesus is no ordinary Messiah.

Two thousand years of Christian history have made the story easier for us to digest, perhaps dulling its sharp edges. Yet, for those experiencing it in real-time, Jesus was nothing short of scandalous. Authentic Messiahs don't get crucified. At least, that's the intuitive belief that Matthew will challenge over the next 28 chapters.

A heedless glance at Jesus's life story—impoverished, no official titles, crucified—does not shout "King of kings and Lord of lords." But Matthew wants us to take more than a heedless glance.

Matthew challenges us to dig deeper to see the culmination of God's incredible, unexpected, long-awaited, redemptive story. Matthew tells a story where God anoints His Messiah, establishes His kingdom, and saves His people, fulfilling all of Israel's hopes and promises and uniting the world into one family. This story is called the gospel, and it's the journey Matthew has in store for us.

To take us on this journey, Matthew carefully and strategically reads Israel's Scriptures alongside the life, teachings, and actions of Jesus. He documents how seamlessly interwoven they are. Matthew demonstrates from Jesus's genealogy that He is the culmination of the story of Israel (Matt 1:1–17). He illustrates how Jesus's life parallels and exceeds renowned Old Testament figures (like Abraham, Isaac, Moses, Joshua, David, Solomon, Elijah, Jonah, etc.).

And he catalogs the myriad of ways Jesus "fulfills" passages from Israel's Bible. Matthew gives the reader confidence that Jesus is no aberration from Israel's Scriptures, but He is the telos of those Scriptures.

Introducing Jesus

Ten times in Matthew's gospel, the author stops the story, proverbially grabbing the reader by the collar, and describes an Old Testament text as "fulfilled." When Matthew does this, he is basically shouting, "Hey reader! In case you were going too fast and missed it, this event in Jesus's life fulfilled an Old Testament passage." In each of these instances, Matthew, the narrator, inserts his own voice to teach the reader how to understand Jesus in light of the Old Testament (and conversely, how to better appreciate the Old Testament in light of Jesus). He adds these illuminating parenthetical notes to demonstrate how Jesus is the culmination of the entire Biblical narrative.

- Matthew 1:22–23 fulfills Isaiah 7:14
- Matthew 2:15 fulfills Hosea 11:1
- Matthew 2:17–18 fulfills Jeremiah 31:15

- Matthew 2:23 fulfills "the prophets"?
- Matthew 4:14–16 fulfills Isaiah 9:1–2
- Matthew 8:17 fulfills Isaiah 53:4
- Matthew 12:17–21 fulfills Isaiah 42:1–3
- Matthew 13:35 fulfills Psalm 78:2
- Matthew 21:4–5 fulfills Zechariah 9:9
- Matthew 27:9 fulfills Zechariah 11:13, blended with Jeremiah 32:6–8

A few interesting facts emerge as we examine these citations. Matthew cites Isaiah more than any other prophet on this list. All but one of these "fulfillment" passages (Ps 78:2) come from the Prophets. None of them come from the Law of Moses. Also, most of these citations appear in the opening chapters of Matthew (Matt 1:22; 2:5–6, 15, 17–18, 23; 3:3; 4:14–16). About half of these Scriptures introduce Jesus's life and ministry, thus impacting how we read the rest of the story. As Richard Hays notes,

> This clustering of fulfillment quotations near the beginning of the Gospel conditions readers to expect that nearly everything in the story of Jesus will turn out to be the fulfillment of something prescribed by the prophets.[1]

By using the Old Testament in this way, Matthew demonstrates that Jesus's life, ministry, and even His death are all compatible with the story of Israel. Not only compatible but necessary. Israel's Scriptures have been pointing and leading to this reality all along. Jesus's death was not an unexpected failure but a carefully planned fulfillment of God's intentions all along.

Apparently, authentic Messiahs do get crucified.

The Old Testament Really Matters

Matthew also uses Scripture in many other ways. Scriptural citations do not only come from the narrator but also from the lips of the characters in the story. They use Scripture in sermons, prayers, conversations, and arguments. Sometimes, these characters use the words "fulfilled/fulfillment," and sometimes they don't: Matthew 2:5–6; 3:3; 4:4–11; 5:17–48; 9:9; 10:35–36; 11:10, 17; 12:7; 13:14–15; 15:8–9; 19:4–5, 18–19; 21:13, 16, 42; 22:32, 37–39, 44; 26:31, 54–56; 27:46, etc.

Additionally, Matthew constantly uses subtle word plays, echoes, allusions, and themes that depend on knowing the Old Testament to be understood. The Old Testament is the lens through which Matthew sees everything he writes. We'll address many of these as we journey through the text of Matthew. We'll spend a good bit of time in the Old Testament. Matthew certainly does. The Old Testament is vital to the story of Jesus.

This is a tough reality for a church that often lacks clarity regarding the Old Testament. We have many questions about the Old Testament. What exactly should we do with it? Is it authoritative today? Should it be read differently than the New Testament? Should we even call it the "Old Testament"?[2]

Some early Christian thinkers (e.g., Marcion of Sinope) wanted to exclude the Hebrew Scriptures entirely from the Christian Bible. Granted, I don't know any Christian who explicitly takes that view today (maybe they are out there). Still, it is common to relegate the Old Testament to second-class Scripture. I recently had a man complain to me that his church wastes too much time in the Old Testament instead of teaching the gospel.

I know of some who believe the Old Testament presents too many moral difficulties to still be useful in our culture (as if our culture simply loves the ethics of the New Testament). They think the Old Testament hurts our apologetics, and Christians should intentionally distance themselves from it to make the gospel message more palatable. Matthew thinks the exact opposite.

The Gospel of Matthew upholds the Old Testament's value, integrity, and authority from beginning to end. Jesus, very explicitly, argues that His intention is not to abolish the Law and the Prophets (Matt 5:17–19). Sometimes, the church has forgotten that. Not the smallest stroke of Moses' pen shall pass away "until heaven and earth pass away" and "all is accomplished." So, we better not "relax one of the least of these commandments."

Jesus views Israel's Scriptures as a source of divine instruction and authority for His disciples. As followers of Jesus, we probably should also. Ultimately, all authority rests with Jesus (Matt 28:18–20), but Jesus has delegated authority to the Scriptures, including the Old Testament.

While it's essential to know that the Old Testament is still authoritative and valuable today, we must consider how its authority works today. Interpreting the Old Testament properly is vital to our adherence to Jesus. Thankfully, He presents us with interpretive strategies and methods of application that help us along our journey. We should read the Old Testament differently after meeting Jesus. Context matters. Just like the interpretation of the New Testament must be done from a contextual framework, the same is true of the Old Testament.

No Christian explicitly obeys every single word of the New Testament. Not only would that be impossible, but in many instances, it wouldn't make any sense. Do I really need to come to Paul soon (2 Tim 4:9)? Or can a woman not braid her hair (1 Pet 3:3)? Must I go to a village to find and untie a colt (Mark 11:2–3)? What about kissing, head covering, and going up to a door in heaven (Rom 16:16, 1 Cor 11:2–16, Rev 4:1)? Some of these examples are silly and are obviously not intended as normative for all Christians, everywhere, always, but the point remains: Context is key to interpretation, and Scriptural authority (even for commands) is impacted by the setting of the writing.

For followers of Jesus, the Old Testament is still authoritative, but in many ways, its context has been changed in Jesus. The setting has been transformed. Through the Messiah, we are invited to read (or reread) Israel's Scriptures anew, with unveiled faces, from a fresh perspective.

Why could Peter, a Jew, "rise, kill, and eat" unclean foods (Acts 10:12–13)? It wasn't because he should reject the teachings of Moses or abolish the Torah. It was because God cleansed the foods (Acts 10:15, Mark 7:18–19). I'd suggest one still shouldn't eat unclean foods, but we should not call unclean what God has cleansed (1 Tim 4:3–5). God changed the context.

Many of the barriers between Jews and Gentiles (Sabbath, temple, food laws, circumcision, holidays, etc.) must be interpreted in fresh ways for the universal, worldwide kingdom of God. Paul spends much of his letters breaking down those barriers while still quoting and upholding Israel's Scriptures. Paul's letters could have been so much shorter had he simply said, "Forget about circumcision; that was Old Testament stuff. It doesn't matter anymore." But that's not how Paul thought or argued. To him, the Old Testament still mattered very much, but the time had come for some fresh interpretations from a Messianic context. Matthew writes the story of how Jesus is changing the context. We'll see how Jesus changes the context of purity regulations (Matt 8:2–3), food laws (Matt 15:16–20), Sabbath (Matt 11:28–12:14), and temple (Matt 21:12–22:14, 24:1–2).

A valuable (though imperfect) illustration is to view Jesus fulfilling the Law and Prophets as a marriage fulfills an engagement. A betrothal can end either with a breakup or a wedding. A breakup severs/abolishes/destroys the relationship, while a marriage fulfills it. Marriage experiences that old relationship in new and beautiful ways. Jesus didn't divorce or break up with the Law and the Prophets. He provided rich, fuller, and beautiful ways to experience the Law and the Prophets. In marriage, the agreements, promises, hopes, commitments, and memories made during the engagement still matter as they come to fulfillment. Similarly, for the church, the agreements, promises, hopes, commitments, and memories of Israel's Scriptures still matter as they come to fulfillment in the Messiah.

Reflection Questions

1. Does the Old Testament matter to Christians? How does it matter? How can knowing the Old Testament help us understand God, Jesus, and the mission of the church? Should Christians teach and preach from the Old Testament?
2. In what ways has Jesus changed how we use the Old Testament? Should we read the Old Testament differently because we are Christians? Is the Old Testament still authoritative? In what ways should we use the Old Testament as our authority?

Endnotes

[1] Richard Hays, *Echoes of Scripture in the Gospels* (Waco: Baylor University Press, 2016), 108.

[2] For the sake of tradition and clarity, I still use the phrase Old Testament in this book. The Bible, however, usually uses words like "Scripture" or "Law and Prophets" rather than "Old Testament." I like the title, "The First Testament," used by John Goldingay in his translation. John Goldingay, *The First Testament: A New Translation* (Downers Grove, IL: IVP Academic, 2018).

REFLECTION 2

PREDICTION AND PROPHECY

"Fulfilled" in Matthew

JESUS CAME TO "FULFILL" the Law and the Prophets (Matt 5:17). Matthew presents Jesus fulfilling Scripture in both His teachings and in events surrounding His life. For example, when Jesus was born, He fulfilled Isaiah 7:14. During His family's brief stay in Egypt, He fulfilled Hosea 11:1. When Herod slaughtered the children in Bethlehem, Jeremiah 31:15 found its fulfillment. These Scriptures were fulfilled by events connected to the life of Jesus.

Jesus also fulfilled Scripture with His teaching. In the Sermon on the Mount, after saying that He came to fulfill the Law and Prophets, Jesus shows a fuller way to understand and apply Moses's teachings. Jesus quotes Moses (and popular interpretations/misinterpretations of Moses), then adds His own "fulfilled" understanding of those passages.

Moses says not to murder (Exod 20:15), yet Jesus amplifies and fulfills the meaning to include not being angry or insulting a brother (Matt 5:22). Moses says not to commit adultery (Exod 20:14), but Jesus says not even to lust (Matt 5:28). In this section of His sermon, Jesus quotes:

- Exodus 20:15 (Matt 5:21)
- Exodus 20:14 (Matt 5:27)
- Deuteronomy 24:1 (Matt 5:31)
- Leviticus 19:12, Numbers 30:2 (Matt 5:33)
- Exodus 21:24, Leviticus 24:20, Deuteronomy 19:21 (Matt 5:38)
- Leviticus 19:18 (Matt 5:43)

The teachings of Jesus fulfill all these passages.

It's interesting that events connected to Jesus's life usually fulfill the Prophets, while His teachings tend to fulfill the Law. Combined, throughout Matthew, Jesus is fulfilling the Law and the Prophets through His life and teachings.

The word "fulfilled" has a wide range of meanings. When Matthew uses this word, it is tempting to assume he means that something predicted in the Old Testament just came to fruition. But not all prophecy is prediction, and Matthew uses the word to include much more than prediction.

Certainly, there are predictions about a future Messiah littered throughout the Old Testament, and we should understand Jesus to be the ultimate actualization of those predictions. However, Matthew uses the word "fulfilled" to describe many texts that are not predicting the Messiah or any future event.

For example, when Jesus fulfills the words of Moses in the Sermon on the Mount, He was not bringing into reality a future predicted by Moses. Likewise, when Jesus fulfills righteousness during His baptism (Matt 3:15), it has nothing to do with a prediction about the future.

Similarly, when Jesus fulfills the Prophets during events in His life, as we will see, He's not bringing predictions to reality.

A New Way of Reading

One easy way to see that "fulfilled" in Matthew is not just about predictions is to go back to the Old Testament and read those supposed predictions. Read the passages that Matthew cites.

Doing so reveals that most of those passages are not predictions at all. They are not even usually about the future. Or at least not about the distant future. Most of them are about circumstances in the prophet's own lifetime.

However, when Matthew cites Micah 5:2 (Matt 2:6), which actually does predict a future ruler arising out of Bethlehem, he does not use the word "fulfilled." That's when we would expect it most! Contrary to our expectations, Matthew does not use the word "fulfilled" to indicate Messianic predictions. Instead, the word "fulfilled" exhibits the congruence between the life of Jesus and the Scriptures of Israel in a new and more full way than was ever expected.

As noted in the first reflection, we should read the Old Testament differently because of Jesus. We should read with Christ-centered eyes of faith. Because we believe that Jesus is God and is the ultimate source of revelation, He holds the authority over our understanding of Scripture. He rightfully changes how we read the Bible. Without Jesus, we would not read the Old Testament the way we do. Neither would Matthew.

Near the end of the Gospel of Luke, two times, the resurrected Jesus has Bible studies with His disciples. The first Bible study is with two disciples on the road to Emmaus. On that occasion, we read, "Beginning with Moses and all the Prophets, he interpreted to them in all the Scriptures the things concerning himself" (Luke 24:27). During the second Bible study, over some broiled fish, Jesus says to his disciples,

> "These are my words that I spoke to you while I was still with you, that everything written about me in the Law of Moses and the Prophets and the Psalms must be fulfilled." Then he opened their minds to understand the Scriptures … (Luke 24:44–45).

I would love to have sat in those Bible studies. Undoubtedly, along with explaining Messianic predictions, Jesus elucidated new ways of reading Scripture with Him at the center of the Law, Prophets, and the Psalms. Luke goes on to give us some of these readings in Acts. But I think we see these new ways of reading throughout the New Testament. And Matthew is full of them.

The resurrection of Jesus must be the foundation of any Christian reading of the Old Testament. In 2 Corinthians 3, Paul describes how nonbelieving Jews read Scripture differently than disciples of Jesus. Paul has expertly read the Bible both ways.

After describing how Moses veiled his face after meeting with the Lord on Sinai, Paul writes,

> For to this day, when they [unbelieving Israel] read the old covenant, that same veil remains unlifted, because only through Christ is it taken away. Yes, to this day whenever Moses is read a veil lies over their hearts. But when one turns to the Lord, the veil is removed (2 Cor 3:14–16).

Paul's point is that Moses used to veil his face to dim the radiating glory of the Lord (Exod 34:29–35). When people read the Old Testament without Jesus, that glory-dimming veil remains. But those who have turned to the Lord take off the veil when they read Moses and the glory of Christ shines through more vibrantly than ever imagined.

Consider what this means. While reading the Old Testament can lead us to Christ (Gal 3:24), the flip side is that turning to Christ is essential to read the Old Testament accurately. We cannot properly understand the Old Testament apart from turning to Christ. Matthew reads the Old Testament with an unveiled face, and his Gospel presents a beautiful introduction to early Jesus-centered biblical interpretation.

Studying with Matthew

I like apologetics. Defending the Christian faith is an important Christian task. However, we must be careful not to make apologetic arguments (even with the best intentions) that do not faithfully represent the Bible. I think this happens more commonly than we'd like to admit. For example, I've heard apologists claim something like: "There are over 300 Old Testament predictions about Jesus, and He fulfills every one of them. The odds of that happening are mathematically impossible if Jesus is not who He claimed to be."

These arguments sound wonderful but are problematic. There are certainly not 300 predictions about Jesus in the Old Testament. There are some straightforward Messianic predictions, but that's not primarily how Jesus fulfills Scripture. In this book, we will examine how Matthew's "fulfilled" passages reveal Jesus's unity with the story of Israel, radical Messianic mission, and mysterious divine identity. These Old Testament passages, understood through the Messiah, draw us deeper into the gospel story.

Matthew's reading of the Old Testament is troublesome for those without faith in Jesus. Matthew does not strictly follow the literal, historical interpretive style we modern readers prefer. It may look like Matthew uses verses out of context. Some accuse him of blindly proof-texting a random, hodgepodge assortment of unconnected and irrelevant passages to bolster his argument about Jesus. But Matthew is not dumb and has no interest in dishonesty.

If Matthew's quotation seems out of context, he is probably well aware. And he is probably doing something you are not expecting. We may need to broaden our Biblical horizons, alter our Scriptural expectations, and expand our restricted interpretive strategies. Matthew's interpretive style is not rooted in classical apologetics, modern historiography, or Western exegetical assumptions but in the miraculous revelation of the resurrected Jesus. The resurrection of Jesus changes everything, even how we read the Bible.

Matthew's methodology, whether we like it or not, is divinely inspired. We may want Matthew to read the Bible like us and do apologetics like us, but he's not going to. He is going to faithfully tell the story of Jesus. Our responsibility is to open our minds to the possibilities within Scripture and let Matthew lead our study. We are going to find out that Jesus fulfilled the Law and the Prophets, and Matthew is going to show us how.

Reflection Questions

1. What is prophecy? Is every prophecy a prediction? Can prophecy be fulfilled through events beyond its original context? Does God view prophecy the same way we do?
2. What is the value of apologetics? What is the value of Bible study? What are some possible ways apologetics might harm our Bible study? How might apologetics help our Bible study?

REFLECTION 3

GENEALOGY AND HOPE: READ MATTHEW 1:1–17

The Book of Genesis

MATTHEW, never too subtle in his use of the Old Testament, begins his gospel with the words: "The record of the genealogy ..." or, more literally, "Book of Genesis ..." Seriously, that's a legitimate translation of the first words in Matthew. The first sentence in Matthew's gospel, which introduces both the genealogy and the entire story to follow, calls itself the "Book of Genesis of Jesus Christ, son of David, son of Abraham" (Βίβλος γενέσεως Ἰησοῦ Χριστοῦ υἱοῦ Δαυὶδ υἱοῦ Ἀβραάμ). What a fitting introduction to the first book of the New Testament.

Let's break down this opening sentence a little. Nearly every single word draws upon the Old Testament. "Book of Genesis" should make readers think of the first book of the Bible.[3] The terms "Christ" (Messiah), "son of David," "son of Abraham," and even "Jesus" (which is another way to translate the name "Joshua") should bring Old Testament characters and concepts to mind.

Matthew is a continuation of the story started in Genesis that reaches fulfillment in Jesus, the Messiah, from the royal line of David, a true descendant of Abraham. None of those words make sense without an Old Testament backdrop. This reminds us that Matthew is not beginning a brand-new story but is continuing the ancient story. The story that started in Genesis did not end in Malachi or 2 Chronicles, but the Genesis story continues in Jesus Christ.

History and Theology

Be honest. Did you read every name in that genealogy? If you're anything like me, it's easy to skim/skip this material. Our eyes gloss over, and we start jumping from line to line until reaching the end. That's sad because Matthew's genealogy is relatively short (imagine your name being recorded forever in Scripture as part of the line of descendants leading to the Savior of the world, and folks skip you because it's boring). Have you ever read the beginning of 1 Chronicles? If so, I am impressed. It is nine chapters of weird names. It is a genealogical marathon. Matthew's is only 15 verses. I think we can make it through.

Biblical genealogies are fascinating. They convey far more than historical facts and names. They trace a line in history from one person to another. They take you from a beginning point to a preferred destination. Along the way, they may skip names or omit generations, but the line reaches its conclusion and often provides theological rather than just historical information.

There are many ways to write a genealogy. Just compare Matthew's genealogy to Luke's (Luke 3:23–38) to see how different they can be. Why does Matthew begin his Gospel with a genealogy? Why did he head the genealogy with Abraham? Why not Tarah? Or Nahor? Or Noah? Or Adam? Why highlight Abraham, David, and Babylonian exile along the way to Jesus? Why structure and arrange the genealogy by sets of fourteen (Matt 1:17)? Why mention five women along the way?

To answer these questions, we must examine the theological purpose of genealogy. This genealogy reveals central themes for understanding the Gospel of Matthew and has theological designs revealed in the details. Let's consider just four of them.

Four Strange Details

1. By beginning with a genealogy, Matthew connects Jesus to the long story of Israel. Each name represents a person, a story, and a life. Genealogy is the quickest way to summarize and retell the story of a family. Each person plays a crucial role in the coming of the Messiah. Jesus does not appear out of thin air to initiate some new religion. Jesus is the culmination of a long, winding, dramatic narrative. As succinctly as possible, Matthew gets the reader from Abraham to Jesus (from Genesis to Messiah), summarizing the entire history of the people of God that leads us to Christ.

2. Matthew includes five women in this genealogy: Tamar, Rahab, Ruth, Bathsheba, and Mary. Take a gander through the other genealogies in the Bible, and you'll see that virtually no attention is paid to women.[4] Matthew's genealogy is different, and we're supposed to notice. As the virgin mother of Jesus, Mary is obviously a key figure. While Tamar, Rahab, Ruth, and Bathsheba are less directly involved, remembering their stories may help us figure out why they are mentioned.

Tamar, Rahab, Ruth, and Bathsheba are all women with questionable reputations. That's not to say they are evil or immoral women. In fact, they are all presented as innocent. But none have a clean, easy, traditional life story. Tamar, after being deceived and deprived of a husband by Judah, her negligent father-in-law, disguises herself as a prostitute and sleeps with him. After becoming pregnant, she shrewdly proved that Judah was the father and demonstrated herself to be more righteous than him (Gen 38:26).

Rahab was a prostitute from Jericho whose faith (and deception) led to her household's survival. Ruth was a Moabite woman who arranged an eyebrow-raising private encounter with Boaz at midnight (which turned out to be innocent, but a risqué setting nonetheless), which led to their marriage. Finally, Bathsheba, the wife of a Hittite named Uriah, was summoned and violated by King David while her husband was away. Matthew omits her name, calling her "the wife of Uriah." Instead of her name, Matthew reminds us of the sordid content of the story.

Think of what these names have in common: each belongs to a woman. Like Mary (pregnant outside of wedlock), each has some "scandal" in her story (even if she is righteous and innocent). Each of these women is either a Gentile or deeply connected to Gentiles.[5] Four scandalous Gentileish women brought about Israel's Messiah. This Savior is not only for Jews but also for Gentiles (a significant theme culminating in the mission to the Gentiles in Matt 28:18–20). Jesus is not only for those squeaky-clean folks with spotless reputations but for real people: the sinful, neglected, mournful, and abused of all backgrounds.

3. Matthew structures this genealogy around the number fourteen (Matt 1:17). This detail might seem random or pointless, but it definitely is not. Many possible explanations float around for why Matthew does this.

One suggestion is that Matthew is nodding subtly to David's royal line. The Hebrew method of calculating the numerical value of certain words and names as a means of interpretation, known as *gematria*, may lie behind the number fourteen.

If I want to write the alphabet, I'll write the English letters "A, B, C, D," and if I want to count, I'll use Arabic numerals, "1, 2, 3, 4." In Hebrew, however, the alphabet also serves as a numbering system. So, each letter in the Hebrew alphabet, *alef*, *bet*, *gimel*, *dalet*, etc., has a numerical value associated with it:

— א- *alef* (1)
— ב -*bet* (2)
— ג -*gimel* (3)
— ד -*dalet* (4)
— ה -*he* (5)
— ו -*vav* (6)
— etc.

Interestingly, the Hebrew name "David" (דוד—*dalet, vav, dalet*) has a value of, you guessed it, fourteen. Perhaps Matthew is illustrating from beginning to end, by the very structure of the genealogy, that Jesus is the son of David.

Another suggestion focuses more on the significance of seven than fourteen. Mathematically, three sets of fourteen are also six sets of seven. Therefore, Jesus was born at the beginning of the seventh seven. Reading this passage along with the Old Testament reminds us of the laws concerning the Sabbath, Sabbath year, and Jubilee (Deut 5:12–15; Lev 25, 27:16–25; see Dan 9:24–27). Jesus enters the story to initiate the seventh seven. He brings the Sabbath of Sabbaths and the Jubilee of all Jubilees: debts are canceled, freedom is guaranteed, and hope is restored! The Messiah has arrived.

4. Matthew highlights Abraham, David, and Babylonian exile leading to the Messiah. Highlighting Abraham demonstrates that Jesus, as a descendant of Abraham, is indeed the fulfillment of promises made to Abraham. Abraham's story leads directly to Jesus. Highlighting David assures us that Jesus is the royal Messianic son of David. David's kingdom leads directly to Jesus.

The Babylonian exile is the strangest detail highlighted by Matthew. It's not a person or a name, so why is it in this genealogy? I think this question is answered by remembering God's promise that David's house and kingdom would endure forever (2 Sam 7:16). However, during the Babylonian exile, David's monarchy came to a sudden and agonizing halt. Nebuchadnezzar sieged Jerusalem, destroyed the temple, and ended David's throne.

Even after returning home and rebuilding their city, no son of David ruled as king. Foreign and pagan powers dominated Israel. God's absence was felt among His people (Ezek 10:4, 18; 11:23). Babylon, Persia, and Greece each held power over Israel. Herod the Great's rise to power and Rome's rule marked the end of the short-lived Hasmonean Dynasty (where Israel tried to gain autonomy again). God's promises to David remained unfulfilled. There is a sense in which, even though Israel returned home from exile, the results of the exile lingered. Instead of domination by Gentiles in Babylon, they were dominated by Gentiles at home. Even in their homeland, exile remained.

The Messiah was supposed to end that royal drought and fulfill God's kingdom promises. Matthew traces the line of Jesus from Abraham (foundation) to David (kingdom) to exile (loss of kingdom) to the Messiah (the kingdom of God restored and expanded to all nations, fulfilling promises made to David and Abraham). The anguish of exile is replaced by the salvation of the Messiah. The most unmistakable sign that exile has ended is that Emmanuel, "God with us," has appeared.

Reflection Questions

1. What do genealogies mean to you? Can you learn anything about yourself from your family history? Why is the genealogy of Jesus so important? Why would Matthew arrange the genealogy in this unique way? What can it mean historically? What can it mean theologically?
2. Why did Matthew mention five women? How is that unique, and how are these women significant? What

does that teach us about the mission of Jesus? What women does Jesus reach out to that could fit on this list?

Endnotes

[3] The Septuagint, or Greek translation of the Old Testament, used the word "Genesis" to title the first book of the Bible. In Hebrew, the title is "Bereshit," which is the first Hebrew word in the book of Genesis, בְּרֵאשִׁית , usually translated "In the beginning." Our English Bibles share the Septuagint title. The word Genesis, γενέσεως is the Greek translation of the Hebrew word toledot, תּוֹלְדוֹת which appears at key moments throughout Genesis: 2:4; 5:1; 6:9; 10:1; 11:10, 27, 25:12, 19; 36:1, 37:2, etc.

[4] Several women are mentioned, however, in 1 Chronicles 1:1–2:4.

[5] Tamar was presumably a Canaanite, although it's not explicitly stated (Gen 38:2–6). Rahab was from Jericho. Ruth was a Moabite. And Bathsheba married a Hittite.

REFLECTION 4

GOD WITH US : MATTHEW 1:18–25

Isaiah 7 and the Virgin Birth

MATTHEW'S FIRST "FULFILLMENT" passage is right after the genealogy and virgin conception of Jesus. Matthew 1:22–23 cites Isaiah 7:14 as a passage Jesus fulfills. For several reasons, Jesus's birth is unlike any other birth in world history. It is a singular, unique event that sets the stage for the transformation of the world. From His birth, Matthew challenges us to see Jesus as "God with us."

As we discussed in earlier reflections, the exact way Jesus "fulfills" passages from the Old Testament can take a variety of shapes. They are far more nuanced than simply predictions coming to pass. Sometimes, Jesus fulfills Scriptures that are not predictions at all. However, in Isaiah 7:14, Isaiah genuinely predicts the future, but it might not be the exact prediction we expect.

In Isaiah 7, three kings face a dark and uncertain fate. They share a powerful and terrifying enemy. That enemy is the stuff of sleepless nights and fevered dreams. That enemy is the mighty, ruthless, and hungry empire called Assyria.

Two of those kings, Pekah (king of Israel) and Rezin (king of

Syria) decided to unite their forces. They then sought an alliance with Ahaz (king of Judah). The more who join the alliance, the stronger the coalition. Ahaz, however, refused to join. This refusal infuriated Pekah and Rezin. Subsequently, they decided to attack Jerusalem, overthrow Ahaz, and set up their preferred king—the son of Tabeel—who would join the alliance and show them loyalty.

Ahaz is stuck with limited options. Ahaz could potentially trust his military and power to fend off Syria and Israel. This wouldn't work well, and he knows it. He could perhaps just join the alliance with Pekah and Rezin, but he does not trust that alliance. He could go to Egypt for help and military protection. This would mean becoming a vassal nation to an untrustworthy Pharoah (Isa 30:1–7). Or he could go straight to Assyria and try to strike a deal with them. This would also be costly. Judah would lose autonomy and pay heavy tribute, but maybe/hopefully, Assyria would be nice to them.

None of these options are God's will for Ahaz, although he ultimately chooses the last one and makes a treaty with Assyria. He goes to Assyria, saying, "I am your servant and your son. Come up and rescue me from the hand of the king of Syria and from the hand of the king of Israel, who are attacking me" (2 Kgs 16:5–9).

The Lord, through Isaiah, came to Ahaz during this stressful time with a message of hope and confidence. Isaiah told Ahaz not to make any alliances or treaties with the surrounding nations but to trust in the Lord. Isaiah says, "Be careful, be quiet, do not fear, and do not let your heart be faint ..." (Isa 7:4). Isaiah predicts that Pekah and Rezin's alliance will be short-lived, and Israel and Syria won't last much longer.

In case Ahaz had any doubts (which he did), God offered to confirm Isaiah's message with a sign. Ahaz could have asked for any sign he wanted, whether as high as the heavens or as deep as Sheol (Isa 7:10–11). Ahaz, feigning respect, refused to ask for a sign. In Ahaz's mind, I think, he knew already he would not listen to Isaiah, and no sign was going to change that. He wasn't going to waste his time.

However, the Lord gives him a sign anyway: "Therefore, the Lord himself will give you a sign. Behold, the virgin shall conceive and bear a son, and shall call his name Immanuel" (Isa 7:14). As the text continues, we discover that "before the boy knows how to refuse the evil and choose the good, the land whose two kings you dread will be deserted" (Isa 7:16). This sign is excellent news for Ahaz.

This sign means God is with Ahaz (even though Ahaz is clearly undeserving). Ahaz does not need to rely on foreign powers or his own might; God will be with him through this ordeal. The sign also means that Ahaz's problems will be short-lived. This sign will come quickly. Just trust God. With a bit of patience, before this child is even old enough to choose between right and wrong, Pekah and Rezin will cease to be a problem.

What Does Matthew See Here?

Now, what in the world does this story have to do with Jesus? That alliance dissolved over 700 years before Jesus was born. How does He fulfill that passage?

Numerous mysteries about this passage have been hotly debated for about two thousand years. I doubt I can satisfactorily settle them now. Many of those debates have centered around the meaning of the Hebrew word הָעַלְמָה (almah – "the young maiden" or "the virgin") and its Septuagint translation ἡ παρθένος (parthenos – "the virgin").

The wording of Isaiah 7:14 in Hebrew does not necessitate a miraculous virgin birth (although it would not necessarily exclude it). The point of the "sign" is the meaning of the name "Emmanuel" and the speed of Pekah and Rezin's downfall. Salvation arrives quickly to Ahaz because God is with him.

When a young woman/virgin has a son who is called "God with us" and who brings salvation, it makes a lot of sense to see a connection between Mary and Jesus in this passage. Jesus may not have been the explicit original referent in the text, but His identity and the circumstances of his birth and life deeply correspond to this text in new, meaningful ways. Jesus adds unforeseen depth and significance to this text, transforming and fulfilling it through His birth and divine presence.

This is the key to understanding how Matthew uses this passage. Mary takes the role of the young maiden (almah) and virgin (*parthenos*), while Jesus fulfills the title "[E]Immanuel." When the citation concludes, Matthew makes sure to translate "Immanuel" as "God with us." That theological idea is ultimately where his focus lies.

The first Old Testament passage quoted in Matthew (and, based on the arrangement, the New Testament) identifies Jesus as "God with us." As God saved Ahaz from his enemies, Jesus "will save His people from their sins" (Matthew 1:21). Emmanuel, God with us, is a sign of that coming salvation.

"God With Us"

From this point forward in Matthew, it is essential to read the actions of Jesus as the actions of God among His people. Through Jesus, God's presence has demonstrably returned to Israel. Jesus's birth fulfills Isaiah 7:14 in vibrant and unexpected ways. Jesus is no mere symbolic representation of the presence of God; Jesus is the incarnation of God.

For example, a recurring theme throughout Matthew is the worship of Jesus. The word προσκυνέω (*proskyneō*), sometimes translated as "worship," is given to Jesus repeatedly in Matthew's Gospel (Matt 8:2; 9:18; 14:33; 15:25; 18:26; 20:20; 28:9,

17). Characters worship Jesus from His infancy (Matt 2:11) to the resurrection (Matt 28:9, 17). Depending on the context, sometimes it is translated as "worship," "kneeling," or "falling down before ..." but make sure you don't miss it. This theme is just one of many indications throughout Matthew that Jesus is "God with us."

With that in mind, remember Jesus's interactions with Satan in the wilderness. Jesus says, "You shall worship the Lord your God, and serve only Him" (Matt 4:10). That word "worship" is προσκυνέω, and it is to be given exclusively to God. Anything else is idolatry. Yet somehow, it's acceptable and obedient to worship Jesus. Why? Jesus is "God with us."

From the earliest moments of the Gospel, the stage is set to worship Jesus. Wise men from the east traverse great distances, reading the stars in the heavens, with valuable gifts to offer, to fall and worship (προσκυνέω) a small child in a house in Bethlehem (Matt 2:2, 8, 11). That's not normal. You don't do this for an ordinary child. But it is fitting when the child is "God with us."

After the resurrection, when His disciples finally see the unrivaled glory of their Lord, they prostrate themselves and worship Him (Matt 28:9, 17). The concluding phrase of Matthew's Gospel intentionally reminds the reader that through Jesus, God is with us. Jesus is born as "God with us," and He departs this world with the promise, "I am with you always, even to the end of the age." No matter what enemy stands before you—whether Pekah and Rezin, Herod, the demonic forces of darkness, the sting of sin, or the pain of grief and death—rest assured that salvation is near. Through Jesus Christ, God is with us and will always be with us.

Reflection Questions

1. What is the value of the virgin birth? What does the virgin birth teach us about Jesus? How does the virgin birth set the stage for what follows in Matthew?
2. How is Isaiah 7:14 a "sign" to Ahaz? How is that passage fulfilled in Jesus? Why is the name "God with us" important to Ahaz? Why is that name essential for us to understand Jesus? How is that name used differently in Isaiah than in Matthew?

REFLECTION 5

THE BIRTH OF A KING: READ MATTHEW 1:18–2:23

Something Big is Happening

THE OPENING CHAPTERS of Matthew demonstrate that something special is happening. The genealogy points to Jesus, the Messiah, as the ultimate son of David and the hope to end Israel's exile. Jesus arrives in a swirl of divine activity.

Matthew 1:18 says, "Now the birth of Jesus Christ was as follows …." The word translated as "birth" is the Greek word "Genesis" (also used in Matt 1:1). A new Genesis is being written, and it will be an incredible story. The advent of Christ is not an accident. God has intricately ordained each part. Take note of these seven incredible events surrounding the Messiah's birth.

First and most remarkable, a virgin conceives a child. This event is entirely unprecedented in world history. The unpredictable nature of this moment significantly heightens its mystery. We have zero historical record of a Jewish expectation for the Messiah to be born of a virgin. Jews believed the events in Isaiah 7 had already transpired seven hundred years earlier. It was not read as a Messianic prediction. But after the virgin birth, Christians began rereading Isaiah 7:14 and found a connection to Jesus (discussed in the previous reflection). This was not the case beforehand, which lends credibility and authenticity to the story.

Think about it this way. A long-anticipated expectation of a virgin-born Messiah would compel followers of Jesus to prove that Jesus was born of a virgin. This compulsion may motivate embellishment or even the invention of a virgin birth story to lend credibility to Jesus. But since there was no expectation for a virgin-born Messiah, there was no reason to make up such a story.

Messiahs do not need to come from virgins. The reason to say Jesus was born of a virgin was that, well, He was born of a virgin. His followers then read the Old Testament and found a deep resonance in Isaiah with this miraculous event. But the event happened first.

Second, with the conception and birth of Jesus comes an influx of heavenly messengers and revelatory dreams (Matt 1:20–21; 2:12, 13, 19, 22). Joseph, who receives several of these dreams, demonstrates his righteousness (Matt 1:19) and proves himself faithful and obedient to the heavenly instructions. God's revelations and Joseph's faith and obedience lead to the salvation of his family.

Third, as earlier reflections have already discussed, Scripture is repeatedly fulfilled in the coming of Jesus. Matthew 1:23; 2:6, 15, 18, and 23 demonstrate that Jesus is walking in step with the prophets of Israel. The Scriptures of Israel find their richest meaning in the life of Jesus.

Fourth, two names are given to Jesus, revealing His identity and destiny. Joseph is told in a dream to "call His name Jesus" (Matt 1:21), and His birth fulfills a passage that says to "call His name Immanuel" (Matt 1:23). While "Jesus" becomes His literal designation, both names have symbolic meanings that detail God's nearness and activity. Jesus is "Immanuel" because, in a mysterious and profound way, He is "God with us." This name demonstrates the presence of God among His people through Jesus.

Immanuel is called "Jesus" because "He will save His people from their sins." This meaning is another hint that the end of exile is found in Jesus. Exile occurs because of sin, and Jesus is coming to save them from these sins. The name "Jesus" comes from the Hebrew name, also translated as "Joshua," which means "Yahweh Helps" or "Yahweh Saves." Jesus's two names mean that God is with His people (Immanuel) and will save His people (Jesus).

Fifth, because of Jesus's birth, mysterious wise men from the East make their long-distance journey to worship a newborn child. This doesn't happen every day. This event signifies that something global is happening. The Gentile wise men worshipping Jesus after His birth, coupled with the Gentile centurion's confession at His death (Matt 27:54), bookend Jesus's life and death and frame His kingdom with worldwide significance. Jesus is not limited to the borders of Israel.

Sixth, Matthew depicts even the stars of heaven pointing to Jesus as the Messiah; creation shouts forth the glory of Jesus from His birth. At His crucifixion, creation trembles with earthquakes and darkness (Matt 27:45–54). From birth to death, physical creation testifies to His lordship and divinity. Heaven and earth bear witness that something extraordinary is taking place at the birth of Jesus.

Seventh and finally, the birth of Jesus causes kings and rulers to quiver with fear. Herod was greatly disturbed because the "King of the Jews" was born. I wonder how many other babies kept King Herod awake at night. Jesus's royal birth sent shockwaves that intimidated the highest levels of authority. The advent of Jesus made the royal proclamation that God is present, working, will save His people from their sins, and will ultimately reign as the true King of all the earth.

Family Turmoil

As always in the life and ministry of Jesus, the good never comes without resistance. Confusion, hardship, and immeasurable evil arise in the early life of Christ. For example, when Mary miraculously becomes pregnant with a child from the Holy Spirit, it sends Joseph's life into a tailspin. He believes she must have been unfaithful and slept with some other man. What else could he think? The pain, confusion, shame, and mistrust that flooded his mind must have been unbearable. Never would he have expected his life to take this turn. He loved her. He trusted her. He thought he knew her. Now, he has some difficult decisions to make.

Betrothal, at that time, was a binding agreement. The commitment was not as light as in our modern engagements, where both parties usually understand that backing out is a viable option. More than a fiancé, a betrothed couple was considered husband and wife. Since they had already promised marriage, divorce was necessary to end a betrothal. The marriage commitment had already begun, even if the reality of married life was still in the future.

Joseph had pledged himself to Mary for life, but now his future is a mess. It's unclear how often this punishment was still practiced in Joseph's day, but according to the Law of Moses, it sure seems Mary had committed a capital offense. Even Roman law allowed the execution of an adulteress. Yet, Joseph decided to deal with this secretly, sparing Mary's honor and perhaps her life.

Joseph's actions play into a theme that will become significant throughout Matthew: God desires compassion and mercy, not sacrifice (Matt 9:13, 12:7; Hos 6:6). Joseph is an example of what this means. Rather than destroying Mary, he acts out of love and mercy (see John 8:1–11). Accordingly, Matthew calls him "righteous" (Matt 1:19).

Rachel Weeping

Jesus's family struggles are not yet over. Joseph soon needs to pack everything and flee to Egypt as a refugee. The Jewish Messiah found safety among the Gentiles in Egypt—how is that for irony? While Jesus lives and grows as an outsider in a foreign land (like Moses), the families back in Bethlehem suffer incredible evil. Remember the ruthless slaughter. Joseph and Mary no doubt knew many of these families. I wonder if Jesus had ever played with any of those children as a baby. The whole town was left in utter devastation as loud sobs and wails filled the night.

These tragic events fulfill a passage from Jeremiah 31:15. Rachel, a wife of Israel (Jacob), looks across time at the misery and death experienced by her children and weeps (Matt 2:18). In Jeremiah's original context, Rachel peers into the future and weeps over her children's destruction and captivity in Babylon. Jeremiah 31 describes the pain and misery of Babylonian exile (the same exile mentioned in Matt 1:11, 12, 17).

Matthew borrows this passage to show that Rachel is still weeping as she observes the horrendous evil that continues to be mounted upon her children. This time by Roman-appointed rulers. Her tears remind us that exile continues. Rome has replaced Babylon, but the nations are still roaming and killing her children. And Rachel still weeps.

Matthew quotes Jeremiah 31:15 about Rachel weeping, but much more is written in Jeremiah 31. Matthew expects us to be aware of the context that he is quoting. This chapter does not end with Rachel weeping but with the promise of a new covenant. The pain of Israel's exile is transformed into great joy (Jer 31:13–14), and Israel will return home (Jer 31:17, 21, 23–25).

Jeremiah 31:31–34 depicts a new covenant, unlike the broken covenant made at Sinai. Exile will end, a new covenant will emerge, God will be merciful to Israel's iniquity, and He will remember their sins no more (Jer 31:34). As Richard Hays puts it, "Jeremiah's image of Rachel weeping is a prelude to his bold prophecy of hope for the end of exile."[6] Jeremiah 31 points to the end of exile. Jeremiah 31 points to Jesus. Rachel has reason to weep, but Jesus is coming to comfort her (Matt 5:4), to offer forgiveness, hope, joy, a new covenant, and salvation to God's people.

Reflection Questions

1. What miraculous events surrounding the birth of Jesus are most meaningful to you? Why did you choose that one? What can you learn from it?
2. How does Rachel weep for the children of Bethlehem? Why is reading the Old Testament citations in their original context helpful to see how Matthew uses them? How does the rest of Jeremiah 31 contribute to our understanding of Jesus's mission?

Endnotes

[6] Hays, *Echoes*, 115.

REFLECTION 6
GREATER MOSES

Moses and Exodus

In Israelite lore, there is nobody quite like Moses. Moses defeated their national enemies, freeing them to become an independent nation. He wrote their law codes, which sanctified them as a nation of priests. He provided divine wisdom by which to live, thrive, and know God. He detailed priestly regulations for their worship and religious life. Finally, he recorded their history, purpose, and destiny in writings that have endured through the ages.

Many Americans look back to their own national founders with respect and admiration. Whether it's George Washington, Thomas Jefferson, or James Madison, these men are revered as almost superhuman in their integrity, courage, intelligence, and foresight. (Clearly, this opinion is not unanimous.) In his book on Exodus, Dr. Ed Gallagher describes Moses as

> like all of those founding fathers rolled into one. Moses was the national hero who rescued Israel from foreign oppression (Washington), he was the sage who contemplated the deep

> things of the universe (Jefferson), and he was the great lawgiver promulgating the Israelite Constitution (Madison).[7]

It was not from his grit and intelligence that Moses accomplished so much and held such lasting influence; it was because of his closeness to Israel's God. God uniquely spoke to Moses "face to face, as one speaks to a friend" (Exod 33:7–11). God protected Moses at his birth, chose him for a crucial mission, and showered him with wisdom, authority, and success. As a result, Moses shared fellowship with God unmatched by his contemporaries.

To appreciate the Gospel of Matthew, knowing the story of Moses is essential. Jesus will be directly linked to Moses repeatedly. We must read Matthew in concert with Exodus because Matthew, in his artistic style, is retelling the story of Exodus with Jesus replacing Moses as the central figure. As we open Matthew, a new Exodus is on the horizon, and Jesus will accomplish it. (The idea of a New Exodus is a favorite motif of Israelite prophets to discuss the end of exile. It's a motif continued in Matthew.)

Jesus Sounds a Lot Like Moses

While Matthew sometimes directly cites passages from the Old Testament, he also regularly tells stories about Jesus, without direct citation, that parallel Old Testament stories. Meaning, Matthew compares and contrasts stories from the Old Testament to the life of Jesus so that the reader can see similarities and differences. Taking the life of Moses as our example, notice how often Jesus and Moses connect in the early chapters of Matthew.

In Exodus 1, a paranoid king (Pharoah) emerges and begins to imagine a problem in his kingdom. He believes that the foreigners in His land (the Hebrews) are too populous. He is concerned they might multiply and, maybe, join Egypt's enemies if a war ever breaks out. Fear drives him to the unthinkable. He enslaves the Israelites, making their lives unbearable, and orders the death of their male newborns.

To carry out these infant executions, Pharoah commissions two brave and shrewd midwives, Shiphrah and Puah. Because they feared God rather than the king, they disobeyed his orders, deceived him, and kept the babies alive. God blessed them for their faith and reverence. As a result, in Pharoah's rage and fury, he commanded every newborn Hebrew male to be cast into the Nile River.

To summarize, in Exodus, an evil and paranoid king wants to protect his throne. He is deceived, and he orders young children to be killed. That is the setting for the birth of Moses. Each of these events re-emerge in Matthew. An evil king (Herod) hears about one who is to be born "King of the Jews." He is greatly troubled by this. His fear of this child runs wild and drives him to do the unthinkable.

Wise men from the east traveled to Jerusalem to find and worship this child. Herod wants to use these men to track down and murder the child. But instead, the wise men deceive Herod, worship Jesus, and travel back home another way. After his plot to kill the Christ child fails, Herod is enraged and commands all the little children in Bethlehem (two and younger) to be killed.

Reading these stories side by side, it's easy to see the connections. Pharoah and Herod are mirror images of one another. Shiphrah and Puah deceived the king to save the children, much like the wise men from the East. The innocent children bore the brunt of the king's wrath as he ordered their slaughter. Moses and Jesus entered this world in terrible circumstances, saved only by divine grace and intervention.

The similarities continue when Moses is rescued in a basket from the Nile River and grows up as a Hebrew in Egypt (in

Pharaoh's household). Jesus is rescued when His Hebrew family flees from Bethlehem to, of all places, Egypt. Eventually, Moses and Jesus (for very different reasons) leave Egypt and return to be with the people of God. They both pass through the water (the Red Sea and Jordan River), fast 40 days and 40 nights (Exod 34:28, Matt 4:1), face temptation in the wilderness (40 years vs. 40 days), and become great teachers of Israel. Much like Moses, Jesus goes up on a mountain to reveal God's word to the people (Matt 5:1). In Jesus's famous Sermon on the Mount, He repeatedly compares His teachings to Moses's. The similarities are everywhere.

Jesus and Moses Diverge

It is also crucial to notice, however, the ways that Jesus and Moses differ from one another. The broad outlines of their lives are the same in the early chapters, but numerous contrasts emerge in the story. For example, Jesus is miraculously born of a virgin while Moses is not. Moses flees Egypt because he killed an Egyptian, while Jesus is still a child when He leaves Egypt. While they both went to the wilderness, only Jesus made it out. Moses ultimately died in the wilderness and was unable to lead Israel into the Promised Land. Jesus victoriously makes it out of the wilderness, overcoming Satan's temptations, and then begins His ministry. Moses's ministry ended in the wilderness, but Jesus's ministry began from the wilderness.[8]

Jesus, while quoting Moses in the Sermon on the Mount (and popular interpretations of Moses), responds with the phrase, "But I say to you ..." (Matt 5:22, 28, 32, 34, 39, 44). Jesus intentionally presents His teachings in the context of Moses's words but highlights them in new ways. Jesus reinforces Moses's teachings but also adds divine clarification and intensification to them.

In Matthew, when Jesus and Moses finally meet at the

transfiguration, they are both on a mountain, and a cloud appears. Remember that cloud Moses followed? It's back in Matthew. The voice of God then booms from the cloud and terrifies the disciples (Matt 17:1–6), just like it did those who heard it in Exodus 20:18–21; 24:15, 16. While Peter wants to equate Moses and Jesus (and Elijah) with three tents, the voice from the cloud distinguishes them, saying that Jesus is His Beloved Son (not Moses or Elijah). Instead of calling the people to listen to Moses (like the cloud in Exodus), we are called to listen to Jesus.

Jesus is presented as being like Moses but also something much more. Jesus is more excellent than Moses. He is Moses 2.0. Just like Moses led Israel out of slavery in Egypt, Jesus will lead His people out of slavery. But Jesus makes it through the wilderness and brings us home to the Promised Land. While Moses was a great and wise leader and teacher, Jesus alone is the divine, virgin-born, sinless, beloved Son of God. Jesus alone conquered the powers of darkness, fulfilling God's purposes in Israel, inaugurating the kingdom of heaven on earth, and bringing salvation to every nation.

Reflection Questions

1. In what ways is Jesus like Moses? How does that shape your understanding of Him and His mission?
2. In what ways is Jesus unlike Moses? How does that shape your understanding of Him and His mission? How might these similarities and dissimilarities contribute to Matthew's "fulfillment" theme?

Endnotes

[7] Ed Gallagher, *The Book of Exodus: Explorations in Christian Theology* (Florence, AL: Heritage Christian University Press, 2020), 4.

[8] Matthew also seems to parallel Jesus and Joshua in several ways. In fact, in the original languages, Jesus and Joshua share the same name.

REFLECTION 7

BETTER DAVID

Son of David and King of the Jews

THE FIRST VERSE of Matthew describes Jesus as "the son of David." Many call Jesus by this title throughout the Gospel (Matt 9:27; 12:23; 15:22; 20:30–31; 21:9, 15). The name David is mentioned about seventeen times (Matt 1:1, 6, 17, 20, 9:27; 12:3, 23; 15:22; 20:30, 31; 21:9, 15; 22:42, 43, 45), and the Messianic title "Son of David" is used ten times. Interestingly, in Matthew 1:20, an angel calls Joseph "Son of David" (by taking Mary as his wife, Joseph legitimizes Jesus's identity as the Son of David).

Matthew emphasizes this title more than Mark, Luke, and John combined (Mark 10:47, 48; 12:35–37; Luke 18:38–39; 20:41, 44; and John never uses it). Using this designation links Jesus to David. But, then, by the end of Matthew, we realize that both this Davidic link and Messianic title are inadequate. David is too small to be compared with Jesus.

As Jesus is far greater than Moses, so also Jesus is far greater than David. Jesus is genealogically the Son of David, but He is much more. Matthew concludes this "Son of David" motif by proving that David calls Jesus, "Lord" instead of "Son" (Matt 22:42–45). While it is appropriate to understand Jesus as a king from the line of David, He is by far the most extraordinary King Israel ever had. He is greater than any who came before Him, including David. In fact, Matthew will eventually compare Jesus to Solomon, the literal son of David and king of Israel. In that section, we are told, "Behold, something greater than Solomon is here" (Matt 12:42). Jesus is not only David's Son; He is greater than David's Son. He is David's Lord.

King of the Jews

Jesus, as Son of David, is the legitimate "King of the Jews." Matthew records four scenes where Jesus is called "King of the Jews." We are going to quickly look at what each reveals about Jesus. The first one occurs right after Jesus's birth. Matthew 2:2 contains a question asked by magi from the east, "Where is He who has been born King of the Jews? For we saw His star in the east and have come to worship Him."

Jesus's kingship was seen in the heavens by those far beyond the borders of Israel. Even wise Gentiles fall in worship before the holy Child. Jesus is not bringing the return of David or David's kingdom but something grander and more cosmic in scope. He is bringing the divine presence of God.

Rulers quake in their boots at the birth of Jesus. Herod, the Roman appointed "king of the Jews," suffers dread at the birth of Jesus. He takes drastic action to kill Jesus, his rival. Every time Jesus is called "King of the Jews" in Matthew, human rulers are trying to kill Him.

Before continuing, I want to add a quick note about Herod's plot against Jesus. In Matthew 2:4–6, Herod consults the chief priests and scribes to discover Bethlehem as the birthplace of the Messiah. Micah 5:2 is cited for this information. What's interesting is that the citation concludes with a line saying He "will shepherd my people Israel" (*ποιμανεῖ τὸν λαόν μου τὸν Ἰσραήλ*). That concluding line is not found in Micah. While Micah 5:4 does mention this future king will be a shepherd, that exact line comes verbatim from 2 Samuel 5:2. And guess who it is talking about? David.

Not only is it talking about David, but contextually, it is about David's ascension to the throne as the rightful king in place of Saul (2 Sam 5:1–4).[9] The Israelites gathered to anoint David as king and said,

> In times past, when Saul was king over us, it was you who led out and brought in Israel. And the LORD said to you, "You shall be shepherd of my people Israel (*ποιμανεῖ τὸν λαόν μου τὸν Ἰσραήλ*), and you shall be prince over Israel."

This passage about David (God's chosen king) coming to power in place of Saul (an unfit ruler) is applied to Jesus (God's chosen king) while Herod (the unfit ruler) attempts to kill Him. It also shows that even while Saul was king, David was leading the people. During the ministry of Jesus, there will be human rulers sitting on thrones, but Jesus is the chosen leader inaugurating the true kingdom.

Herod is certainly portrayed as a Pharaoh-type figure in Matthew. But, albeit more subtly, he is also portrayed as like King Saul.[10] Like Saul, Herod believed he was the rightful King of the Jews, but God handed the kingdom to another (1 Sam 13:14, 15:26). Like Saul, Herod tried to kill his rival (1 Sam 18:10–11, 19:9–10). Like Saul, Herod failed and died (2 Sam 1:1, Matt 2:19). Both kings, Saul and Herod, were powerless to stop the Lord's anointed from reigning.

The mixture of quotations in Matthew 2:6 not only describes the birthplace of the Messiah but also foreshadows the inevitable transition from an inadequate king to God's chosen Messiah.[11] The story of Jesus becoming king is what Matthew will spend the rest of this book writing about. No matter what schemes Saul or Herod concoct, God's chosen ruler "will shepherd my people Israel."

Now, back to the phrase "King of the Jews." The three other scenes where Jesus is called "King of the Jews" are in the Passion Narrative. When Jesus is on trial, Pilate asks, "Are you the King of the Jews?" Jesus responds, "You have said so" (Matt 27:11). When the Roman soldiers beat Jesus, they place a crown of thorns on His head, a scarlet robe on Him, and a reed in His right hand. Laughing and mocking, the soldiers cry out, "Hail, King of the Jews!" (Matt 27:29). When the plaque is placed on the cross above Jesus's head, detailing the charge against Him, it reads: "This is Jesus, the King of the Jews" (Matt 27:37).

These four scenes depict attempts to murder Jesus, charges laid against Him, beatings He suffered, and His crucifixion. Apparently, "King of the Jews" is a dangerous phrase. From birth to death, attempts have been made against Jesus's life by the rulers of this world. Kings of the earth do not want God's kingdom or chosen Ruler. Therefore, they use deception, violence, and death to stop the enthronement of Jesus as "King of the Jews." But, despite their vain efforts, they only bring God's plans to fruition.

The cross is the definitive picture of the upside-down kingdom of heaven. Kings exalt themselves to lofty thrones wearing expensive, gaudy crowns and garish jewelry. Their robes are made of the rarest materials, the finest linens, and the costliest dyes. Their coronations are excessive celebrations of power, excellence, and prestige. They parade their greatness before all.

Jesus Christ was enthroned upon a shameful cross. He was stripped naked. His crown was made of thorns, decorated with pain and mockery. His coronation was a haunting display of bitter envy and malice. God doesn't need a throne to become King; He can use a cross. On the cross, Jesus aligned with the sick, the poor, and the powerless while satirically hailed "King of the Jews." This irony was no accident. The paradox of the cross is the dishonorable, offensive, scandalous means by which God established His kingdom, enthroned His Son, and blessed His people.

King of All Nations

The story of Jesus does not conclude on a cross. Instead, after His victorious resurrection, His (doubting) disciples worshipped Him (Matt 28:17) on a mountain. The final words of Matthew's Gospel remind us that Jesus is indeed the Son of David and King of the Jews, but also something so much more: "All authority in heaven and on earth has been given to Me." Jesus lives and reigns on high to this day.

David's kingdom had borders, and the Jews were one people among many peoples. Jesus began His ministry by gathering followers from the regions previously ruled by David (Matt 4:24–25). By the end, the borders of His kingdom have been removed, and all heaven and earth are under the authority of Jesus. There is no nation or realm where He does not reign.

The gospel is the proclamation of His administration. The gospel is the announcement of good news that Jesus is indeed King. The time has come for the world to recognize His Kingship. Jesus reigns with all authority whether humans and nations accept it or not. The reality of the reign of Jesus is not dependent upon human agreement, submission, or belief.

Jesus reigns with divine authority over heaven and every nation on earth. At His birth, Gentiles from distant nations worshipped, and at His death, a Gentile Roman centurion declared, "Truly this was the Son of God!" (Matt 27:54) These moments hint toward the worldwide authority of the Lord

Jesus Christ. In the Great Commission, Jesus makes His all-encompassing authority explicit. Neither the Roman Empire, the power of Satan, nor the sting of death can overcome the kingdom of heaven. Therefore, disciples must go into every nation and make more disciples.

Citizenship in the kingdom of God is not about where you live or what government rules but about allegiance to King Jesus through baptism and obedience. As leadership over God's people transitioned from Pharaoh to Moses, Saul to David, and Herod (or Caesar, or any human king) to Jesus, so in baptism and obedience, we shift the rule of our lives to Jesus. Our allegiance belongs to the Lord of lords and King of kings whose followers constitute our true family and whose kingdom is our borderless nation.

Reflection Questions

1. In what ways is Jesus like David? How is Jesus the "Son of David"? How does this shape your understanding of Jesus and His mission?
2. In what ways is Jesus unlike David? How is Jesus not the "Son of David"? How does this shape your understanding of Jesus and His mission? How might comparing Jesus to David contribute to Matthew's "fulfillment" theme?

Endnotes

[9] Another interesting note about this passage is that David was "thirty years old when he became king" (2 Sam 5:4). While Matthew does not tell us Jesus's age, Luke lets us know that Jesus was about thirty years old when He began His ministry (Luke 3:23).

[10] As you keep reading Matthew, in chapter 14 another Herod is connected to King Ahab and Ahasuerus.

[11] Hays, *Echoes*, 146.

REFLECTION 8
FAITHFUL ISRAEL

Jesus and Israel

THE JESUS/OLD Testament parallels do not end with Moses or David. You can find them all over the pages of Matthew's Gospel with many Old Testament figures, including the nation of Israel as a whole. Jesus not only parallels and completes the stories of specific individuals, but Jesus also completes Israel's purpose and calling.

Matthew presents Jesus as the faithful Israelite whose life recapitulates the story of Israel and whose deeds accomplish everything God called Israel to do. In Jesus, Israel's failures find successes, her sins receive redemption, her Scriptures are fulfilled, her hopes are assured, and her destiny is realized and secured.

Jesus is unimpressed with the leaders of Israel, and part of His Messianic vocation will be to revitalize the mission of Israel and reform where she has lost her way. In some ways, this is a reformation movement. Jesus will call twelve men (like the sons of Israel) to share in and continue this reformed Israel movement. This will not happen by breaking or annulling Israel's Law and Prophets but by obeying and fulfilling them. As Israel was to be "a light for the nations, that my salvation may reach the end of the earth" (Isa 49:6), so Jesus will call His disciples to be the "light of the world" (Matt 5:14) and send them with a message of salvation to all the nations of the earth (Matt 28:16–20).

Again, this will become more apparent as we journey through Matthew, but let's briefly notice a few clues to help us read with this theme in mind. Matthew opens with a genealogy that leads from Abraham to Jesus. This genealogy briefly summarizes Israel's story from her founding, through her monarchy, beyond her exile, and to her Messiah. Jesus is where her story has been aimed all along.

Remember, secondly, that Jesus is constantly fulfilling Scripture. Looking back at those Scriptures is insightful. For example, read Matthew 2:14–15. After fleeing to Egypt to escape the wrath of Herod, Jesus "remained there until the death of Herod. This was to fulfill what had been spoken by the Lord through the prophet: 'Out of Egypt I called My Son.'"

This passage parallels the story of Moses's life, but also directly connects Jesus to Israel. The Scripture that Jesus "fulfilled" was not about Moses or a prediction about the Messiah. Instead, it was a passage about Israel and the Exodus out of Egypt. It comes from Hosea 11:1: "When Israel was a youth, I loved him, And out of Egypt I called My son."

Hosea 11 is a tragic retelling of God's relationship with Israel as a loving Father who suffers continual rejection from a rebellious son. God loved Israel and called His son out of Egypt (Hos 11:1, Exod 4:22, 23). Yet even though God called Israel, "they kept sacrificing to the Baals" (Hos 11:3). God taught His son, Israel, to walk, held him tight in His arms, and healed him. God led Israel with bonds of love, but they "are bent on turning from Me" (Hos 11:6). Yet, God looks at His son, saying, "My heart is turned over within Me, All My compassions are kindled" (Hos 11:8). As rebellious as Israel had been, God determines not to give up on His son (Hos 11:9).

Hosea 11, describing God's love for His rebellious son is somehow fulfilled in Jesus. How? Israel was called out of Egypt as God's son (Exod 4:22–23, Hos 11:1), but they rebelled in that role. Jesus, as an Israelite, came up out of Egypt to reignite God's story with Israel. As God's unique Son, Jesus succeeded wherever Israel failed. Jesus came as that Son Israel was always supposed to be. The story of Israel is relived and renewed in Jesus, and He fulfills it the right way.

Through the Wilderness

This connection is deepened when Jesus is tempted in the wilderness. Already, like Israel, Jesus spent His early years in Egypt. Then, in Matthew 4:1–11, He enters the wilderness for 40 days to mirror Israel's 40 years. Before entering, Jesus went through the waters of baptism. Similarly, Moses and Israel went through the waters of the Red Sea before the wilderness (See 1 Cor 10:1–4). It is noteworthy that Jesus was baptized "to fulfill all righteousness" (Matt 3:15). Whose righteousness? Throughout Matthew Jesus fulfills the righteousness that Israel lacked. As Israel's representative, Jesus fulfills their divine mission, their Law and Prophets, and their lacking righteousness.

The first time God's son (i.e. Israel, Exod 4:22–23) went to the wilderness, they grumbled at God because of hunger (Exod 16), they tested God at Meribah (Exod 17:1–7), and they turned to idols (Exod 32:1–10). These three sins happened almost immediately as they entered the wilderness in the book of Exodus.

Then, incredibly, in the book of Numbers, they cycle through each of these sins again! They grumble because of hunger and manna (Num 11:1–9), they tested God at Meribah (Num 20:2–13), and they again worshipped false gods (Num 25:2–3). Israel's wilderness experience is marked by failure from beginning to end. An entire generation, including Moses, died in the wilderness. If the first "son of God" could sin, fail, and die in the wilderness, Satan is hopeful the next Son of God will also.

The key to unlocking the meaning behind Jesus's wilderness temptations is found in Jesus's quotations from Deuteronomy 6–8. Those chapters recount the failures of Israel in the wilderness. The temptations will be discussed further when we get to Matthew 4, but for now, know that Jesus's responses to Satan reveal His successful understanding of lessons Israel failed to learn in the wilderness. He will not make the wilderness mistakes they did.

Why did God feed manna to Israel? Deuteronomy 8:3 answers,

> He humbled you and let you be hungry, and fed you with manna ... that He might make you understand that man does not live by bread alone, but man lives by everything that proceeds out of the mouth of the Lord.

Clearly, Jesus understands this lesson because this is the passage He quotes.

Jesus also quotes, "You shall not put the Lord your God to the test, as you tested Him at Massah" (Deut 6:16, see Exod 17:7 and Num 20:2–13). Israel put the Lord to the test continually, but Jesus has learned not to. Finally, Jesus quotes, "You shall worship the Lord your God, and serve Him only (Matt 4:10, Deut 6:13). While Israel repeatedly feared, served, and worshipped other gods, even in the wilderness, Jesus refused to worship the source of all idols, even when it would have given Him wealth, fame, and kingship over all the world.

The wilderness was a school for Israel. They were supposed to learn these lessons and graduate before entering the promised land. Frustratingly, they did not learn their lessons and brought their wilderness failures into the promised land with them. Jesus, as an Israelite, went back to the wilderness on Israel's behalf. He defeated temptation and graduated with honors. Israel's story is now back on track and being relived with Jesus at the center. Their failures are replaced with His successes. He came up from Egypt, successfully navigated the wilderness, and will be faithful in the promised land.

Suffering Servant

As a final example of how Matthew presents Jesus as the renewed successful Israel, note how Matthew 8:17 quotes Isaiah 53:4: "He Himself took our infirmities and carried away our diseases." These words in Isaiah describe God's servant who suffers and dies for His people. Matthew equates that servant with Jesus. We usually associate the phrase "took our infirmities" with the removal of sins. Yet, Matthew used it in the context of Jesus's healing ministry.

Additionally, in Matthew 12:17–21, Jesus fulfills the role of God's chosen, beloved, well-pleasing, Spirit-indwelled servant (see Isa 42:1–3). Jesus's baptism provides a similar glimpse of Jesus as God's beloved Son, who receives the Holy Spirit, and in whom God is well pleased. Matthew 8:17 and Matthew 12:17–21 directly link Jesus to the Servant depicted in Isaiah.

In Matthew 20:28, Jesus describes the "Son of Man" who came "to serve, and to give His life a ransom for many." Since Matthew has already directly linked Jesus with Isaiah's servant, we should be aware of that theme as we continue reading. The one who "serves" and "gives His life a ransom for many" should certainly remind us of the Suffering Servant of Isaiah 53.

During His trial, Jesus behaves just like the servant of Isaiah 53. That servant "opened not his mouth ...." While being "oppressed," "afflicted," and "led to the slaughter," he was "silent ... so he opened not his mouth" (Isaiah 53:7). Jesus, while facing oppression, affliction, and impending slaughter, "remained silent" (Matt 26:63), "He gave them no answer" (Matt 27:12), and "He gave him no answer, not even to a single charge" (Matt 27:14). Matthew not only cites specific passages linking Jesus to the Suffering Servant at the trial, but Jesus imitates and carries out the destiny of that servant.

So, who is that servant? It must be Jesus, right? Isaiah 40–55 contains many references to a "servant" (41:8–9; 42:1, 18–19; 43:10; 44:1–2, 21, 26; 45:4; 48:20; 49:3–7; 50:10; 52:7–53:12). Surprising to many Christians, Isaiah usually identifies this servant as "Israel" (41:8; 44:1, 21; 45:4; 49:3). Sometimes, however, beginning around Isaiah 49:5–7, Isaiah's servant is not specifically Israel, but also One who acts on behalf of Israel.

It seems to me that this is precisely what Matthew is doing with Jesus. In Matthew, Jesus both represents Israel and lives and acts on behalf of Israel. Jesus represents Israel by reliving their story and succeeding where they failed. He acts on behalf of Israel as their Savior who takes their suffering upon Himself to actualize their forgiveness, salvation, and the fulfillment of their vocation to bring the rest of the world together in obedience to God.

It may be helpful to think of Jesus as an Olympic gold medal winner who brings victory to his country. While describing the same race, one could say, "Usain Bolt holds the world record in the 100m sprint" or "Jamaica holds the world record for the 100m sprint." Both are true.

Similarly, Israel's commission to be God's faithful Son and God's righteous servant finds its actualization in Jesus. God called Israel for a specific purpose, which they failed to live out. So, God Himself came, in the person of Jesus, to fulfill Israel's purpose in the world. Jesus is the true, faithful Israelite who represents Israel and fulfills her call and destiny. Jesus is the gold medal-winning climax of the story of Israel.

Reflection Questions

1. In what ways is Jesus like Israel? How does this shape your understanding of Jesus and His mission? How do they shape Matthew's use of Old Testament prophecy?
2. In what ways is Jesus unlike Israel? How does this shape your understanding of Jesus and His mission? How does this comparison contribute to Matthew's "fulfilled" theme?

REFLECTION 9

BAPTIZED BY JOHN: READ MATTHEW 3:1–17

Introducing John

MATTHEW INTRODUCES John the Baptist as a wilderness man. He's a radical who upsets the status quo. John is a preacher, a prophet, and the second coming of Elijah, "the troubler of Israel" (1 Kgs 18:17). King Ahab gave Elijah that unflattering moniker, and he didn't mean it as a compliment. Elijah rejected the title. He told King Ahab, "I have not troubled Israel, but you and your father's house have, because you have forsaken the commandments of the Lord and you have followed the Baals" (1 Kgs 18:18).

Elijah, while controversial, did not consider himself to be Israel's troubler. It was the sins of the kings of Israel that caused the trouble. John the Baptist will face similar problems and enemies. Matthew 3 describes John using several allusions back to Elijah. They both spent time in the wilderness (1 Kgs 19:4). Their clothing is strikingly similar (2 Kgs 1:8). Plus, they both prophesied a challenging message of repentance to Israel.

Supposing these allusions go unnoticed, later, Jesus will explicitly say, "John himself is Elijah who was to come" (Matt 11:14). Matthew 11:7–15 presents a short commentary on

Matthew 3:1–12. Both passages discuss John in the wilderness (Matt 3:1–2, 11:7). Then his clothes are described (Matt 3:4, 11:8). John's prophetic message is noted (Matt 3:3, 5–12, 11:9–10). Then Jesus directly links John to Elijah (Matt 11:14). We should read John and Elijah's lives as paralleling one another.

They both preached righteousness, stood up against kings, and put their lives on the line (Matt 14:1–12, 1 Kgs 21:20–24, 2 Kgs 1:15–16, etc.). King Ahab was to Elijah what Herod was to John the Baptist. Several significant differences emerge, however, as we compare their lives. Perhaps the most noticeable is that Elijah was protected from the king and ascended into the heavens (2 Kgs 2:11). In contrast, John was murdered in a lonely dungeon (Matt 14:10).

This contrast reminds us that John is not only paralleled with Elijah but also with Jesus. John and Jesus both preached, "Repent, for the kingdom of heaven is at hand" (Matt 3:2, 4:17). They both refer to their opponents as a "brood of vipers" (Matt 3:7, 12:34, 23:33). They both warn about trees that do not bear good fruit (Matt 3:10, 7:19). Unlike Elijah, they both faithfully suffer violence and death at the hands of world powers.

Additionally, Elijah was violent and killed his enemies (1 Kgs 18:40). In stark contrast, John and Jesus preach the peaceable, nonviolent kingdom of heaven. They die rather than kill. They suffer for their enemies rather than make their enemies suffer. The teaching and demonstration of nonviolence, from the Sermon on the Mount to the cross at Calvary, is a central ethical theme in Matthew's gospel.

Repentance Realized

As John preaches and baptizes, many come out to see all the hubbub. Among the crowds are Pharisees and Sadducees (Matt 3:7). As they approach John, we get a few soundbites revealing his message.

- John is not impressed with the Pharisees and Sadducees that come out to him. He immediately calls them a "brood of vipers." These groups, by and large, did not believe in John's message or baptism (Matt 22:23–27). It is rare to see the Pharisees and Sadducees—who were divided on many issues—come together for anything. But they are united in their rejection of John—and their attitudes toward Jesus (Matt 16:1, 6).
- John believes that wrath is coming. John is not specific about what this "wrath" is, but he does connect it with fire and destruction (Matt 3:7–12).
- Repentance should lead to a change in actions. John tells them to "bear fruit worthy of repentance." One cannot fake this repentance because the evidence is in the fruit. When people change their minds about the kingdom (Matt 3:1), they should live out the teachings of the kingdom. They should bear fruit for the kingdom (Matt 3:8, 7:17–20, 13:23). The Sermon on the Mount presents the essence of this fruit-bearing life.
- God's judgment is based on fruit, not family. If anyone could have felt superiority or security with God based on genealogy, it would be the Israelites. They were God's chosen people. Yet, John declares that it doesn't matter who their fathers were. Nobody is approved or disqualified before God based on nationality, ethnicity, race, or genealogy. God can make people who look, think, dress, and talk like us out of stones. God is looking at our fruit. This passage is another indication, of many in Matthew's Gospel, of the coming worldwide mission of God.

- Separation is imminent. John preached that "the kingdom of heaven is at hand" (Matt 3:1), that wrath is coming (Matt 3:7), and that "even now the axe is laid to the root of the trees" (Matt 3:10). Verses 10–12 illustrate this separation in several ways: those who bear good fruit and those who do not, those baptized in the Holy Spirit and those baptized with fire, and those who are wheat and those who are chaff. The word "fire" appears in all three verses. The first and final references describe judgment. It is most likely that the middle reference is also about judgment. These are pictures of the "wrath" mentioned in Matthew 3:7.
- The One who brings this ultimate separation, Jesus, is mightier than John. Jesus also provides a different baptism. John's baptism was not about the Holy Spirit (Acts 19:1–7), but the baptism Jesus offers very much is.

The Baptism of Jesus

Jesus coming to John for baptism creates some interesting dilemmas. For one thing, John isn't worthy to even carry the sandals of Jesus (Matt 3:11). So how can he baptize Him? In the minds of many, this is a reversal of what should happen. The teacher should baptize the student. The spiritual leader should baptize the spiritual infant, right? But, like everything else in the kingdom of heaven, the roles are reversed. This reversal of roles stuns John, and he even tries to prevent Jesus from receiving baptism. It feels inappropriate.

A second dilemma is that Jesus has no need to repent and no sins to confess, which seemingly makes this baptism unnecessary. John believes Jesus should be the one baptizing him.

Jesus is the superior person who provides the superior Holy Spirit baptism. John just said as much in Matthew 3:11.

It would have been fascinating for Jesus to have stopped and baptized John instead. That could have really sent a message about His superiority; Jesus even baptized the baptizer! But Jesus does the opposite. He humbly submits to John's baptism, which provides a beautiful model for us and an even more important message. Baptism should always be a passive act of submission and humility.

So, why did Jesus do it? Why did He come to John and receive baptism even when He had no sins to confess? Even when He had nothing to repent of? When John confronts Jesus about this, Jesus explains it is to "fulfill all righteousness" (Matt 3:15). That phrase is unique to Matthew and provides an answer, but it is still ambiguous. How is Jesus fulfilling all righteousness?

Jesus may be "fulfilling all righteousness" in several ways. One may simply be by obeying God. John's baptism comes from God (Matt 21:25–27), and Jesus is responding to God with obedience. If Jesus refused John's baptism, He would be refusing something that came from God. Instead, Jesus offers an example of obedience and righteousness. Furthermore, Jesus demonstrates the legitimacy of John's baptism.

Another way Jesus may be "fulfilling all righteousness" is understood by His identification with Israel. He is embodying Israel, reliving their story, and fulfilling God's call to Israel. Jesus came up from Egypt (Matt 2:19–21), went through the water (baptism/Red Sea), overcame temptation in the wilderness (Matt 4:1), and taught righteousness from the mountain (Matt 5:1). He has purposefully reenacted the story of Israel, and where Israel has failed regarding righteousness, He succeeded. By receiving baptism, Jesus is fulfilling Israel's righteousness.

God demonstrates His approval of Jesus by opening the

heavens, pouring out His Holy Spirit, and declaring His good pleasure for His beloved Son. These events should bring several Old Testament passages to mind: Exodus 20:18–21, Psalm 2:7, Isaiah 42:1 (Matt 12:18). God's voice (like on Mount Sinai and on the Mount of Transfiguration) thunders from the heavens.

This voice declares Jesus to be the beloved Son of God. Isaiah 42:1 describes God's servant (discussed in the previous reflection) as the One who has God's Spirit upon Him and is the One in whom God delights. The servant will also bring justice to the nations (a hint towards the coming Great Commission). Jesus, who baptizes with the Holy Spirit (Matt 3:11), in a surprising reversal, now receives the Holy Spirit when John baptizes Him.

Applying this passage today, it is fascinating how many gifts and gracious acts of God come together at baptism. The New Testament combines rich theology and deep symbolism to depict Christian baptism. Like John's baptism, our baptism is rooted in repentance and receiving the forgiveness of sins (Acts 2:38). Like Jesus's baptism, we receive the Holy Spirit and are declared children of God (Acts 2:38; Gal 3:26–28).

Baptism is the humble, passive act of receiving God's gifts rather than active work to earn them. In baptism, we are as active as a dead man being lowered into a grave. When we are pulled out of that grave, God imbues us with new life. Like the resurrection, which is the beating heart of our faith, baptism is God's powerful work, which brings forgiveness to the sinner, hope to the wretched, direction to the lost, and new life to the deceased.

Reflection Questions

1. How is John the Baptist like Elijah? How is John different than Elijah? How is Jesus greater than

both? How is the kingdom proclaimed by Jesus and John different than the kingdom proclaimed by Elijah?

2. What is the connection between baptism and repentance? What does repentance mean? How is repentance a one-time act, and how is it a continual act? Why did Jesus need to be baptized?

REFLECTION 10

CONQUERING TEMPTATION: READ MATTHEW 4:1–11

Temptation #1: Stones to Bread

AT THE END of Matthew 3, God declared from the heavens, "This is My beloved Son" (Matt 3:17). This must have sent a cold chill down Satan's spine. Those words form the basis of his attack in Matthew 4:3, "If you are the Son of God, command that these stones become bread."

To Satan, Jesus does not look like the Son of God. He is weak and starving in some miserable wilderness. A good father provides food and shelter for his children. If Jesus is God's Son, why isn't God providing? Even more confusing, why is God, through the Spirit, leading Jesus to danger and temptation? "Jesus was led up by the Spirit into the wilderness to be tempted by the devil" (Matt 4:1). Jesus is intentionally "led" by God "to be tempted."

The phrasing of Matthew 4:1 reminds me of the end of the Lord's prayer, "And do not lead us into temptation, but deliver us from evil [the evil one]" (Matt 6:13).[12] In the wilderness, Jesus was led into temptation to overcome the evil one. He did the same thing on the cross. Throughout this reflection, we will see how these wilderness temptations connect thematically and linguistically directly to the cross. Something valuable, perhaps essential to the mission of Jesus, takes place during these temptations.

Satan believes the best way for Jesus to prove that He is God's Son would be to miraculously turn stones into bread. At first glance, it's not apparent why turning rocks into bread is a sin. Later, when Jesus is again in a wilderness,[13] He miraculously makes bread out of, well, not stones, but smaller amounts of bread. Still, miraculous bread-making in the wilderness isn't a sin. In fact, it's what God did for Israel with manna.

So why is it a sin? Perhaps Jesus was not supposed to use miracles selfishly. In Exodus 16 and Matthew 14, the miraculous bread/manna was made to serve others. If Jesus did turn stones into bread, it'd be hard to say He was tempted in all points as we are (Heb 4:15). I mean, I can't turn stones into bread when I'm hungry.

But maybe something else is also happening here. Satan presents Jesus with the possibility of "saving Himself" instead of faithfully enduring hardship. If Jesus is going to endure the cross, this is the very thing He must not do. Satan's temptations are eerily similar to the words used to mock Jesus during the crucifixion, "*If You are the Son of God*, come down from the cross ... He saved others; He cannot save Himself. He is the King of Israel; let Him now come down from the cross, and we will believe in Him" (Matt 27:42). These words at the crucifixion should remind the reader of Satan's words in Matthew 4. Overcoming these temptations in the wilderness is the preparation Jesus needs to overcome the temptations on the cross.

Also, we need to remember that Jesus is reliving and successfully fulfilling the story of Israel. When Jesus responds to Satan in these three temptations, He always cites Scripture (Matt 4:4, 7, and 10). That's a good model for us. Having Scripture in our heads can help us hear and remember the voice of

God when temptation strikes. However, these scriptural citations are also interpretive keys for understanding these temptations. Each Scripture comes from Deuteronomy 6–8 and illustrates what Israel was supposed to have learned in the wilderness.

In the wilderness, Israel found itself with no bread. But, unlike Jesus, they groaned and complained against God because of it (Exod 16:2–3). They did this again in Numbers 11:1–9. They longed to abandon their deliverance and hoped to rebelliously turn back for Egypt. They demonstrated no trust in God or His word. However, God still graciously provided bread for them.

In Deuteronomy, Moses explains God's purposes in these events:

> He humbled you and let you be hungry, and fed you with manna ... *that He might make you understand that man does not live by bread alone, but man lives by everything that proceeds out of the mouth of the Lord* (Deut 8:3).

Jesus understands that man does not live by bread alone. The message Israel failed to grasp in the wilderness is the message Jesus uses to overcome temptation in the wilderness. Jesus demonstrates the humility and reliance upon God that was needed from Israel. Through Jesus, the Israelite, and Messiah, Israel now has a faithful wilderness experience.

Temptation #2: Testing God's Love

Satan and Jesus then leave the wilderness for the pinnacle of the temple in Jerusalem. Satan challenges Jesus, saying,

> *If you are the Son of God*, throw Yourself down; for it is written, "He will command His angels concerning you" and "On their

> hands they shall bear you up, so that You will not strike Your foot against a stone" (Matt 4:6).

Just as a good father shouldn't let his son starve, a good father would catch his son if he fell. I have two young boys; I spend a lot of time trying to catch them. I'd definitely try to catch them if they were falling off a building. But I'd also be pretty upset if they purposefully jumped off just to test me. We are not called to "test" God but to "trust" God. Satan is trying to blur that distinction.

Just as refusing to turn stones into bread prepared Jesus for the cross, so did this temptation. Could Jesus have called angels to save Him from falling off the temple? I suppose so. But Jesus must not get into the habit of calling angels to save Him from injury or death. Matthew 26:53–54 explicitly states that Jesus could have called angels to save Him from crucifixion. Again, however, that's the very thing He must not do.

While being crucified, those who mocked Jesus cried out, "He trusts God; let God rescue Him now ... for He said, 'I am the Son of God'" (Matt 27:43). They are basically saying, "If Jesus is the Son of God, God should rescue Him!"

Notice that the logic and even the wording of Matthew 27:40–43 closely match the logic and wording of Satan's temptations. In fact, both Satan and the mockers quote Psalms (Ps 91:11–12 and Ps 22:8). Satan and the mockers are teammates in these attacks.

This temptation echoes forward to the cross, but it also echoes backward to Israel in the wilderness. When Satan tempted Jesus to leap from the pinnacle of the temple, trusting angels to rescue Him, Jesus responded, "You shall not put the Lord your God to the test" (Matt 4:8). That is a quote from Deuteronomy 6:16, which if you go back and read it, ends with the phrase, "as you tested Him at Massah."

Israel tested God at Massah (Exod 17:7; see Ps 95:7–11). In

Exodus 17, Israel complained about water right after complaining about the lack of bread. Israel regretted leaving Egypt because water was scarce in the wilderness. They do this again in Numbers 20:2–13. God responds to their faithlessness by graciously giving them water from a rock. But that place became known as the location where Israel quarreled with and tested God. Jesus does not test God in the wilderness. Jesus faithfully endures. He fixes Israel's failure.

Temptation #3: The Easy Way to Kingdom

Finally, Satan takes Jesus up on a high mountain, shows Him all the kingdoms of the earth and all their glory, and says, "All these things I will give You, if You fall down and worship me" (Matt 4:9).

If Jesus is God's Son, He should be a king (2 Sam 7:13–14; Ps 2:6–7). Shouldn't Jesus be ruling the kingdoms of the world? Shouldn't He share in their glory? Since apparently God is not offering that, Satan will. Satan provides a shortcut to power and glory. Like the world's kingdoms, all Jesus must do for this power is give allegiance to Satan (Rev 13:1–4).

Last night, I talked with my six-year-old son, Oliver, about these temptations. I told Him that Satan offered to make Jesus king over all the kingdoms of the earth. All Jesus had to do was worship Satan rather than God. Oliver looked at me and said, "But Jesus already is king over all the earth." I liked that response.

What Satan missed is that Jesus is an inaugurated king. His kingdom is not like Rome, Babylon, Egypt, or any other violent worldly power. Unfortunately, many people have missed, and still miss, this fact about Jesus. While on the cross, the chief priests said, "He is the King of Israel; let Him now come down from the cross, and we will believe in Him" (Matt 27:42). They could not be more misguided in this statement. Jesus is king precisely because He did not come down from the cross.

After His self-giving death and glorious resurrection, Jesus says, "All authority has been given to Me in heaven and on earth ..." (Matt 28:18). Satan offered a cheap, knock-off version of this authority. Jesus rejected Satan's offer and faithfully served His Father even through death. Through the cross and resurrection, Jesus defeated the powers of darkness, fulfilled the promises made to Israel, opened the door of salvation to the world, established God's kingdom on earth as in heaven, and now reigns supreme.

When Jesus rejected Satan's offer, responding, "You shall worship the Lord your God, and serve Him only" (Matt 4:10; Deut 6:13), He again connected His life to the story of Israel in the wilderness. This third quotation from Deuteronomy is a call to solely worship God and not to "follow other gods, any of the gods of the peoples who surround you ..." (Deut 6:14).

Almost immediately after entering their covenant with God (Exod 24:1–8), promising to serve only Him and make no other gods (Exod 20:1–6), Israel made a golden calf. They said, "This is your god, O Israel, who brought you up from the land of Egypt" (Exod 32:4). They worshipped other gods again in Numbers 25:1–3. Idolatry was a weakness for Israel throughout their relationship with God, and it started early. In the wilderness, Jesus rejected idolatry and the power and riches that came with it and committed Himself to love, worship, and give His sole allegiance to His Father.

Whereas Israel died in the wilderness, Jesus made it through successfully. As He reenacted their story, bearing their experiences on Himself, Jesus gave them victory instead of failure. Jesus rewrote Israel's history in the wilderness, and He rewrites the story of humanity through His death and resurrection.

Reflection Questions

1. How was Jesus tempted in all points as we are? How can He relate to us through this experience? Why did Satan tempt Jesus in the wilderness? How does Satan tempt us? Why is the use of Scripture helpful in this story?
2. What do these temptations teach us about the mission of Jesus? What do they teach us about the kingdoms of earth? How do these temptations connect to Israel's past? How do they prepare Jesus for the cross?

Endnotes

[12] Although the Greek word for "led" ἀνήχθη in Mathew 4:1 is not the same as the word "lead" εἰσενέγκῃς in Matthew 6:13, the idea is similar.

[13] See Matthew 14:13 and 15, the word translated "secluded" or "desolate" is ἔρημον, translated as "wilderness" in Matthew 4:1.

REFLECTION 11

A LIGHT IN THE DARKNESS: READ MATTHEW 4:12–5:2

The Son of God Settles in a New City

AFTER OVERCOMING THE WILDERNESS TEMPTATIONS, three events take place. First, angels come and minister to Jesus (Matt 4:11). Jesus did not ask them to catch Him after leaping from the temple or to rescue Him from the cross, but lest we ever doubt God's love for His Son, the angels do come and serve. Second, while God's love is precious, it does not mean we will live without hardship. Jesus soon hears the troubling news that John the Baptist has been arrested (Matt 4:12). This event receives a fuller explanation in Matthew 14:1–14. Third, Jesus withdraws into Galilee and finds a new place to settle (Matt 4:12–13). Jesus moves from Nazareth to Capernaum.

This change in location is significant to Matthew. Geographically, Capernaum is "located by the sea, in the region of Zebulun and Naphtali" (Matt 4:13). This is not just some pointless geographical tidbit. Matthew sees theological significance in this change of scenery. It immediately reminds him of a passage from Isaiah, which He quotes to explain the meaning of Jesus's move:

> "The land of Zebulun and the land of Naphtali, By the way of the sea, beyond the Jordan, Galilee of the Gentiles—The people who were sitting in darkness saw a great Light and those who were sitting in the land and shadow of death, upon them a Light dawned" (Isa 9:1–2, as quoted in Matt 4:15–16).

Several important points emerge from this quotation. This area is called "Galilee of the Gentiles." This is another pointer that Jesus's kingdom will have an impact reaching far beyond the borders of Israel. Jesus will have "all authority in heaven and on earth" and will have disciples of "every nation." The second half of this quotation reveals an essential aspect of Jesus's coming ministry. Matthew says that those sitting in darkness and the shadow of death will see a great light dawn. That description of light breaking into darkness introduces Jesus's ministry and preaching in the next verse (Matt 4:17; see Matt 3:2, 10:7).

Jesus's preaching and ministry are about light dawning upon those sitting in darkness and death. Jesus immediately begins to preach, "Repent, for the kingdom of heaven is at hand." This kingdom will be a source of light to a world of darkness. In fact, all who follow Jesus are asked to participate in shining and embodying that light. In the next chapter, during the Sermon on the Mount, Jesus challenges His followers with these words:

> You are the light of the world. A city set on a hill cannot be hidden; nor does anyone light a lamp and put it under a basket, but on the lampstand, and it gives light to all who are in the house. Let your light shine before men in such a way that they may see your good works, and glorify your Father who is in heaven (Matt 5:14–16).

While Jesus is the Light, through His ministry, He is

spreading that light to His followers. We are to become that light also. We are to continue shining the light of Christ on those who sit in darkness. This Isaiah quote is a profound introduction to the ministry of Jesus. It reveals the ultimate Gentile reach of His ministry (which is also seen in the expression "you are the light of the world") and that through His ministry, the light will reach those in darkness. This light-shining mission, by the way, again links Jesus's identity with Israel and the Servant who was called to be a "light for the nations, that my salvation may reach the end of the earth" (Isa 49:6). Jesus is completing Israel's work.

"A Son is Given ..."

However, to appreciate this quotation even more, we should go back to Isaiah and see what the context of this citation reveals. Isaiah 9:1–7 offers a message of hope and assurance through Israel's doom and anguish. Isaiah 8:22 says, "Then they will look to the earth and behold, distress and darkness, the gloom of anguish; and they will be driven away into darkness." This is a horrible message for Israel. The "distress," "darkness," "gloom," and "anguish" come from a mighty enemy, Assyria, whom God is using to punish Israel. But Isaiah 9 assures the reader that God's wrath will not last forever. A great day is coming when "there will be no more gloom for her who was in anguish...but later on He shall make it glorious ..." (Isa 9:1). This is the passage Matthew wants us to think about.

As we keep reading Isaiah 9, we find that this light will shine upon those in darkness and "increase their gladness; They will be glad in *Your presence*" (Isa 9:3). So, this light will accompany God's presence among His people. And God's presence will be experienced through the arrival of a great king and ruler:

> For a child will be born to us, a son will be given to us; And the government will rest upon His shoulders, And His name will be called Wonderful Counselor, Mighty God, Eternal Father, Prince of Peace. There will be no end to the increase of His government or of peace, On the throne of David and over his kingdom, To establish it and uphold it with justice and righteousness From then on and forevermore (Isa 9:6–7).

It is this glorious kingdom, upheld by justice and righteousness, that Jesus begins to preach in the next verse: "Repent, for the kingdom of heaven is at hand." If Matthew was looking for an Old Testament passage to excite His readers about the coming kingdom of heaven and the Light of God's presence through the person of Jesus, I think He found it. Don't skip the geographical info. Matthew uses even a seemingly trivial geographical detail about Jesus moving to a new town to further the plot and introduce the power and hope of God's kingdom. This is another example of why you should always go back and read the Old Testament context of Matthew's Scriptural citations. Matthew knows the context and expects his readers to also.

His Ministry Begins

As Jesus preaches the inbreaking kingdom of heaven on earth, He begins to gather disciples who will join Him in that message and spread that light. Matthew 4:18–22 details the call of Simon, Andrew, James, and John. These four fishermen immediately leave their boats, nets, and even a father behind to follow Jesus. This is a brief glimpse of a truth that will become clear in Matthew. Nothing, not a career, possessions, or even family, is more important than heeding the call to follow Jesus: "Everyone who has left houses or brothers or sisters or father or mother or children or farms for My name's sake, will receive many times as much, and will inherit eternal life" (Matt 19:29).

Along with preaching about the kingdom, Jesus shines His light on the world by living out the kingdom's message. The kingdom is not only heard in His words but is seen in His actions. His miracles and healings are a profound demonstration of the reign of God (Matt 4:23–25). When God is King, and His kingdom is on earth, His will is done (Matt 6:10). It is God's will for the sick to be healed and those suffering to have peace. Preaching the gospel must always be combined with demonstrations of the gospel.

Jesus is "proclaiming the gospel of the kingdom" (Matt 4:23). The reign of God (kingdom) is good news (gospel). Matthew often combines preaching "the gospel of the kingdom" with healings and miracles. In fact, Matthew 4:23–24 is almost exactly quoted again in Matthew 9:35:

> Jesus was going through all the cities and villages, teaching in their synagogues and proclaiming the gospel of the kingdom, and healing every kind of disease and every kind of sickness.

When Jesus sends His disciples to preach the arriving kingdom of heaven, He says, "And as you go, preach, saying, 'The kingdom of heaven is at hand.' Heal the sick, raise the dead, cleanse the lepers, cast out demons, freely you received, freely give" (Matt 10:7–8). Jesus preaches but also heals, and He sends His disciples out to do the same. Israel's mission to be a Light shining in darkness is to be picked up and carried by Jesus and His followers. We are called not only to bask in the light of Jesus but to become that light (Matt 4:16, 5:16, 10:27). Preaching the gospel is essential, but like Jesus, it should be combined with demonstrations of the gospel. Why should people trust us about the age to come if we don't care about them in this present age? The gospel needs to be more than preached but lived, experienced, and shared. Jesus did not rely on words alone but on actions. If the church is not a source of help, blessing, encouragement, healing, generosity, and the sacrificial love of God, then the church has no right to preach about those things.

As Jesus's ministry began, "Large crowds followed Him from Galilee and the Decapolis and Jerusalem and Judea and from beyond the Jordan" (Matt 4:25). This geographical area is quite similar to the boundaries of David's old kingdom. Jesus, the Son of David, is shepherding God's people in the same regions as David. The renewed and improved Davidic kingdom is arriving in the Messiah. The crowds came to Jesus because of His actions. He earned this audience. Upon seeing these crowds, Jesus goes up a mountain and preaches the most challenging, transformative, and significant sermon ever spoken, heard, or written.

Reflection Questions

1. Why does it matter that Jesus moved from Nazareth to Capernaum? How is that theologically significant? How does this move fulfill Scripture? What does it tell us about Gentiles? What does it tell us about the identity of Jesus?
2. How do Jesus's miracles relate to His teaching? How do the miracles and His teaching demonstrate the kingdom of heaven? How should the church apply this model of helping and teaching?

REFLECTION 12
DIVINE TEACHER

Teaching with Authority

MATTHEW PRESENTS a multifaceted picture of Jesus, illuminating His identity and mission in fascinating detail and beautiful imagery. Jesus is Immanuel. He is the presence of God among His people. Jesus is a new and improved Moses who guides, teaches, and leads God's people. Jesus is the true King of the Jews and the Son of David. He makes Roman-appointed rulers tremble with fear. Jesus is Israel's representative, fulfilling her mission and destiny in His life as the climax of her story. Each of these identity markers bears witness to the unprecedented authority of Jesus. This poor Galilean laborer speaks with the authority of a king and the sovereignty of God.

Establishing this authority is essential for comprehending many of the stories in Matthew. Jesus is introduced as "Messiah," "son of David," and "God with us" (Matt 1:1, 23). That introduction behooves us to adhere to all that follows. At His baptism and Transfiguration, the voice of God thunders from above to declare the supremacy of Jesus (Matt 3:17, 17:5). Jesus teaches with divine authority and unparalleled wisdom. He often leaves the crowds in awe, "for He was teaching them as one who had authority, and not as the scribes" (Matt 7:28).

Even a VIP Roman military man recognizes the authority of Jesus. A centurion, who commands respect and obedience, feels unworthy in the presence of the authoritative Christ (Matt 8:8–10). Jesus, unlike any mere human, has the divine authority to forgive sins (Matt 9:6–8). He can waltz into the temple, flip tables, and stop all the proceedings because, after all, it is His Father's house (Matt 21:23–27). Jesus can share and delegate His authority to give others command over the dark spiritual underworld and power over physical ailments (Matt 10:1).

This authority is demonstrated from the beginning of Matthew, reinforced throughout His ministry, and reaches culmination in the resurrection. Matthew concludes, saying,

> All authority in heaven and on earth has been given to me. Go therefore and make disciples of all nations, baptizing them in the name of the Father and of the Son and of the Holy Spirit, teaching them to observe all that I have commanded you. And behold, I am with you always, to the end of the age (Matt 28:18–20).

As the true King and ruler over every nation on earth, Jesus has the authority to command humans of all nations. He is taking over the world. Borders do not limit His reign. The uncontrollable, unstoppable, unlimited, divine authority of Jesus is central to the Gospel of Matthew.

Five Major Speeches

This authority is the foundation of Jesus's teachings. The authoritative words of Jesus explain the life, ethics, and theology of the kingdom of heaven in five primary blocks of instruction (5:1–7:27, 10:5–42, 13:1–52, 18:1–35, 23:1–25:46). These five major speeches organize and set the structure of the Gospel of Matthew.

Matthew intersperses Jesus's actions with His teachings so that together, they inform the reader about the kingdom. In other words, Matthew cycles through sermons that teach the kingdom and stories that demonstrate the kingdom. This cycle repeats five times throughout Matthew's Gospel. The introduction to Jesus's life and ministry (Matthew 1–4) and the Passion narrative (Matt 26:30–28:20) bookend these five cycles.

Each speech is a capstone to the actions of Jesus that led up to it. Matthew concludes each of these five speeches with these recurring phrases: "When Jesus finished these sayings" (7:28); "When Jesus finished instructing his twelve disciples" (Matt 11:1); "When Jesus had finished these parables" (13:53); "When Jesus had finished these sayings" (Matt 19:1); and "When Jesus had finished all these sayings" (Matt 26:1).

This recurring conclusion is reminiscent of how the teachings of Moses in Deuteronomy conclude before he offers a final blessing for Israel: "And when Moses had finished speaking all these words ..." (Deut 32:45). This phraseology is another connection back to Moses. In fact, these five speeches may purposefully parallel the five books of Moses and communicate, again, that Jesus is a new and improved Moses.

The five speeches center around the kingdom of heaven:

1. These speeches begin with The Sermon on the Mount (5:1–7:27). This sermon serves as the foundational political document for God's kingdom. It is a "Declaration of Independence" from worldly ethics and a "Constitution" for how to live under God's rule. In the Sermon on the Mount, Jesus details what life in His kingdom should be like. The practical question of how to live as part of a brand-new society with God as King is answered. The

upside-down nature of the kingdom and the revolutionary ethics of the Messiah make this sermon one of the most challenging texts in the Bible. Attempting to apply the Sermon on the Mount will change you forever.

2. The second speech, sometimes called the "Mission Discourse," is recorded in 10:5–42. This speech prepares the disciples for the dangerous mission of proclaiming the kingdom of heaven (10:7). Before sending the disciples out on this mission, Jesus imparts His authority to them (10:1). This speech emphasizes the unavoidable struggles and hardships foundational to the kingdom. The kingdom of heaven is not for the timid or faint of heart. While this speech is given to prepare His disciples for their first short-term mission trip, it foreshadows their ultimate mission for the kingdom of heaven after His ascension.
3. The "Parables Discourse" in 13:1–52 reveals the secrets of the kingdom of heaven (13:11). These parables bring either clarity or confusion to the listener. They describe the unexpected nature of the kingdom in both its messiness and unsurpassed value. Significant themes include human rejection of God's kingdom, Satan's interference, the potential for dramatic kingdom growth, the unparalleled value of the kingdom, and the separation of the righteous from sinners at the consummation of the ages.
4. Referred to as the "Discourse to the Church," the fourth speech (18:1–35) focuses heavily on forgiveness and humility in the kingdom of heaven. An unforgiving spirit, the offspring of pride and self-righteousness, is among the most challenging

roadblocks to the kingdom. This speech is connected to the "church" because it contains one of Jesus's only uses of the word "church" (ἐκκλησία) in the Bible (Matt 16:18 being the other). No other Gospel uses the word "church" (Luke, however, starts using it in the book of Acts).

5. Finally, after arriving in Jerusalem, Jesus offers His final discourse in 23:1–25:46 to prepare His disciples for the coming judgments of God. Harsh condemnations of the scribes and Pharisees, warnings about the destruction of Jerusalem, and ultimate judgment are the main topics. This speech closes with parables and warnings describing the awaited—but long-delayed—coming of the Lord.

The phrase "kingdom of heaven" (or just "kingdom") is littered throughout each of these five speeches: Matthew 5:3, 10, 19, 20; 6:10, 33; 7:21; 10:7; 13:11, 19, 24, 31, 33, 38, 41, 43, 44, 45, 47, 52; 18:1, 3, 4, 23; 23:13; 24:14; 25:1, 34. Jesus began His ministry by preaching, "Repent, for the kingdom of heaven is at hand" (Matthew 4:17). These speeches reveal the content and challenge of His kingdom message.

Obedience, Wisdom, and the Reign of God

The Sermon on the Mount concludes with a call to obedience. It is not those who say "Lord, Lord" who enter the kingdom, but those who do the will of God (Matt 7:21). The road of obedience, while narrow and difficult, leads to life (Matt 7:13–14). Wisdom and eternal life are gained by those who follow that narrow road and put the teachings of Jesus into practice. They are like the wise man who builds his house firmly on the rock (Matt 7:24–27). The wisdom gleaned from obeying Jesus fortifies us to weather all the storms of life.

According to Jesus, wisdom is not gleaned by hearing, listening, or memorizing these words. Wisdom is not attained by learning from Jesus; wisdom emerges through obedience to Jesus. It is not enough to say the right words, call Jesus "Lord," or become a Christ-centered intellectual. Instead, we must be transformed by putting His words into practice. We become participants in the reign of God by trusting and obeying the teachings of Jesus.

The first speech in Matthew concludes by focusing on the themes of life, wisdom, obedience, and the authority of Jesus (Matt 7:12–27). It is Matthew's intention for readers to remember those themes for each successive speech. For every word and action of Jesus that follows, the reader must remember His authority and obey His message. Jesus is more than the wise sage on a mountaintop; He is the King, Lawgiver, and incarnation of God who can lead us to wisdom and eternal life. The challenge of discipleship is not just to hear Him but to do what the authoritative Jesus says.

Reflection Questions

1. How does the authority of Jesus relate to His teaching? How many major speeches does Jesus give in Matthew? What is the key idea that unites these speeches? How does Matthew use these speeches to organize the book?
2. In what ways are the words of Jesus authoritative for the church today? How do we apply His teachings to our lives? How do we relate His teachings to our culture? How is Jesus's teaching connected to wisdom?

REFLECTION 13

THE KINGDOM OF HEAVEN

Kingdom of the World or Kingdom of God?

THE KINGDOM of heaven is a major theme in Matthew. There is a constant tension between the "kingdoms of the world" and the "kingdom of heaven." Satan tries to entice Jesus with "kingdoms of the world and their glory" (Matt 4:8), but Jesus has a different type of kingdom in mind. Empires of the world attempted to murder Jesus as a baby. They beheaded John. They nailed Jesus to the cross as an adult. Jesus's designation as "King of the Jews" positioned His life, from birth to death, in conflict with the kingdoms of this world.

Explicitly, Jesus charges His disciples to be different than those who rule the world's kingdoms:

> You know that the rulers of the Gentiles lord it over them, and their great ones exercise authority over them. It shall not be so among you. But whoever would be great among you must be your servant, and whoever would be first among you must be your slave, even as the Son of Man came not to be served but to serve, and to give his life a ransom for many (Matt 20:25–28).

Jesus was crowned with thorns and enthroned upon a cross. Under His rule, the first is last, and the last is first. If you desire heaven's kingdom to exhibit the power, wealth, and coercive techniques of the kingdoms of this world, you will miss Jesus. The church has done that in her history with dire consequences. If you find hope in the politics or kingdoms of this world, you may have already given Satan what he asked for (Matt 4:8–9). Jesus calls us to something different.

Kingdom of God or Kingdom of the Heavens?

So far in this reflection, we've referred to the "kingdom of heaven." If we were studying Mark, Luke, or John, we'd be talking about the "kingdom of God." But that's not Matthew's preferred vocabulary. Matthew talks about the "kingdom of heaven" or, more literally, the "heavens." Matthew is the only author to write about the kingdom of heaven, and he mentions it a whopping 32 times. So, what does he mean by it? He does not simply mean "heaven" or "going to heaven." Saying, "The kingdom of heaven is like a merchant in search of fine pearls" (Matt 13:45) is not the same as "going to heaven after you die is like a merchant in search of fine pearls." Or that the merchant is searching to go to heaven one day. Matthew speaks of "heaven" as the current dwelling of God, not the future eternal home of disciples. God is often called the "Father in heaven" (Matt 5:16, 45; 6:1, 9, 14; 7:11, 21; 10:32, 33; 16:17; 18:10, 14; 23:9, etc.) or "heavenly Father" (Matt 5:48; 6:14, 26, 32; 15:13; 18:35, etc.).

In Matthew, the kingdom of heaven is a current reality (Matt 5:3, 10). It is also "near" or "at hand" (Matt 3:2, 4:17, 10:7). There is also the hope of dining in the "kingdom of heaven" on some future day (Matt 8:11). Jesus speaks about the "kingdom of heaven" existing "from the days of John the Baptist until now" (Matt 11:12). The kingdom of heaven is experienced on earth in the past, present, and future. Clearly, something else is meant in these passages than a spiritual home after death.

As noted above, Matthew writes, "kingdom of heaven," whereas Mark, Luke, and John say, "kingdom of God." Why does Matthew make this switch? One popular suggestion is that these phrases mean the same thing, but Matthew chooses to reverently avoid the word "God," so he substitutes "heavens" as a euphemism. It's true that sometimes "heavens" is a euphemism for God, but this suggestion seems unlikely. While rare, Matthew still does use the phrase "kingdom of God" four times (Matt 12:28; 19:24; 21:31, 43); he also uses the word "God" over fifty times in other contexts. Matthew has no problem with saying "God."

Instead, Matthew says "kingdom of heaven" for theological and didactic reasons. Matthew wants us to see a contrast between the kingdom of heaven and the world's kingdoms. In short, the kingdom of heaven is what heaven is like, where the Heavenly Father dwells. God rules and reigns in heaven with supreme authority. We also want God's reign and supreme authority to envelop the earth. We want God's kingdom to spread from His heavenly dwelling to our earthly abode, which is what Jesus's kingdom mission is about.

Thus, Jesus prays, "Your kingdom come, Your will be done on earth as it is in heaven ..." (Matt 6:9–10). When God's will is "done on earth as in heaven," we glimpse the heavenly kingdom. So, the phrase "kingdom of heaven" reminds us that God's heavenly kingship is making its way to earth through Jesus. While this kingdom was breaking into the world in the days of Jesus and is still experienced today, it won't be fully realized until the age to come.

"Kingdom of heaven" language may also, like the "Son of Man" language, come from a relevant passage from Daniel 7. The book of Daniel is essential reading to appreciate what

Jesus is doing in Matthew. Ed Gallagher notes this connection when he writes,

> Remember that in Daniel 7, the kingdoms of the earth are represented as nasty beasts, and then "one like a son of man coming with the clouds of heaven" receives a kingdom from the Ancient of Days (7:13–14). The fact that the earthly kingdoms are pictured as beasts, whereas the kingdom of the Ancient of Days is handed over not to a beast but to one like a son of man, establishes a strong contrast between God's kingdom (ruled by a son of man) and earthly kingdoms (ruled by beasts).[14]

Daniel and Matthew share a similar story. The God of heaven rules a heavenly kingdom. He delivers that kingdom to the "Son of Man" while the predator beasts (earthly kingdoms), who seem to rule this world, terrorize, destroy, and attack God's world. But God's heavenly kingdom ultimately wins. It takes root on earth, ends the reign of those dreaded beasts, and welcomes "all peoples, nations, and languages" into God's presence (Dan 7:14, Matt 28:18–20). This important narrative framework stands behind many of the writings in our Bible (including the book of Revelation).

The beasts show their teeth when Herod slaughters the children of Bethlehem. The beasts devour and destroy when John the Baptist is beheaded. The terror of the beasts is fully displayed when Jesus is nailed to the cross. The beginning, middle, and end of Matthew show the beasts' true colors. But, Jesus, through love, sacrifice, and the power of God, took the full brunt of the beasts' wrath and emerged victoriously with all authority and an everlasting kingdom for all people and all nations (Matt 28:18–20).

Beware the Beast

When Jesus teaches about the kingdom of heaven, He teaches about God's heavenly reign. Jesus wants that heavenly reign to extend to His creation. So, let's think for a moment. How much anger, hatred, insult, lust, adultery, divorce, deceit, retribution, and violence does God desire in heaven? I'm thinking none. Those are inconsistent with His heavenly reign. This is the logic of the Sermon on the Mount and all the teachings of Jesus. We're participating in heaven on earth when we obey Jesus. It is incumbent upon us not to bring these earthly vices, the tools of the beast, into heaven's kingdom (Matt 5:21–48).

Jesus challenges us to live now as if we were in heaven, where our heavenly Father dwells. Through our lives and obedience to God, we are offering a glimpse of heaven to the world. God's reign should be seen in us. When this happens, we become the salt of the earth. We shine as lights in the darkness. We become a city set on a hill (Matt 5:13–16). We are to live as a foretaste of the glories God has in store.

In reality, since we are not in heaven, this will create conflict. Heaven is unwelcome by the beasts. That's why Jesus must prepare His followers for persecution, slander, and violence (Matt 5:10–12; 10:16–18, 26; 24:9–14, etc.). It's why He is nailed to the cross.

But we must never forget our allegiance is to the Lordship of Jesus and the kingdom of heaven. Christianity, when avowing its loyalty to the beasts, has harmed this kingdom-centered mission. The beasts so often turn us against each other. Unlike Jesus, the beast does not love its enemies. When we insult others, support violence, and rage against the enemies of our particular beast, we darken our radiance as God's light. We hide it under a very powerful bushel.

The beast can use politics and even moral impulses to divide us for Satan's glory. Do not let the beast, with his sly deceptions, fool you into thinking that supporting him is God's work (Rev 13:3–8, 11–17). Do not let the beast define your enemies or manipulate you into hating them. Do not let the beast blind you into believing that violence is the answer or that wealth is the solution. That is how Satan, even without incense or man-made idols, receives our praise and gains a foothold in our world.

The beasts of this world and the kingdoms they rule will never bring about the kingdom of heaven. Satan raises them to steal your loyalty. Our mission is to work for heaven's kingdom, showing the goodness of the reign of God to a dark and sinful world. Do not turn Christ's heavenly, eternal, glorious kingdom into a weapon wielded by a temporal, nationalistic political party. The beast is too small, and God is far too big.

Reflection Questions

1. How would you describe the politics of Matthew? Who is the true King? Who is the beast? How should we view the kingdoms/nations of this earth? Are there still "beasts" today? What makes a nation a beast? How should the kingdom of heaven impact our politics?
2. Why does Matthew use the phrase "kingdom of Heaven" instead of "kingdom of God"? Do those mean the same thing? How does the kingdom of heaven compare to the kingdom of David or Israel?

Endnotes

[14] Ed Gallagher, *The Sermon on the Mount: Explorations in Christian Practice* (Florence, AL: Heritage Christian University Press, 2021), 7.

REFLECTION 14

THE SERMON ON THE MOUNT: READ MATTHEW 5:1–7:29

"Up on the Mountain"

"The mountain" is a crucial setting in Matthew's Gospel (Matt 4:8; 5:1; 8:1; 14:23; 15:29; 17:1, 9; 21:1; 24:3; 26:30; 27:33; 28:16). Jesus just came down from a mountain with Satan, where He saw and rejected the kingdoms of this world (Matt 4:8–10). Now, He goes back up a mountain to show and invite humanity into the kingdom of heaven. Satan offered the kingdoms of the world while Jesus declared the kingdom of heaven.

The Jesus/Moses motif is a principal interpretive key for reading the Sermon on the Mount. Jesus going up this mountain, after the constant parallels with Moses, should bring Moses on Mount Sinai to mind. Moses went up the mountain to experience the presence of God, receive divine instruction, and teach God's Law to Israel. Moses's experiences on the mountain were so transformative that coming down, "the skin of his face shone because of his speaking with Him (God)" (Exod 34:29). His shining face was such a bizarre sight that Aaron and all the sons of Israel were afraid to come near him. Moses had to veil his face to dim the glory it revealed (Exod 34:33–35).

In Matthew 17:1–8, over 1000 years later, Moses again appears on a mountain. This time, he is talking to Jesus, but instead of Moses, it is Jesus's face that "shone like the sun" (Matt 17:2). And Jesus's clothes, from head to toe, "became white as light." The glory once on Moses's face has expanded and transferred to Jesus's whole body, and with Jesus, this glory was now unveiled.

That great cloud Moses followed in the wilderness, which rested on the mountain, also reappears in the Transfiguration (Matt 17:5). But this time, instead of calling people to Moses, the voice says to listen to Jesus, God's beloved Son (Matt 17:5). And just like the voice terrified the Israelites (Exod 20:18–21), the disciples now fall in terror at the voice of God (Matt 17:6). The mountain symbolizes that the glory and authority of Moses now belongs, in even greater proportions, to Jesus Himself.

This idea is amplified when we get to the end of the Gospel of Matthew, and Jesus again appears on the mountain. This time, after His resurrection, He is worshipped on top of the mountain by the disciples (Matt 28:17). Moses was not worshipped on the mountain. Moses encountered God on the mountain in the burning bush and in the cloud. From that burning bush, Moses was commissioned to free God's people from Egypt. On the mountain with Jesus, His disciples are commissioned to free God's people among all the nations. This image does not present Jesus as Moses but as the God who called Moses. After all, Jesus is "God with us."

The mountain reminds us of the unparalleled authority, glory, and divinity of Christ. This must guide us as we go back and read the Sermon on the Mount. In this sermon, Jesus does not receive His Law from the cloud; Jesus stands on the mountain with God's authority within Himself. Throughout this sermon, Jesus quotes words and ideas from Moses (and popular/misguided interpretations of them), but then He will set His own words alongside them (Matt 5:21–48). If you have listened to Moses, listen even more to Jesus.

On this mountain with Jesus, we are invited to an even more extraordinary Sinai moment, with a greater Moses, giving even wiser teaching. This is not to say that Jesus is supplanting or contradicting the Law of Moses (Matt 5:17), but instead that Jesus is explaining, fulfilling, and interpreting the heart of the Law of Moses to correct common misunderstandings and to frame God's Law in a new light. As Israel took the Law of Moses on Mount Sinai as the center of their obedience to God, Christians should read the Sermon on the Mount as the heart of our response to God.

Righteousness and the Kingdom of Heaven

Two key ideas of this sermon are "righteousness" (or "justice") and the "kingdom of heaven." These words are repeated throughout. We are called to practice righteousness/justice (Matt 5:6, 10, 20, 45; 6:1, 33), and when we do, we demonstrate the kingdom of heaven (Matt 5:3, 10, 19–20; 6:10, 33; 7:21). God's justice offers a glimpse of His kingdom. Our ultimate aim is to "Seek first His kingdom and His righteousness" (Matt 6:33). This sermon is how we do that.

This sermon is what a transformed society living for God's kingdom looks like. It presents the foundational ethical values (justice) of the kingdom of heaven. Certainly, we must make individual applications of it, but the sermon offers a communal way of life. Jesus describes a city on a hill, not just a bunch of individual people standing on their own hills. You will not be the light of the world individually; no single person can live this sermon perfectly, but communally, living this sermon presents a powerful witness to the kingdom of heaven on earth. As Christians, we carry the challenge of this sermon together.

If followers of Jesus commit to living this transformed life, we will become a new kind of humanity, a little taste of heaven in a world so full of hell. We will be salt and light. We will stand out like a city on a hill. That's what it means to be part of the "kingdom of heaven." This sermon shows what it means for the reign of God in heaven to invade earth.

Seeking His kingdom and righteousness must become the priority of our lives (Matt 6:33). It will be rejected by the masses (Matt 7:13–14). Even those saying, "Lord, Lord," may fail to live out these ideals (Matt 7:21–23). I mean, look at the church (and, indeed, yourself) and answer these questions:

How many of us rejoice in persecution? Have we given up anger, lust, and dishonesty? In all their forms? Do we turn the other cheek when struck? Do we genuinely love our enemies? All of them? Any of them? Can we say we give, pray, and fast without desiring acknowledgment from others? Who among us does not store up treasure on earth? Who among us does not worry about our lives? Are we truly as understanding, sympathetic, and graceful to others as we are to ourselves? Or our friends?

Living this unique, challenging, counterintuitive, and Christ-focused life, which projects God's future in this present age, extends His goodness and holy character through our actions, and demonstrates His heavenly reign and light in a world devastated by sin and darkness, is central to our mission as followers of Jesus. It is a difficult road and a narrow gate. It is a demanding call. Yet, it is the call of "righteousness."

Thus, our righteousness must surpass the scribes and Pharisees. It must show the world something different and special. Our light must shine before men to God's glory (Matt 5:16), and our communities must bear good fruit in His name (Matt 7:16–17). We are God's billboard. Our lives advertise His Kingship. We carry God's reputation, and this sermon instructs us how He wants it done.

Wisdom and Obedience

Jesus concludes this sermon not by telling His disciples to hear, learn, or memorize these words but to obey them (Matt 7:24–27). Wisdom is not attained by understanding Jesus's ethical ideals but by practicing them. Accumulation of divine knowledge is good, but Jesus wants actualization. Obedience is how we become wise and build upon a solid foundation that will hold, sustain, and protect us.

The disheartening fact we all face is that Jesus demands such an intense level of obedience that we will all be failures. If you read the Sermon on the Mount and self-righteously pat yourself on the back, you either didn't pay attention or you've never looked intently in a mirror. To know yourself is to know your failures. Those who finish this sermon feeling confident in themselves have deceived themselves.

That is not to say we have no confidence. But our confidence is not found in our righteousness or ability, but in Jesus. We're not saved by perfectly living this sermon; we're saved by the One who preached it. It is Jesus's obedience to His own sermon that led Him to the cross. If He didn't love His enemies, He wouldn't have died for them. It is in the cross that we find our confidence before God. Jesus embodied this sermon throughout His life. Jesus is the supreme and perfect interpretation of this sermon. And it cost Him His life.

The Sermon on the Mount is challenging but not devoid of grace. We absolutely must offer God obedience. There is no other way. But even at our best, it will be imperfect obedience. So, when you fall while practicing this sermon, get back up, dust yourself off, and try again. This sermon is training us. We will not get it right the first time, and we will never live it to perfection on this side of heaven.

Our obedience is critical but not central. Jesus's obedience is central. His obedience is the heart of our hope. His perfection is how we know that even if we were His enemies, He would still love us. Even though we crucified Him, He is still forgiving. Even when we fail, He does not abandon us. The self-sacrificial, painfully generous, all-consuming, indiscriminate love we are called to extend is the very love God graciously pours out on us. It's the love Jesus showed on the cross. It's the love that saves the world.

Reflection Questions

1. What is the significance of "the mountain" in Matthew? How does the mountain connect Jesus back to Moses? How does the mountain connect Jesus to God? What significant moments in Biblical history took place on mountains?
2. What is the connection between justice/righteousness and the kingdom of heaven? What are the most challenging aspects of this sermon? What are some of the benefits and costs of living this way? How important is it to obey the Sermon on the Mount?

REFLECTION 15

DISAGREEING WITH JESUS: READ MATTHEW 5:1–7:29

It's Hard to Always Agree with Jesus

I SOMETIMES DISAGREE WITH JESUS. I wish I didn't. I wish everything Jesus said made perfect sense to me. Basically, I wish He thought more like me. Occasionally, I have difficulty seeing His wisdom. For example, when I see people mourning, and I witness their pain, heartache, and tears, I don't usually think of them as blessed (Matt 5:4). Jesus says the persecuted are blessed (Matt 5:10–12), but I still wouldn't want to trade places with them. Does that mean I don't want to be blessed? Or do I disagree with Jesus about who is blessed?

When Jesus says, "Do not resist the one who is evil" (Matt 5:39), I worry about that. I hear a recipe for letting evil people run amok over this world. Shouldn't Christians stand against evil? Shouldn't we resist injustice, oppression, immorality, violence, theft, and many other terrible plagues that infect our world? Shouldn't we stop people from perpetrating those sins?

Jesus offers several examples of "not resisting an evil person," and with each one, I have a visceral reaction against it. My gut says these are not right. If someone slaps me on the face

(Matt 5:39), there is no way my automatic response is to accept it, turn the other cheek, and open myself up to another slap.

If someone sues me for my tunic (Matt 5:40), well, that'd be odd because I don't own a tunic. But in our modern lawsuit-happy world, I bet I'd be frustrated. I'd be stressed about money, lawyers, meetings, court dates, and all the rigmarole. I'd probably be mad. I certainly wouldn't want to give them more than they tried to take.

Suppose the USA was invaded, conquered, and occupied by ruthless hordes of bloodthirsty Canadians who became our national overlords, charged us unbearable taxes, stole our autonomy and freedoms, enforced unjust laws, and inflicted harsh penalties upon us. In that case, I doubt I would be a big fan of Canada. And if some Canadian soldier came to my home on a Saturday afternoon in October, during the 2nd half of a football game, and forced me to carry his luggage for a mile or be arrested (Matt 5:41), I'd be furious. But I'd probably stand up, grab his stinking bag, and walk that ridiculous mile. But I wouldn't want to carry his bag an inch farther than legally required.

Frustratingly, Jesus critiques my instinctive response in every instance. He says if someone slaps me on the cheek, turn the other to him. If someone sues me, give more than was asked. If someone forces me to go one mile, go two. In my experience, whether we admit it or not, most of us disagree with Jesus.

Bluntly, I don't like several things Jesus says in the Sermon on the Mount. I doubt this would actually work. It might be a nice, wistful, pie-in-the-sky dream that evil people, without resistance, will voluntarily cease injustice, and goodness will prevail, but our world is filled with counterexamples. Sometimes, people are treated like garbage, suffer immensely, and die without justice. Sometimes, people are abused, traumatized, and harmed, while no good comes from it. So, I'm sorry, but suggesting that we don't resist evil people feels completely wrong.

Listening to Jesus

Here comes the big question: "What should I do when I disagree with Jesus?" I have several options. #1. I could ignore Him. Many do. #2. I could diligently analyze the text and so over-contextualize and creatively interpret His words that I never have to face them. I could dilute them with my wisdom and exegetical prowess so they become nice ideas without real-world application. We're pretty smart. If we think hard enough, we can find enough differences between our 21st-century world and what Jesus said so long ago that we can read this sermon unscathed. #3. I know if I pull out a Bible concordance, I can justify myself by finding other, less radical, Bible verses that fit my preexisting worldview better: "David sure didn't turn the other cheek with Goliath, and neither will I!" That way, I can ignore Jesus and still claim to follow the Bible!

But at this point, I must stop. Though easier and well-trod, that road leads to dangerous places (Matt 7:13–14). If we're going to be followers of Jesus and call Him "Lord," we must take what He says seriously, no matter how uncomfortable. Even when we disagree. Or, perhaps, especially when we disagree.

Our comforts, instincts, gut feelings, intuitions, emotional reflexes, and natural inclinations do not equal God's will. In fact, they are probably not much different than other people. I'm a product of my culture, like everybody else. And so are you. My thoughts are not more trustworthy than Jesus's words and the kingdom of heaven is not when my will is done on earth. When we approach Jesus, we all must slow down, give up control, take a long internal look, and instead of changing Him, allow Him to change us.

There is a paragraph in Alexander Pope's famous *Essay on*

Man that I like to carry around with me. It is an important reminder about my place in this cosmos. I am not God. I'm not above God. When I judge God based on how well His words and actions correspond to my beliefs, I have placed myself above Him. I have become His judge. I have become God's god.

Pope writes:

> *Go, wiser thou! and, in thy scale of sense*
> *Weigh thy opinion against Providence;*
> *Call imperfection what thou fanciest such,*
> *Say, here he gives too little, there too much:*
> *Destroy all creatures for thy sport or gust,*
> *Yet cry, if man's unhappy, God's unjust;*
> *If man alone engross not Heav'n's high care,*
> *Alone made perfect here, immortal there:*
> *Snatch from his hand the balance and the rod,*
> *Rejudge his justice, be the God of God.*[15]

When we judge, critique, and correct the words of Jesus, we make ourselves His Lord. Now, we're good at this. And we can be nuanced with it. We don't outright say Jesus is wrong; we just strategically interpret His words so they become less jarring and a little more palatable with the result that we diminish His role in our lives.

Please don't read the Sermon on the Mount, striving to apply it in the least intrusive ways possible. Don't look for how it doesn't apply. Don't make it comfortable. Let His words be intrusive. Let them be hard. I don't know if anyone can universally apply them, but certainly don't try to minimize them. Let them create tension within you and a battle in your heart. If the Sermon on the Mount is easy, you're doing it wrong.

How to Read the Sermon on the Mount

I struggle to agree with Jesus because I want this sermon to be something it's not. I want everything Jesus says to work in the real world. I want it to be practical, rational, and helpful. Here's what I want: If I turn the other cheek, I want my enemy to be so impressed by my meekness and example of love that he amends his ways, becomes a disciple of Jesus, and the kingdom of heaven expands! The problem is that it doesn't usually happen like that. I might just get hit again. And laughed at. And he will walk away. And the world won't be any better.

But what if that's the wrong goal for the Sermon on the Mount? What if Jesus is not showing us how to change the world but how to live in it? What if He is not showing us the way the world works but the way God works? What if our job is not to make the world good but to demonstrate God's goodness in the world? What if my call is to be faithful even when the world isn't?

In their book *Resident Aliens: Life in the Christian Colony*, Stanley Hauerwas and William Willimon challenge us to read the Sermon on the Mount differently. They offer a helpful perspective:

> The basis for the ethics of the Sermon on the Mount is not what works but rather the way God is. Cheek-turning is not advocated as what works (it usually does not), but advocated because this is the way God is—God is kind to the ungrateful and the selfish. This is not a stratagem for getting what we want but the only manner of life available, now that, in Jesus, we have seen what God wants. We seek reconciliation with the neighbor, not because we feel so much better afterward, but because reconciliation is what God is doing in the world in the Christ.[16]

When we remember that Jesus's goal is not for us to change the world but for the persecuted, cruciform, upside-down kingdom of heaven to break into this world, we should not be surprised when His words make life hard. We won't see the universal conversion of the world based on our actions. Living Jesus's words might not change others, but it will change us. We may never mold our persecutors by praying for them. Our enemies may still hate us. Our offer of peace may be rejected. Like the prophets, we may be ignored or hated by the masses. Thus, we are called to carry our cross.

Only God can transform the world. At the end of the sermon, Jesus informs us that most people will not repent or obey (Matt 7:13–27). We should not expect them to. The Sermon on the Mount "works" by showing God's light in a world of darkness (Matt 4:16). Yes, some may see it and "glorify" the "Father who is in heaven" (Matt 5:16). That is a wonderful outcome. Most will reject, hate, and persecute you for it. Jesus experienced both. We rejoice either way (Matt 5:10–12).

Reflection Questions

1. Do you ever disagree with God? In what ways? How do you handle that? What does it mean if someone always finds exactly what they want when they read the Bible?
2. How does the Sermon on the Mount work? How does it teach us about the nature of God? If everyone lived this way, what would the world be like? Why don't people live this way?

Endnotes

[15]Alexander Pope, "An Essay on Man," In *The Bedford Anthology of World Literature: The Eighteenth Century, 1650–1800*. Edited by Paul Davis, Gary Harrison, David M. Johnson, Patricia Clark Smith, and John F. Crawford (Boston: Bedford, 2003), 263.

[16] Stanley Hauerwas and William Willimon, *Resident Aliens: Life in the Christian Colony,* exp. 25th-anniversary ed., Nashville: Abingdon Press, 2014), 85.

REFLECTION 16

WHO IS BLESSED?: READ MATTHEW 5:1–12

Rethinking Blessing

WHENEVER WE ENCOUNTER JESUS, we need to expect the unexpected. We should look for the first to be last, weak to be strong, and the greatest to be servants of all. Our King is the One with nowhere to lay His head. The One who washes feet. The One who is beaten, stripped naked, shamed, and crucified. Jesus calls the uncallable and blesses the unblessed. His kingdom is upside-down, backward, and inside-out. Thus, Jesus begins the Sermon on the Mount with the perfect introduction to the kingdom of heaven.

We know Jesus has been preaching, "Repent, for the kingdom of heaven is at hand" (Matt 4:17). To repent is to have a complete change of mind and direction. Our view of the world must change to see God's kingdom. In the Sermon on the Mount, we discover what this repentance entails. For Jesus, the starting point for seeing the world with a heavenly kingdom vision is to rethink who the blessed ones are.

Who would you say are the most fortunate people in the world? Imagine you've never read the Sermon on the Mount.

Don't try to come up with pious, spiritual-sounding answers. Instead, just ask yourself, who has the good life? Is it the rich and famous? The good-looking? Is it the world's greatest athletes? The most talented people? Those who travel the most? The most intelligent?

Christians have so Christianized the word "blessed" that it dulls the shocking way Jesus begins this sermon. This puts us at an interpretive disadvantage. If we read these beatitudes as a list of spiritual virtues that God will reward, we will walk away thinking it all makes sense. It's common to read these words as saying nothing more than "spiritual virtues lead to spiritual rewards" or "God blesses you if you do good things." That all seems to be in order. But it misses the point of what these beatitudes are all about.

What are the Beatitudes?

The beatitudes (from the Latin word *beatus*, meaning "blessed") are not commands to be obeyed. Instead, they are shocking statements about reality in God's kingdom. If you read the word "blessed" as "happy," "flourishing," or "fortunate," you can better see how surprising some of these statements are. Especially, "blessed are those who mourn" and "blessed are those who have been persecuted" (Matt 5:4, 10). We don't usually consider those people fortunate or flourishing. These beatitudes are often recipes for being trampled in this world.

If you want to get ahead in sports, business, or politics, these beatitudes will not help you. I'd love to say that being "poor in spirit," "merciful," and "pure in heart" will help you get the promotion you want or become the starting linebacker, but they won't. In fact, outside of the kingdom of heaven, most of these descriptions are not virtues people strive for. They are not strengths in our world.

Gentle, merciful peacemakers are, at best, not taken seriously and, at worst, are viewed with scorn as weak, timid, or spineless. Gentle, merciful peacemakers who hunger and thirst for righteousness are not usually elected president or made CEO. They may not be rich or well-known. But God sees and loves them. Scot McKnight summarizes Jesus's meaning: "A 'blessed' person is someone who, because of a heart for God, is promised and enjoys God's favor regardless of that person's status or countercultural condition."[17]

Jesus begins this sermon by singling out and drawing to Himself those weaklings who are most likely to be ignored and rejected by society. Jesus has a place for them. Their disposition is of no consequence in the world but is honored in the kingdom of heaven. Jesus has use for them. God favors them. They may not matter to the elites, but they matter to God.

A pure heart won't make you famous, but you'll see God. Gentleness may not make you money, but you'll inherit the whole earth. Hunger and thirst for righteousness may not fill your belly, but God will satisfy you. You may be poor in spirit and even be persecuted, but the kingdom of heaven is yours. You are blessed. You are fortunate. Though the world may be blind to it, you live the good life.

Structuring the Beatitudes

When comparing Matthew's and Luke's beatitudes, it is noteworthy how spiritualized Matthew's are. For example, Luke writes, "Blessed are you who are poor," while Matthew writes, "Blessed are the poor in spirit" (Luke 6:20, Matt 5:3). Luke writes, "Blessed are you who are hungry now," while Matthew writes, "Blessed are those who hunger and thirst for righteousness" (Luke 6:21, Matt 5:6). Luke focuses on material poverty and hunger for food, while Matthew emphasizes spiritual poverty and the hunger for righteousness. Both matter to God.

Luke also makes explicit what is probably implicit in Matthew. Luke records "woes" on those not included in the beatitudes. In Luke, not only are the poor and hungry blessed, but "woe to you who are rich, for you have received your reward," and "woe to you who are full now, for you shall be hungry" (Luke 6:24–26). While Matthew does not have a "woe section" in the Sermon on the Mount (Matthew records Jesus's woes in Matt 23:13–36), we can infer that the reverse of everything Jesus says is also true.

Each beatitude listed has three parts: the pronouncement of blessing, an attribute describing the blessed person, and a message of hope which explains the blessing.

The first and the last beatitudes (verses 3 and 10) describe the "poor in spirit" and those "persecuted for the sake of righteousness." These mirror each other and help frame all the beatitudes. They share the same blessing: "For theirs is the kingdom of heaven." These bookend the entire list. The people described in between them—mournful, meek, hungry and thirsty for righteousness, merciful, pure in heart, and a peacemaker—will likely be "poor in spirit" and "persecuted." The kingdom of heaven is for them all.

The phrase that begins and ends the list, "theirs is the kingdom of heaven," contains a present tense verb describing a current reality. Whereas the beatitudes in the middle (in verses 4–9) have an eschatological message of hope for the future:

- "They shall be comforted."
- "They shall inherit the earth."
- "They shall be satisfied."
- "They shall receive mercy."
- "They shall see God."
- They shall be called sons of God."

These verbs are future and passive—except for "they shall see God," which is future and middle. These beatitudes reveal that God's favor and kingdom, through the present struggle, will one day have unprecedented benefits. Their humble state will experience a radical reversal of fortune in the coming age.

Verses 11 and 12 differ a bit from the verses that come before. It's difficult to say whether verse 11 is intended as its own beatitude or if it is a further elaboration of verse 10. For one thing, it comes after the "bookend" phrase, "for theirs is the kingdom of heaven." So, it breaks the structure. It also switches from the third person, "they" and "those" (which is in every other beatitude), to the second person, "you." So, grammatically, it stands out and personalizes the conclusion of the beatitudes.

With this change, Jesus directs the message specifically to those standing before Him. He no longer talks about "they," but as He gets into His sermon, He switches to "you" (Matt 5:11–12). From here, He says, "You are the salt of the earth" and "You are the light of the world" (Matt 5:13–14). So, we ought not to think of how this sermon applies to "them" anymore; we must see how it applies to ourselves.

Reflection Questions

1. What is shocking about the beatitudes? How well do they describe you? Which ones relate to you the most? The least?
2. How would you connect the beatitudes to the life of Jesus? What moments in His life correspond to the beatitudes? How do the beatitudes prepare us for the kingdom of heaven and the rest of the Gospel of Matthew?

Endnotes

[17] Scot McKnight, *Sermon on the Mount. The Story of God Bible Commentary* (Grand Rapids: Zondervan, 2013), 35.

REFLECTION 17

THE BEATITUDES, PART 1: READ MATTHEW 5:1–12

*Blessed are **the poor in spirit:*** Who are the poor in spirit? What does it mean to be poor in spirit? This phrase is often associated with humility. I think that is basically right. Several Old Testament passages use phrases similar to "poor in spirit": 1 Samuel 1:15, Psalm 34:18, Proverbs 29:23, Ecclesiastes 7:8, and Isaiah 66:2. These can shed light on the meaning for us. While the phrase is connected to humility, it usually occurs because of humble circumstances. Some interpreters connect it back to the Hebrew word *anawim*,[18] which is translated as "humble," "poor," "needy," or "afflicted" (Ps 22:6, 25:9, 34:2, 76:9, 147:6, 149:4; Isa 11:4, 61:6; Amos 2:7; and Zeph 2:3). Consistently in the Old Testament, these people are deemed as useless and afflicted by society but are loved and cherished by God.

These people would be the opposite of "rich in spirit" or "proud in spirit" (Eccl 7:8). Boasting, arrogance, brashness, and overconfidence in one's own opinion are the antithesis of "poor in spirit." If you want to find good examples of "poor in spirit," you should definitely stay off of political discussions on Facebook and X. Those cesspools rarely demonstrate the spiritual poverty Jesus is talking about. In my estimation, one good way to interpret "poor in spirit" is to look at the rest of these beatitudes. Those people are "poor in spirit," and the kingdom of heaven is for them. Jesus Himself, introduced by Matthew as "God with us," is the perfect example of the poor in spirit.

Blessed are those who mourn: Who are these mourners, and why are they mourning? Remember, Matthew's beatitudes tend to emphasize the spiritual significance of these words (differently than Luke's). Indeed, Matthew may mean mourning the loss of a loved one. If so, "they shall be comforted" alludes to the resurrection, where death is conquered and eternal life reigns. But I wonder if the "mourning" may reference (or at least include) lamenting the spiritual condition of the world (and oneself). In this case, those who mourn the sin, evil, oppression, violence, and injustice around us and within us will be comforted in the age to come when all wrongs are made right. Jesus promises a reversal of fortune, and comfort is in the future of those who mourn now.

The book of Isaiah ends with an encouraging word for those who weep and mourn over Jerusalem (Isa 66:10–13). Isaiah records God's promise of comfort, saying, "As one whom his mother comforts, so I will comfort you; As you will be comforted in Jerusalem" (Isa 66:13). When God sees His people mourning, whatever may have caused it, He wants to comfort them. As a father, I also want to comfort my children in their sorrow. But alas, I'm always cast aside for their mother. Moms have a special way of comforting. In a message of hope, God, our Father, offers the comfort only a loving mother can provide.

Mourning, weeping, lamentation, and sorrow are all natural parts of life and essential aspects of faith. While living in a fallen world, mourning is a proclamation of truth. There is reason to mourn. There is no use hiding, stifling, or denying it. Until that final day, when God "will wipe away every tear from their eyes; and there will be no longer any death; there will no longer be any mourning, or crying, or pain ..." (Rev 21:4), mourning and grief will mingle with hope in the heart of a believer. But a day of comfort is coming.

Blessed are the meek: This blessing does not originate with Jesus. Jesus is quoting Psalm 37:11, "The meek shall inherit the land and delight themselves in abundant peace." I mentioned earlier that some associate *anawim* with "poor in spirit," but a better link would be here. *Anawim* is the Hebrew word translated as *meek* in Psalm 37:11. What does it mean to be meek? In Psalm 37, the text Jesus uses, the "meek" are tantamount to those who "cease from anger and forsake wrath" (37:8), those who "wait on the Lord" (37:9), and the "righteous" (37:16). They are described in contrast to the "evildoer" (37:1, 9) and the "wicked man" (37:10). "The wicked have drawn the sword and bent the bow to cast down the afflicted and the needy ..." (37:14). Those who use their might to oppress others are the opposite of the meek. The meek live peaceably, humbly, and patiently with God and men.

In our world, the ruthless, powerful, and violent take the land. They use their power for selfish gain, regardless of whom they trample. How did Assyria, Babylon, Persia, Greece, Rome, the beasts and kingdoms of this earth, expand their empires? It wasn't with meekness. They used fierce savagery and bloodshed to accumulate land for themselves. God promises something else in His kingdom. The earth/land is not conquered by the ruthless but is inherited by the meek. In contrast to the evildoers who will be "cut off" (Ps 37:9, 34), the meek will "dwell in the land" (Ps 37:3) and "inherit the land" (Ps 37:9, 11, 22, 29, 34). The meek and humble will rule this earth, and God will be glorified.

Blessed are those who hunger and thirst for righteousness: Sometimes, we mistakenly interpret "those who hunger and thirst for righteousness" as "those who are righteous." But those don't mean the same thing. I don't usually feel hungry or thirsty after eating a huge meal and guzzling water. I'm quite satisfied then. I hunger and thirst when I am lacking. More specifically, I hunger and thirst when I recognize my lack. This will become a central theme in Matthew's gospel, but those who believe they are righteous do not hunger and thirst for righteousness. When we see our sinful selves in an accurate light and come face to face with who we truly are, we long and strive for something better.

While internal righteousness is important, this passage also expresses an outward desire for justice. When we see injustice/unrighteousness in society and the world around us, we hunger and thirst for something better. We want to see justice roll like waters and righteousness like an everflowing stream (Amos 5:24). We want the righteous God to act and execute His will.

Those who hunger and thirst for righteousness long for the day wherein God acts as the perfect Judge. Isaiah 11 describes a God who "with righteousness He will judge the poor, and decide with fairness for the afflicted (*anav*) of the earth" (Isa 11:4). Those who hunger and thirst for God's righteousness (see Matt 6:33) can rest in the assurance that righteousness and justice will have the final say in God's glorious future.

Blessed are the merciful: Those who extend mercy to others will also receive it. A similar idea emerges right after the Lord's Prayer in the next chapter: "For if you forgive others for their transgressions, your heavenly Father will also forgive you. But if you do not forgive others, then your Father will not forgive your transgressions" (Matt 6:14–15). The extension of our mercy is rooted in the merciful character of God. Conversely, "in the way you judge, you will be judged" (Matt 7:2). If we are harsh and condemning, we can expect a harsh and condemning God. If we are merciful and forgiving, then God will give mercy and forgiveness to us. Throughout Matthew, God notes how we treat others and returns that treatment to us (Matt 18:21–35, 25:31–46).

The word "merciful," a translation of ἐλεήμονες, is used many times to describe God in the Old Testament (LXX): Exodus 22:25–27, 34:6–8, 2 Chronicles 30:9, Nehemiah 9:31, Psalm 103:8, 111:4, 116:5, 145:8, Jeremiah 31:2, Joel 2:13, Jonah 4:2. If you read those Old Testament passages, you'll see that God's mercy extends to those suffering both because of sin and poverty. You'll also notice that many of those passages borrow the language of Exodus 34:6–8, which is a pivotal description of the nature and character of God:

> The Lord, the Lord, a God merciful and gracious, slow to anger, and abounding in steadfast love and faithfulness, keeping steadfast love for thousands, forgiving iniquity and transgression and sin, but who will by no means clear the guilty, visiting the iniquity of the fathers on the children and the children's children, to the third and the fourth generation.

Those who extend mercy to others will receive mercy from a merciful God. If we know our own sinful state and recognize our need for mercy, then we better make certain to share mercy with others. I want God to be as merciful as possible to me. I need that. The whole world needs that. So, let's join God in offering and extending mercy to others. Mercy is multiplied when God reigns.

Reflection Questions

1. Can you think of times in your life that you have been poor in spirit? Mourning? Meek? Hungering and thirsting for justice? Merciful? Can you think of people you know who exhibit these qualities? What do these look like in the real world?

2. How do the beatitudes connect to the resurrection and the age to come? In what ways do they give you hope? When will mourners be comforted? How will the meek inherit the earth? Who will satisfy those hungering and thirsting for righteousness? When will the merciful receive mercy?

Endnotes

[18] Randy Harris, *Living Jesus: Doing What Jesus Says in the Sermon on the Mount* (Abilene: Leafwood Publishers, 2012), 28.

REFLECTION 18

THE BEATITUDES, PART 2: READ MATTHEW 5:1-12

Blessed are ***the pure in heart:*** We often think of the word "pure" in terms of avoiding sexual misconduct or the filth of this world. Those are good and necessary ambitions. However, the idea of "pure in heart" means a bit more than that. The pure in heart are those whose hearts are not diluted with many desires, passions, and aims that divide our loyalty or detour our pursuit of God. Those distracting passions may be sexual. But they may also be greed, pride, or revenge. The expression "pure in heart" describes a singularity of focus that leads to simplicity in life. Pure hearts are aimed towards God, and in Him, we find our value, our purpose, and our well-being (Ps 73:1, 13, 25–28). Old Testament pictures of this idea are found in Psalm 24:3–4 and David's prayer of repentance in Psalm 51:10–13.

The ultimate aim of one who is pure in heart is to be with God. This is why Jesus promises, "for they shall see God." Scot McKnight contrasts being "pure in heart" with "being pure in hands, or in observances, or in reputation (15:1–20; 23:25–28)."[19] Throughout Matthew, we'll see people who seek purity based on washings, greetings, or other externals. They wash the outside of the cup to make everything look pure, but inside, the heart is full of filth. They say long prayers in the street to look clean, but their heart reveals pride and the desire for praise. They seek the honor of men rather than God.

McKnight suggests, "The best commentary on 'pure in heart' is 6:1–18, where religious actions are done not for the praise of others but in order to engage with God, and 6:21, where the disciple is not shaped by wealth or possessions."[20] Even our "acts of righteousness" can betray an impure heart if done for accolades. When the distractions of lust, wealth, reputation, honor, and praise are abolished, and our hearts are left in the pure, singular pursuit of God, Jesus assures us we will see Him (see Exod 33:11, 20).

Blessed are the peacemakers: Peacemaking is not always a recipe for peace. It's never a recipe for comfort. Sometimes, an attempt to make peace places one in the middle of warring parties. Sometimes, those warring parties join forces against that peacemaker in the middle. Peacemaking is burdensome. Peacemaking can inadvertently become enemy-making. But even then, if we listen to Jesus, the peacemaker loves his enemies and pursues peace.

The world aims for peace in some pretty nasty ways. Nations often seek peace by eliminating enemies: "We can only have peace when we get rid of the people who are wrong." Think about the Pax Romana (Roman Peace), which lasted about 200 years, including the time of Jesus and when the New Testament was written. Rome had peace! But how? Well, they destroyed or enslaved their enemies. I don't think that's the peacemaking Jesus is going for here.

Ironically, the Colt Single Action Army was a popular pistol used in the US Army and was a staple in the old Wild West in the late 19th century. It was affectionally referred to as the "Peacemaker." If you want peace, get a gun and know how to use it. At least, that's how this world's kingdoms tend to think about it. That's how Satan may want us to view peace. But God's kingdom is quite different.

In the kingdom of heaven, we respond to a strike on the cheek by turning the other (Matt 5:39). This method of peacemaking isn't enjoyable. We are not called to be peacemakers because it is fun or easy. Or even because it will always work (Rom 12:17–18). Remember, the Sermon on the Mount won't always work. We strive for peace because God is a God of peace, and heaven is the realm of ultimate peace.

Peacemakers will be called "sons of God" because they live and act like their Father. In imitation of God, we make peace. Love your enemies and pray for your persecutors: "so that you may be called sons of your Father who is in heaven; for He causes the sun to rise on the evil and the good, and sends rain on the righteous and the unrighteous" (Matt 6:44–45). If you want a good recipe for peacemaking, keep reading the Sermon on the Mount (Matt 5:21–48).

Blessed are those who are persecuted for the sake of righteousness: Living out the divine mission of the kingdom of heaven comes with difficulty and persecution. Do not let that throw you off course. Do not quickly give up amidst persecution like the seed on the rocky soil (Matt 13:20–21). Instead, do the unthinkable and accept persecution with joy because the kingdom of heaven is yours. If you are persecuted, beaten, insulted, or libeled, "rejoice and be glad, for your reward in heaven is great; for in the same way they persecuted the prophets who were before you" (Matt 5:12).

God is watching from heaven and will reward you with far more than you lost during this persecution. In Hebrews, early Christians "accepted joyfully the seizure of your property, knowing that you have for yourselves a better possession and a lasting one" (Heb 11:34). You are also in good company when you suffer persecution. You share in the life and experiences of Jeremiah, Elijah, Zechariah, and Abel (Matt 23:34–35).

You share in the sufferings of Jesus as well. Rejoicing through suffering and persecution is a defining feature of early Christianity. Acts 5:40–42 describes the disciples "rejoicing that they had been considered worthy to suffer shame for His name." Paul writes that God has gifted us "not only to believe in Him, but also to suffer for His sake" (Phil 1:29). He links faith and suffering together as gifts from God. This is after describing his joy even while suffering in prison (Phil 1:12–18).

Peter writes,

> To the degree that you share in the sufferings of Christ, keep on rejoicing, so that also at the revelation of His glory you may rejoice with exultation. If you are reviled for the name of Christ, you are blessed, because the Spirit of glory and of God rests upon you...if anyone suffers as a Christian, he is not to be ashamed, but is to glorify God in this name (1 Pet 4:12–19).

It is common to thank God that we live in a time and place where we have freedom and can worship God openly and without fear. I hear this prayer often. It's a good prayer, and I am thankful for the same things. But remember that Jesus says to thank God when persecution, insults, and suffering come your way. In fact, thank God because of those things. Those who are persecuted, in the words of Jesus, are living the good life.

Reflection Questions

1. Can you think of times in your life when you have been pure in heart? A peacemaker? Persecuted for the sake of righteousness? Can you think of other people who exhibit these qualities or have shared these experiences? What do you appreciate about them? What do these look like in the real world?

2. In what ways do the promises associated with these beatitudes give you hope? What is beautiful about the promise to "see God"? Why are the peacemakers called "sons of God"? What reasons should we rejoice in persecution?

Endnotes

[19] McKnight, *Sermon*, 45.

[20] McKnight, *Sermon*, 45.

REFLECTION 19

ELEVATED RIGHTEOUSNESS: READ MATTHEW 5:13-20

A New Righteousness

JESUS DEMANDS a lot of His followers. He calls His people to have a righteousness that surpasses the scribes and Pharisees. The scribes and Pharisees were considered the most righteous people of the day. Yet, Jesus was unsatisfied with them. Jesus saw the need for reformation in Israel. He wanted His disciples to provide a path forward that surpassed the righteousness of the religious leaders and gained access to the reign of God.

He wanted to take those mentioned in the beatitudes, considered to be the bottom of the social and spiritual barrel, and demonstrate through them a righteousness superior to the elites. Imagine walking through the stands of an NFL football game and hand-selecting the small, the weak, the slow, the uncoordinated, the fragile, the untrained, and the inexperienced and assembling them into a football team that would beat the Super Bowl champs. That's what the Sermon on the Mount does for our walk with God.

Jesus is taking the ignored and overlooked and assembling them into a people who will become the salt of the earth, the light of the world, a city unlike any other, whose righteousness is elevated above anyone else's. He's making them a *polis* on a hill that cannot be missed. This is what Israel was always supposed to be for the world. God freed slaves in Egypt, gave them a Law, and called them to be a kingdom of priests and a light to the nations. Jesus thinks that Israel has fallen off course, and through His disciples, He plans to set things right. The scribes and Pharisees are not getting it done. This is no easy task.

One of the problems Jesus notes about the Pharisees is their insistence on outward demonstrations of righteousness while forgetting to internalize God's commands (Matt 23:25–28). Jesus wants us to be as clean on the inside of the cup as the outside. We become more righteous than the scribes and Pharisees, not with external appearances, but by internal faithfulness. Many chocolate Easter bunnies look the same, but some are hollow inside, while others are solid chocolate. Jesus doesn't want empty disciples. He wants us filled solid with His righteousness.

Jesus wants us, for instance, not only to give up the external act of murder but also, internally, to give up anger. We should step back for a moment and address the internal reasons for murder: unmitigated anger, hurtful words, and unresolved conflicts that lead to hatred. Jesus gives six examples of how internalizing God's word surpasses the righteousness of the scribes and Pharisees (Matt 5:21–48). Jesus demands an internal change of heart that produces the external change in actions (Matt 15:8–9, 15–20).

Fulfilling, Not Negating

Jesus is clear that this righteousness will not be obtained by ignoring or annulling the laws of Moses. That's not how Israel, or His reformed Israel, will accomplish God's will. Jesus is not breaking or disregarding Moses's teachings but interpreting and intensifying them. Jesus explicitly states that He does not intend to abolish the Law or the Prophets. If we think He is, we are misreading Him. (For more discussion of this idea, go back and reread Reflection #1).

Jesus fulfills the Law and Prophets by fulfilling passages about the coming Messiah. But He also fulfills the Law by teaching a fuller, more authentic way to live and apply the Law. Jesus is criticizing the manner in which His contemporaries have understood and applied Moses. Moses's Law was supposed to transform us from the inside.

Jesus wants us to see the Law and the Prophets in their fullest essence. If you only refrain from murder because the Law forbids it, well, good. I'm glad no one was murdered. However, if your heart remains embittered, vindictive, and hateful, then the Law hasn't transformed you. It only stopped your external murderous actions. The Law of Moses was meant to change hearts and actions.

This fulfillment does not occur by annulling the letters and strokes of the words in your Bible. That's the opposite of what Jesus does. Deleting what Moses said will not lead to righteousness. But neither will adherence only to the bare minimum technicalities of the Law. Complete immersion into the Law as understood, interpreted, and lived by Jesus is our pathway to righteousness that surpasses the scribes and Pharisees. It's our pathway to the kingdom of heaven.

In Matthew, Jesus fulfills the Prophets through events in His life (Matt 1:22–23; 2:15, 17, 23; 4:14), righteousness in His baptism (Matt 3:15), and the Law in His teachings and exposition of Moses (Matt 5:17–20, 21–48). None of these things negates Moses, righteousness, or the Prophets, but it does offer a new perspective on them. He is the *telos* to which the Old Testament has been pointing. His life and words bring ultimate fulfillment to all that went before.

Salt, Light, and a City on a Hill

What Jesus says is not normal. Most people don't murder, but just about everyone insults and harbors anger. Many folks don't commit adultery, but lust runs rampant. Have you seen any divorce statistics lately? Lying is a daily activity for most people. So again, for most people, violence, vengeance, and hatred of enemies are not only normal (if the situation calls for it) but are defended both personally and politically.

Do you know what is not normal? To love enemies, turn the other cheek, and always speak the truth. Being noticeably different is an essential part of this sermon. If Jesus produced the same fruit as the scribes and Pharisees, then according to His own standard, He should not be trusted (Matt 7:16–20). The fruit must be different, or His message loses its appeal. The church must travel a separate, more difficult road than the masses (Matt 7:13–14).

Jesus calls for distinguished obedience several times in this sermon:

> For if you love those who love you, what reward do you have? Do not even the tax collectors do the same? If you greet only your brothers, what more are you doing than others? Do not even the Gentiles do the same? (Matt 5:46–47).

Jesus wants us to love and greet others, pray, and view wealth differently than the Gentiles (Matt 5:47; 6:7, 32). Our fruit must be different. Our actions must contrast with the Gentiles, tax collectors, hypocrites in the synagogues and streets, scribes, and Pharisees (Matt 5:20, 46–47; 6:2, 5, 7, 16, 32, etc.).

Jesus does not want our standard of righteousness to come from culture, the wider Gentile world, or even the religious leaders of our day. He wouldn't want it coming from politically partisan ideologies, nations, or the beasts. Instead, he wants our righteousness to come from God's reign in heaven.

Our lives reflect God's image, and our reputation directly impacts Jesus's reputation. So many people only know Jesus through what they hear and see in us. Do not make Jesus look like the follower of some common way of life. His worldwide kingdom is so much more than that.

We are a city set on a hill. If our city believes and behaves like the cities around us, our King appears no different than their kings. The cities at the bottom of the hill are the darkness needing our light. They'll never see it when we hide it under the bushel of worldly attitudes or allegiances. They'll never see our city if we abandon it to join them at the bottom of the hill.

Reflection Questions

1. What does it mean to internalize the teachings of Jesus? Did Jesus abolish the Law of Moses? How did Jesus fulfill the Law? How is Jesus the key to interpreting the Law?
2. What does it mean to be salt, light, and a city? Why is it so crucial to be separate and to stand out? How do people often judge Christianity and the church?

REFLECTION 20

ANGER AND RECONCILIATION:
READ MATTHEW 5:21–26

Do Not Murder

I DON'T MEAN to brag or anything, but in my entire life, I've never murdered anyone. Not even once. It's one of the Ten Commandments I have a perfect track record of keeping. I wish Jesus would pat me on the back and say, "Job well done. Let's move on." But no, Jesus doesn't let us off that easily. Like always, He digs deeper into this commandment to find what we want to overlook. Then, He turns this simple command into a lifelong battle we must grapple with daily.

Jesus wants this commandment against murder to change us from the inside out. Not only should this commandment keep our hands from killing, but it should keep our lips from insulting. It should keep our hearts from anger. It should motivate us to seek reconciliation with our enemies as a greater priority than even worship.

Let's break down Jesus's words and see what steps we can take to apply them to our lives. Obeying the Sermon on the Mount is a journey. Hopefully, we're farther along now than we were years ago, and prayerfully, we'll be closer to the goal next year than now. But, unfortunately, there has yet to be a community of faith or a person, except for Jesus Christ, who has rested at the destination. Like an instrument that only Jesus has played perfectly, we should spend every day practicing.

So, let's start practicing what Jesus says about anger. Jesus begins with two ancient declarations: "You shall not commit murder" and "Whoever commits murder shall be liable to the court." The first statement is from the Ten Commandments, the foundational law code for ancient Israel (Exod 20:13). The second statement is not a direct quotation of any one passage from the Torah. Still, it's something no doubt people have heard and believed. It's a fact about crime and its consequences.

Scot McKnight sees this second statement as a summary of several texts in Israel's law: Numbers 35:16–34 and Deuteronomy 17:8–13; 19:1–14.[21] Murder is a crime settled in courtrooms. Being found guilty, in ancient Israel, would mean the death of the murderer. The avenger of blood usually meted out this punishment. So, in short, the ancients were told not to murder and that murder had dire consequences.

The Cause of Murder

Instead of only looking at murder and its consequences, Jesus wants us to back up and look at the root causes of murder. Shockingly, Jesus says there are consequences for the actions that lead to murder, even before the murder takes place. Or even if literal murder is never committed (like the Tom Cruise movie *Minority Report*). In Jesus's courtroom, even one innocent of physical murder can be found guilty of crimes in the heart and words from the tongue.

Jesus says anger can bring you to court (verse 22). Some translations temper these words by adding the phrase "without cause." That is super nice of them. I like that better. I mean, I can always come up with a cause. People enjoy emphasizing that part of the verse and feeling justified about their anger. However, the problem is that Jesus probably didn't say "without cause." That line is missing in our earliest manuscripts, and it's easy to figure out why scribes added it. Some Christians thought Jesus needed some nuance here. Yet, the fact remains that the Sermon on the Mount doesn't have a lot of nuance. And we must deal with that.

Our anger usually feels natural and justified because, well, anger is natural, and there are legitimate problems in this world. But does anger solve those problems? Does anger end injustice or bring about the peaceable kingdom of heaven? Does anger help us think more clearly? Does anger give us wisdom in our speech? According to Jesus's brother, "the anger of man does not achieve the righteousness of God" (Jas 1:20). Anger allows Satan to slither his way into an already escalating problem (Eph 4:27). "Outbursts of anger" are one of those "works of the flesh" that set its desire against the Spirit of God (Gal 5:16–21).

Instead of looking for ways to justify our anger, what if we tried to quench it? Anger will probably flare up from time to time in your life. When that happens, remember Jesus's words here. We are expert apologists for our wrath. We can always defend it. Don't. Add no fuel to it, and don't defend it. Let it die. Instead, respond to injustice and frustration with thoughtful action that produces good for God's kingdom.

Anger is the first step toward murder. The next step is for anger to seep out through our words (verse 22). Insults generally appear in between anger and murder. Jesus condemns two examples of insults. We shouldn't think He is providing an exhaustive list. Jesus isn't saying, "Go ahead and insult others, but don't use the word 'Raka' or 'Fool.'" These are examples of words that dehumanize or devalue another person. Remember that all humans are created in the "likeness and image of God," so insulting another person is to blaspheme the God they image. Implicit behind every word of Jesus is every individual's God-given value.

The two examples Jesus gives are "*Raka*" and "*Fool.*" *Raka* (ῥακά) translates several possible ways: "good-for-nothing," "empty head," or "idiot." It's basically saying, "You're so stupid you offer nothing of value." For this offense, Jesus says one will stand before the "supreme court" or "council," which is the Greek word συνεδρίῳ (or Sanhedrin). Anger takes you to the general court, but "*raka*" takes you to the Sanhedrin court. The last insult Jesus mentions, μωρέ, translated as "You fool," will land you in a court with authority to cast you into hell.

We should be careful not to push these court images too far. In neither our modern legal system nor ancient Israel will a person be taken to court for anger alone. You probably won't face the highest courts for calling someone an idiot. But we all will stand before God, which is the main point here. Jesus borrows imagery from their legal system to make a grander point. He moves from concern about the courts of the land to consider the eschatological courtroom on that final day. The ultimate Judge has declared not only should we avoid murdering, but crimes of anger and insult, precursors to murder, should be kept in check. Every step, from anger to insult to murder, leads to the destruction of our souls.

The Mission of Reconciliation

While it's easy not to murder, giving up anger and insults is harder. That takes a complete transformation from the inside. However, that transformation is incomplete until we actively seek the other person's good. It is one thing to avoid murder, insults, and anger; it is another to turn and positively pursue reconciliation. This turn is an essential step in the arduous journey that results in loving our enemies (Matt 5:43).

Jesus offers two examples of reconciliation. The first example demonstrates the need to prioritize brotherly reconciliation even over and above the worship of God. Like the other ethical teachings of Jesus, these actions depict the reality of the kingdom of heaven. In the coming age, we will both worship God and live in harmony. To ignore brotherly harmony and only practice worship fails to embody heaven's full ethics. So, the present kingdom of heaven on earth must integrate unity among brothers with the worship of God. God does not want divided worship among fractured people.

The God of Israel repudiates the worship of unloving, unjust, and disobedient people. Isaiah laments that God wholly rejected Israel's offerings and worship because they failed to treat one another with justice (Isa 1:10–17). God tells Israel, "Bring your worthless offerings no longer" (Isa 1:13). God does not want their worship until they make these adjustments: "Wash yourselves, make yourselves clean; remove the evil of your deeds from My sight, cease to do evil, learn to do good, seek justice, reprove the ruthless, defend the orphan, plead for the widow" (Isa 1:16–17). As long as the city behaves like a harlot, neglects justice and righteousness, commits violence, accepts bribes, and ignores orphans and widows (Isa 1:21–23), their worship is meaningless. In Amos, God refuses burnt offerings, sacrifices, songs, and assemblies until His people "Let justice roll down like waters and righteousness like an ever-flowing stream" (Amos 5:21–24).

Worship is the overflow of a life of obedience and justice. Worship does not redeem injustice; instead, injustice pollutes our worship. Jesus applies this prophetic teaching to relationships among His followers. If you have wronged somebody who now harbors anger against you, don't ignore it. Do not worship as if your relationship with God is unrelated to your relationship with your brother. We enter the house of worship through the door of reconciliation.

Further, Jesus adds that even with one not explicitly called a brother, even with your opponent at law, seek friendship. That "friendship" is best understood as harmony or an alliance rather than a new camping buddy or someone you enjoy hanging out with. However, the idea is pragmatic and beneficial. If you continue in hostility, a judge may sentence you to prison. You may end up owing more than you can pay. Do not leave your future in the hands of a judge to decide between enemies. Take matters into your own hands and settle this dispute quickly as a friend.

Reconciliation may delay worship or halt legal proceedings, which is perfectly okay with Jesus. To Jesus, reconciliation is of foremost importance. Murder, anger, and insults are roadblocks to human harmony and the peace Jesus calls us to realize. As followers of Jesus, we must remove these roadblocks and barriers to pave a smooth path with justice, peacemaking, and the pursuit of reconciliation. In that way, we must stand out as lights in this world.

Reflection Questions

1. How do you internalize the command not to murder? How should the command not to murder impact how we view others? What does it teach us about insults? What does it teach us about anger, hatred, and enmity?
2. How is Jesus's teaching practical and beneficial? How is it difficult? How important is reconciliation

and unity to God? Is there anyone with whom you are angry now? Who do you slander or insult? Who do you need to be reconciled to?

Endnotes

[21] McKnight, *Sermon*, 77.

REFLECTION 21

REDEFINING ADULTERY, PART 1:
READ MATTHEW 5:27–32

Adultery Destroys Lives

WARNINGS AGAINST ADULTERY fill the Bible. In Proverbs, a father repeatedly warns his son to avoid an adulteress and pursue "wisdom" instead. Proverbs personifies "Wisdom" and the "Adulteress" as two women who represent two paths for a young man. Wisdom leads to life, and the adulteress leads to death. Life, wisdom, knowledge, discretion, and understanding are found away "from the adulteress who flatters with her words ... for her house sinks down to death and her tracks lead to the dead" (Prov 2:10–11, 16–19). The adulteress woman appears regularly throughout the first nine chapters of Proverbs. She is alluring and increasingly tempting, yet deadly. "For the lips of an adulteress drip honey ... her feet go down to death, her steps take hold of Sheol ... keep your way far from her" (Prov 5:3–8). Consider this question: "Why should you, my son, be exhilarated with an adulteress? ... He will die for lack of instruction" (Prov 5:20–23). The father explains that God's commandments, teachings, and reproofs keep one

> from the smooth tongue of the adulteress. Do not desire her beauty in your heart, nor let her capture you with her eyelids ... whoever touches her will not go unpunished ... the one who commits adultery with a woman is lacking sense; He who would destroy himself does it" (Prov 6:23–35).

Chapter 7 contains the lengthiest description of this adulteress in Proverbs. While wisdom and understanding "keep you from an adulteress" (Prov 7:5), this woman is hard to resist. She is more pleasurable than wisdom. She kisses and entices, saying, "I have come out to meet you ... I have sprinkled my bed with myrrh, aloes and cinnamon. Come, let us drink our fill of love until morning; let us delight ourselves with caresses ..." (Prov 7:13–18). She promises that her husband is far away and will not return soon. "With her flattering lips she seduces him," however, "Her house is the way to Sheol, descending to the chambers of death" (Prov 7:21–27).

This dangerous woman appears again in Proverbs 9:13–18. She is boisterous, sitting at her doorway and calling out to those who pass by. The naive and foolish man enters, "but he does not know that the dead are there, that her guests are in the depths of Sheol" (Prov 9:18).

In our world, adultery often arises more subtly than this woman. It begins with a friendly glance and pleasant conversation. Soon, one is daydreaming, texting, and sharing private messages. You laugh together. You share frustrations. You console one another as friends. A hand is placed on the shoulder. Eye contact is prolonged. You feel a flutter in the belly. Flirting becomes common, risqué jokes are made, innocent meet-ups begin, and eventually, not-so-innocent meet-ups. Things go too far, and you swear it'll never happen again. But it does. And it goes further. Once that door opens, it is hard to close. This happens at work. This happens at church. Only after seeing your ruined marriage, the pain in your children's eyes, and your severed relationships do the foolish steps along the path become clear.

In the Law of Moses and many ancient law codes, adultery literally brought death. Not only is adultery condemned in the Ten Commandments (Exod 20:14, Deut 5:18), but other biblical law codes prescribed capital punishment for the crime: "If a man is found lying with a married woman, then both of them shall die, the man who lay with the woman, and the woman; thus you shall purge the evil from among you" (Deut 22:22).

In the Prophets, adultery was a vivid depiction of Israel's covenant unfaithfulness. The first three chapters of Hosea describe Israel's infidelity in graphic detail through the story of Hosea and his unfaithful wife. She constantly pursued other men as Israel chased other gods. Ezekiel 16 shares a similar illustration. In Jeremiah 3, after giving Israel a certificate of divorce because of her adultery (Jer 3:8), God contemplates divorcing Judah as well. Babylonian exile reminds us that covenant adultery led to banishment, destruction, and death.

Adultery through Lust

In the Bible, adultery is a grievous sin. Adultery occurs in literal and symbolic ways, but in every way, it brings about pain, severed relationships, and death (physical, spiritual, or both). However, none of those passages define "adultery" as Jesus does in Matthew 5. The Sermon on the Mount is unique here. Jesus knows the causes and results of adultery. He also knows that many can technically avoid literal adultery while still letting the sin run rampant in the heart.

Regarding the cause of adultery, Jesus knows it starts with the eyes and the hardening of the heart. Like anger leading to murder, looking at a woman with lust is a crucial step toward adultery. Rather than following that lustful path to its deadly destination, Jesus calls His disciples to avoid taking a single step in that direction. Attempts to stop adultery should not begin at night in a dimly lit room with a woman you desire. Failure is pretty much guaranteed at that point. Jesus wants us to avoid adultery by averting our gaze on day 1.

The 10 Commandments agree with Jesus. Not only is adultery condemned, but so is coveting your neighbor's wife (Exod 20:17, Deut 5:21). The word "lust" (ἐπιθυμῆσαι) in Matthew 5:28 is the same word the Septuagint uses for "covet" (ἐπιθυμήσεις) in the 10 Commandments. Jesus is unique in defining "lust" or "coveting" as adultery, but He is not unique in condemning it.

Jesus defines lust as internal adultery. Just because one hasn't yet physically acted on it, or maybe one never will be able to act upon it, the same hardening and adulterous sins are already taking place in the heart. If one covets/desires/lusts to be with another woman, regardless of success, that heart is already in the wrong place. While lust is a form of adultery that is easier to hide, it will still ruin you. It will destroy from the inside out.

Later in Matthew, Jesus teaches that foods entering a man's body cannot defile, but "out of the heart come evil thoughts, murders, adulteries, fornications, thefts, false witness, slanders. These are the things which defile the man" (Matt 15:18–20). The destructive sins we commit begin by internally harming our hearts before they reach out to ruin others.

Like anger, insult, and murder, this sin ignores God's image in another. Lust is problematic not only because it harms the heart and ruins others but also because it fundamentally denies the image of God in another person. God created every human with divine value and worth. Lust causes us to forget that. Lustful eyes see the sister on the pew, the coworker across the office, the neighbor in the yard, or the woman on the screen, not as a human with purpose, dignity, and divine worth but as an exploitable tool designed for selfish gratification. Lust turns the image of God into an object of pleasure. Lust is idolatry.

Righteous Amputation

Jesus then depicts the extremes His disciples must undertake to avoid adultery. If lust equals adultery, and adultery leads to hell, then whatever one would do to avoid hell should be done to avoid lust. Would you lose a hand to escape hell? Would you lose an eye? If so, you should be willing to lose those fundamental parts of yourself to avoid lust. It is better that you are harmed than you degrade another person. It is better for your body to be destroyed than your body and soul (Matt 10:28).

An important note: be careful whom you condemn while reading this passage. It's common to use this passage to rebuke immodesty. That's an easy way to shift responsibility to another. It's easier to condemn the object of my lust than myself. But I'm quite certain this passage does not tell a man to objectify a woman and then blame her for it, all the while claiming victim status as the innocent bystander who fell prey to her immodesty. That's nonsense. Many men act as if they are helpless and have no control. And even worse, they'll indirectly blame God for this. I've heard from Christian pulpits that "men are visual creatures." It is as if men cannot possibly control their eyes and minds when something enticing is before them.

Read that passage again. While immodesty may be an important topic, it is not the topic here. Jesus is addressing men, and He doesn't offer easy excuses for them. He condemns the eyes that lust rather than the body that is seen. Jesus denounces the heart that objectifies rather than the person who is objectified. Remember, the person you covet is the victim of your adulterous heart, not the cause. Take personal responsibility, and don't look for easy ways to shift blame to others.

Who is responsible for pornography? While it is undoubtedly a sin to create pornography, it is no worse than creating the demand for pornography. Yes, it is a sin to make pornography, but would it be created if nobody watched? Who is responsible for the success of the industry? If you watch it, then it's you. Lustful eyes created the demand.

It's easy to lust and then blame others for it. But the man of God needs to be self-controlled, taking responsibility for his eyes, heart, and internet searches. What others wear and do is beyond our control; our lust is not. So rather than yelling about someone else's shorts, start gouging out your own eyes and cutting off your own hand. At least, that's what Jesus says to do.

Now, just as calling someone "Raka" will not land you before the real Sanhedrin court, Jesus probably does not want His disciples walking around without hands and eyes. We should stand out as salt, light, and a city on a hill, not amputees. But being that salt, light, and elevated city will require sacrifice. Avoiding lust will require sacrifice.

What sacrifices will you make for the kingdom? Jesus here speaks about cutting off hands and gouging out eyes. Jesus later describes those "who made themselves eunuchs for the sake of the kingdom of heaven" (Matt 19:12). Ultimately, Jesus gave up His whole body on the cross for the kingdom's sake. What about you? Would you be the oddball who lives without a smartphone? Could you survive without the internet in your house? Could you distance yourself from a relationship that you know is impure? What cross will you carry as you follow Jesus?

Reflection Questions

1. Why would Jesus focus on internal sins like lust instead of external and more visibly harmful sins?

How is lust harmful to others? Yourself? Society? The kingdom? How is it harmful to objectify women? Why are so many quick to blame women for male lust? Why doesn't Jesus do this?

2. Is it possible to get rid of lust from your life? In what ways are Jesus's words literal, and in what ways are they metaphorical? What steps can you take to get rid of lust? Could this teaching apply equally to women?

REFLECTION 22

REDEFINING ADULTERY, PART 2:
READ MATTHEW 5:31–32

From Lust to Divorce

LUST IS the foundation of so many horrible and degrading sins. Adultery, fornication, rape, trafficking, slavery, pedophilia, harassment, divorce, and so many other painful experiences enter this world when lust germinates and grows within a person. Pornography and much of our entertainment serve as fuel to feed and nurture our passions until they become nearly impossible to control.

Pornography thrives off sexual abuse, revenge, trafficking, and dehumanization for the sake of the lust of the masses. If lust were expelled from the human heart, how many sexual crimes would exist? How many people would suffer sexual abuse? Conversely, how many marriages would endure and thrive? In the kingdom of heaven, lust, the root of so many sexual sins, finds no place. We must reject and eliminate it at all costs.

Lust is one significant reason so many marriages come to an end. It's no accident that Jesus sandwiches His words about divorce between His teachings on lust and oath-breaking. Those topics—lust, divorce, oath-breaking—are all interrelated. What Jesus says about anger (21–26) and retaliation (38–42) also impacts the discussion of marriage. Anger, lust, oath-breaking, retaliation, and hatred are all marriage destroyers. The Sermon on the Mount is not specifically a marriage guide, but obeying what Jesus says can save your relationship. What Jesus says about divorce (31–32) is uniquely structured in this sermon. Jesus discusses anger in 6 verses (21–26), lust in 4 verses (27–30), oaths in 5 verses (33–37), revenge in 5 verses (38–42), and love in 6 verses (43–48). In each of those, Jesus follows a particular pattern. He says, "You have heard" (Ἠκούσατε), and He quotes Scripture, then provides His "but I say unto you" intensification, and then concludes with radical and specific applications. Jesus does not do this with divorce.

Regarding divorce, He does not use the word Ἠκούσατε, "You have heard," which is how He introduces every other scriptural citation in this list (5:21, 27, 33, 38, 43). That word is a key indicator that Jesus is shifting subjects. He does quote Scripture (Deut 24:1) and adds His "but I say unto you" intensification, but He does not elaborate with specific application. Perhaps this explains the desire to invent elaborations on how to apply this. It's also probably why so few interpreters agree on those elaborations. Jesus's words only cover two verses. We tend to make it more complex by adding to what Jesus said.

I think Jesus discusses divorce more briefly than the other subjects because it is not a new subject. Jesus is still commenting on adultery from Exodus 20:14: "You shall not commit adultery." Rather than a new topic, what Jesus says about divorce is part of His application of the adultery text. My Bible arranges the text to place 27–30 (four verses) under the heading "Lust" and 31–32 (two verses) under the heading "Divorce." I think it makes more sense to read all 27–32 (six verses) as a two-fold application of "You shall not commit adultery." This is why the divorce passage does not contain a specific application. It is itself an application of the adultery text.

Jesus applies the adultery text to lust/covetousness and divorce. Adultery was a capital crime in the Old Testament, but lust and divorce certainly were not. These actions were never treated as equals. Nobody thought one committed adultery by lust or divorce and remarriage. I mean, divorce and remarriage is a legal way to avoid adultery. This is the practice Jesus is going to challenge.

Avoiding Adultery

While adultery is a serious crime punishable by death, people have always found ways around it. Some simply had multiple wives. That's polygamy rather than adultery. It's a convenient way to sleep with multiple women without fault. Or, if you didn't want to commit adultery and you didn't want another wife, get yourself a concubine. That's another convenient evasion. A dominant view in ancient Israel was that adultery was a "female" crime. This meant that a married man could sleep with other women, like concubines or even prostitutes, but married women were exclusively the sexual property of their husbands.

This last view is quite common. Now, a man can still potentially commit adultery, but not by sleeping with any woman other than his wife. A man commits adultery only by sleeping with someone else's wife. Adultery was stealing another man's wife/property (see Exod 20:17). Sleeping with a prostitute or a concubine didn't qualify.

In the Law of Moses, notice how adultery is defined and condemned in these passages: Leviticus 20:10–12 condemns having sex with a man's wife: your neighbor's wife, your father's wife, or your son's wife. Deuteronomy 22:22–24 condemns having sex with another man's wife or a girl betrothed to be married "because he has violated his neighbor's wife." Leave another man's wife alone!

In the passages from Proverbs (quoted in the previous reflection), the warnings against adultery were about having sex with another man's wife. That adulteress was married to someone who was out of town. After David abused his authority and stole Bathsheba from Uriah, no one rebuked David for cheating on his other wives. What about them? His sin was taking Uriah's wife. In ancient Israel, married men could sleep around without much repercussion, but not with a married woman. She belonged to someone else.

Another way for a man to sleep with multiple women was to divorce his wife and replace her with another wife. Perhaps someone he desired/coveted. Men were doing this in the days of Moses. It became so common that Moses had to regulate a small aspect of it in Deuteronomy 24:1–4. He tells men that if they divorce their wives because of some indecent thing and hand her a divorce certificate, and she marries someone else, then they are never able to take her back. Even if she gets divorced again or that second husband dies. The divorce certificate was binding, and she could freely remarry and be free of you forever.

This passage, particularly the interpretation of "some indecent thing," was hotly debated in Jesus's day. What amazes me is that the Law of Moses, which covers so many aspects of human life, law, custom, family, worship, and justice, says so remarkably little about divorce. No clear passage tells men or women if, when, or why they can divorce. We only have this law about a specific situation in which a man cannot take back a divorced wife after she remarries. Exodus 21:10–11 and Deuteronomy 22:28–29 also shed a little light on some marriage and divorce particularities, but there is surprisingly little divorce regulation in the Law of Moses. But the Deuteronomy 24 regulation was an important one.

That "certificate of divorce" was a real blessing to the divorced woman. It made the divorce official and legitimate. God gave her complete freedom and protection from her previous husband. He could not command her to return if he later changed his mind (Deut 24:1–4). He had no rights to her. She had the liberty to remarry and start a new life. It gave her a future and a family.

A Better Solution

Jesus, however, sees a problem here. It's great to have a certificate that provides freedom for a woman and ensures she can legally remarry and enter a new family and have protection and security. But that certificate is only necessary if her first husband rejects her, fails to keep his promises to her, and breaks his covenant with her and God. It's only needed if her first husband fails to love and provide for her. Rather than a law to protect the woman who had been disowned, how about a law to protect a woman from being disowned? Jesus wants to protect women, not with a certificate of divorce after they have been discarded, but with a loving, faithful, and committed husband so that they never become discarded.

Jesus teaches that a certificate of divorce, which is so often selfishly abused to satisfy the lusts of the husband, does not prevent adultery. On the contrary, giving her the certificate indicates that her husband's heart has already committed adultery. Husbands, instead of finding ways to replace and upgrade your wife, commit to your wife, love her, honor her, be faithful to her, and stand by her.

In a critique of His culture, Jesus teaches that husbands can commit adultery, and it is not limited to having sex with someone's wife. It's not just about stealing property. Husbands can commit adultery through lust even if they never touch another woman. Adultery occurs in the heart, and even if you go through all the legal paperwork, you're still making her an adulteress when you divorce her. You also cause whoever marries her to commit adultery. So, through lust, divorce, and remarriage, everyone gets caught up in adultery.

Jesus wants something different for His disciples. He wants us to be the light of the world, and one way to do that is through committed, loving, life-long marriages. Our marriage can be a testament to the unfailing love of God. Marriage is a recurring image of God's relationship with His people. Divorce among God's people destroys that beautiful image. God loves us when we are deserving and when we are not. As God does not give up on us, we should not give up on our spouses. Marriage is an opportunity to receive and dispense love, forgiveness, and grace.

Reflection Questions

1. How does lust lead to adultery? Why is divorce harmful? How have people tried to get away with adultery before? How does Jesus critique His culture? How was Deuteronomy 24:1–4 a blessing to women?
2. How is marriage a blessing? How does society benefit from committed, loving marriages? What can be done to strengthen and support marriages? What kindness can you offer to your spouse today?

REFLECTION 23

REDEFINING ADULTERY, PART 3: READ MATTHEW 5:31–32, 19:1–12

Divorce in the Gospels

JESUS'S INTERPRETATION of Deuteronomy 24 is developed further in Matthew 19. Matthew 5:32 doesn't actually say it's wrong to divorce your wife. Read Matthew 5:31–32 and notice that the man who divorced his wife is not called an adulterer. Or a sinner. There is no critique of him at all. In these verses, only the divorced wife and the man who marries a divorced woman are adulterers. However, in Matthew 5:28, Jesus says that lust, which seemingly starts the whole process, is where one finds the husband's adultery.

In Matthew 19, Jesus more explicitly pulls the rug out from under the husband, and we find out that not only can he commit adultery, and not only does it happen through lust, but even a legal divorce will not absolve him of it. His adultery started with his lust, progressed through his divorce, and culminated in his remarriage (Matt 19:9).

This teaching of Jesus is also in Mark and Luke. But, fascinatingly, Matthew 5:32 and 19:9 add a critical little phrase to this discussion about divorce that is missing in those other Gospels. It is commonly called the "exception clause." Without this phrase, every divorce and remarriage is considered adultery. With this phrase, only divorce and remarriage, "except for fornication," is considered adultery. This vital clause is absent in Mark 10:11–12 and Luke 16:18. Consider how significant it is to either add or omit those words. A doctrine so divisive that many churches have fought, condemned, and split over exactly how to teach it isn't even taught the same way among the Gospels!

If we only read Mark and Luke, we'd have no idea they were not exhaustive or comprehensive in their dealings with divorce. The most natural reading would leave us thinking there were no exceptions. They present unconditional prohibitions of divorce. After reading Matthew, however, we realize that Mark and Luke do not offer a complete theology on divorce and remarriage. It at least makes us wonder how complete Matthew's presentation is.

We know for a fact that Jesus does not address every question concerning divorce. Paul ran into a complicated situation regarding divorce that Jesus had not addressed (1 Cor 7:12). Jesus spoke to a Jewish audience before Pentecost and didn't address the potential problems that would arise once the gospel reached Gentile cities. Some people accepted the gospel, some rejected it, and sometimes those people were married. Jesus engaged in an intra-Jewish debate about Deuteronomy 24. Paul's issues in Gentile Corinth were quite removed from that debate. As Paul addressed circumstances surrounding mixed-faith marriages, he stated that his teaching comes from himself, "not the Lord" (1 Cor 7:12). Jesus didn't address it, but Paul needed to.

Comparing these divorce passages within the synoptic Gospels is illuminating. Go ahead and do that: Matthew 5:32 and 19:9; Mark 10:11–12; Luke 16:18. Matthew adds an exception for fornication, which is missing in Mark and Luke. Mark adds a sentence addressing the possibility of a woman divorcing her husband, which isn't in Matthew or Luke. Mark, also unlike Matthew and Luke, never says a man commits adultery by marrying a divorced woman. Luke never mentions that a divorced woman is an adulteress. In a shocking reversal of norms, Luke only explicitly ascribes adultery to men. Carefully comparing the texts reveals quite a few differences. Try it!

Teaching with Humility

What is going on here? Why does each Gospel writer present Jesus's teaching differently? If Jesus didn't mention an exception for fornication, why would Matthew say He did? Conversely, if Jesus did note the exception, why on earth would Mark and Luke omit an essential part of this doctrine? Couldn't it destroy lives and souls if people get this wrong? Presenting partial truth on this issue gets a preacher fired, but each gospel writer only presents partial truth. And still, Paul finds himself with issues bubbling up that Jesus did not address.

How do we get to the bottom of all this? Remember, of the 613 laws in the Torah, none of them address when or how to get divorced. None explicitly forbids divorce (except in the instance of Deut 22:28–29). That is a shocking lack of divine instruction on what feels like a hugely important topic. Questions of exact right and wrong regarding divorce are not new. They have always existed, and I won't be able to answer them now.

If we comb through the New Testament, adding all the bits and pieces from each text and gluing them together like a collage, will one fully comprehensive teaching emerge? Is that how we answer every question? Maybe. But please approach this topic with utmost humility. Be careful. Unanswered questions will emerge. Don't force answers. Please do not harass the text into saying more than it does. Don't destroy lives because of what you "think" a passage "might" imply. Beware when you have left Jesus's words and are presenting your deductions about the possible implications of those words. At least recognize that, while these biblical teachings are true, none offer a fully comprehensive theology. And perhaps you might not either. Much like Paul had to do, the Gospel writers present the teachings as needed for their audience. Perhaps the community to which Matthew wrote struggled with moving forward after a man divorced his wife because of fornication. If they only had Mark, that man would be an adulterer. So, Matthew adapts and clarifies Jesus's teaching for his audience. Perhaps Mark was written in an area like Rome, where women could initiate divorce, and so adapted Jesus's teaching to the needs of his audience. The Holy Spirit inspired each of the words written in these passages. If adaptation took place, it would be Spirit-inspired and God-approved.

That process leaves us with quite a few questions. Are there ever any other possible exceptions? The texts do not say. How does one repent if they have already committed this sin? The texts do not say. Does it matter if one spouse is a believer and another is not? That's the question Paul had to answer, which Jesus didn't address. I worry when we provide over-confident answers to these questions, add to what Jesus said, condemn anyone who disagrees, and split churches if there isn't uniformity.

Leading up to this passage, Jesus says that if you get angry or insult someone, you go to court. One who lusts should cut off hands and gouge out eyes. Most Christians do not do these things even though Jesus explicitly states them. They are (rightly) interpreted hyperbolically. If we're honest, as a whole, we're not great at applying this sermon. Most won't turn the other cheek and accept a second slap. Most won't give freely to a person suing them. Tragically, most don't genuinely love their enemies. Instead, we find convenient evasions and interpretations to comfortably ignore these teachings of Jesus.

Yet, regarding divorce, some Christians do the opposite.

They add consequences to Jesus's teachings that did not originate with Him. The Sermon on the Mount is hard enough without that. Don't create unstated repercussions and then bind them on people, all while refusing baptism, expelling from the church, and splitting the body of Christ over them. Don't condemn as false teachers any who hesitate to follow suit. As a humble word of caution, that's not a biblical or consistent way forward.

Taking Jesus Seriously

To take Jesus seriously, we must firmly commit to our marriages. To divorce your spouse and marry someone else is adultery. That comes from Jesus. To even lust for someone else is adultery in the heart. We must commit to a higher righteousness than that. The world around us pursues every form of lust. They fall in and out of love, divorce, get married again, try to find happiness, and if they cannot, they start the whole process over. It should not be that way among us.

Marriage is a life-long covenant that we ought not to break. Again, this goes back to the image of God in each person. When you pledge the rest of your life to a person created in God's image, remember that their purpose, meaning, and value are not defined by how well they please you. Your spouse is not an object created to make your life better.

If your car isn't working and you can afford a new one, fine, get another one. Your spouse is not a car, though. Some people forget this, but a spouse is far more valuable than a car. Don't ignore that "check engine" light in your marriage. Pour your time, money, effort, and energy into your relationship. Get tune-ups and pay attention to maintenance. Pray, hold hands, talk, make time for each other, go on dates, laugh, discuss the Bible, dream about the future, weep together, hug and kiss and make love, go to counseling, talk to mentors, eat together, go to bed together, read books or watch shows together, worship together, and value your spouse as a human with eternal worth.

God created your spouse on purpose. God joined your marriage intentionally. Do not let anger, lust, or selfishness get in the way. Do not let a "certificate of divorce" hold more authority than the word of God, which joined you together in the first place. Do not tear apart what God joined together. Honor your vows with integrity, cleanse your heart with purity, and protect your marriage with tenacity.

To take Jesus's words seriously, churches should offer as many resources as possible to conquer lust and protect marriages. Confession, accountability, biblical teaching, and counseling must be part of the church's mission. Build relationships and don't let marriages suffer in isolation.

The church must also begin to view adult celibacy more positively. As Jesus and Paul did, committing oneself to celibacy for the kingdom's sake is a realistic option that can bless the kingdom. Not everyone has to be married. Celibacy isn't just for Catholic priests. Churches should prioritize creating room in their fellowship for such Christians. We should look for ways to minister, create fellowship, and give meaningful ministry responsibilities to those who are unmarried and even divorced. Unmarried Christians are valuable assets to the kingdom (1 Cor 7:8, 11, 32–35).

In the ethics of the kingdom, if lust is the problem, a concubine won't solve it. Likewise, taking multiple wives isn't the solution. Even divorce and remarriage, which is legal and seems culturally defensible, fail to honor and obey the call of Jesus. The solution is to stop the lust. The solution is self-control. The solution is grace. The solution is selfless love. The solution is to honor your marriage and remain committed to your spouse.

Reflection Questions

1. Why does the Bible teach about divorce and remarriage differently in every passage about it? What are the benefits of this multifaceted approach? Why is this an issue so few people agree on?
2. How can the church support those impacted by divorce? How can we honor Christ's teachings? How can we be more united on this difficult issue? Does the Bible answer every question regarding divorce and remarriage? What do we know with certainty regarding this topic in the Bible? In what areas are we doing guesswork?

REFLECTION 24

INTEGRITY AND TRUTH: READ MATTHEW 5:33–37

The Folly of Oaths

JESUS'S WORDS about divorce set the perfect introduction to His words about oaths. Marriage is a vow you should keep before the Lord. Marriage is a life-long promise of faithfulness and commitment to another person through good and bad. The words we speak on our wedding day matter. We should keep that oath. But, as Jesus says, you should keep all the words from your mouth, even without a vow or an oath.

Why do we feel the need to make oaths? Why must we make a big, fancy, wordy promise to our spouse in front of witnesses on the wedding day? Why do we place our hand on a Bible and say, "I swear to tell the truth, the whole truth, and nothing but the truth, so help me, God"? Why does the President take that "Oath of Office," saying,

> I do solemnly swear (or affirm) that I will faithfully execute the Office of President of the United States, and will to the best of my ability, preserve, protect and defend the Constitution of the United States?

Is lying good and acceptable so long as an official oath is not taken? Of course not. So why make the oath? What does it accomplish? The purpose of oaths is to add credibility to our words. But why do our words need extra credibility? If lying wasn't a problem, we wouldn't need oaths.

Oaths commit us to be serious about truth, but they are beneficial only if we are not already serious about truth. In a community of lies, oaths serve a necessary purpose. But in the community of Jesus, where lying finds no home, oaths are useless. If you're 100% honest without an oath, then an oath has nothing to add. Therefore, oaths don't exist in heaven because every word spoken is true. This is how it should be among God's people on earth. If we remember that all people are created in God's image, we should speak to them with honesty, integrity, and respect. This leads to an interesting question in my mind. I totally get saying, "Be honest. Truth makes oaths unnecessary." But Jesus takes it further than that. Jesus says, "Do not take an oath at all," and anything beyond "yes" and "no" is "of evil." That final phrase could be translated as "of evil," "from evil," or "of/from the evil one." That is much stronger than simply saying they are unnecessary. Why are oaths evil? Well, let's think about it.

The logic of an oath invites evil. It sets us up for failure because an oath is just words. It is the addition of more words to a statement. But if we do not keep our words, how will adding more words help? If our words carry no weight or truth, adding more words won't help. If you refuse to dig, having two shovels is no better than one. If you don't mean your "Yes" or "No," adding a "But I swear!" won't make them true. Jesus wants us to demonstrate our truthfulness through actions that vindicate our words. Satan wants us to add more words. Oaths are a shortcut to artificial credibility. Disciples are called to take that long, slow journey of building credibility with steadfast truthfulness day after day. Jesus wants our integrity and actions to prove the credibility of our words. More words won't do it. Would two oaths be more convincing than one? What about five? Or twenty? Where does it end? At what point must one tell the truth? If one word isn't trustworthy, 500 more won't help. Credibility comes from a reputation of honesty, sincerity, integrity, and truthfulness.

The Misuse of Oaths

The evil one likes oaths because they encourage varying levels of honesty. However, absolute honesty makes an oath useless. Adding oaths manipulates the listener. Oaths serve to increase someone's trust and confidence by mere talk. This has often been used strategically to smuggle in dishonesty.

This manipulation was happening in Jesus's day. Consider His words later in Matthew:

> "Woe to you, blind guides, who say, 'Whoever swears by the temple, that is nothing; but whoever swears by the gold of the temple is obligated'... And, 'Whoever swears by the altar, that is nothing, but whoever swears by the offering on it, he is obligated'" (Matt 23:16–22).

Some used oaths as gimmicks to make promises, manipulate trust, and garner credibility but then found some irrational technicality that absolved them of their obligation.

Oaths are unnecessary at best and fodder for manipulation and dishonesty at worst. As you read through Matthew, you'll find several oaths offered, none of which are pleasing to God. Herod executed John the Baptist with an oath (Matt 14:7–10). The scribes and Pharisees deceived the people with rules about oaths (Matt 23:16–22). Peter denied Jesus with an oath (Matt 26:72–75). It's no wonder they come from the evil one.

The evil one also likes oaths because they lack humility.

They exaggerate the potential of human knowledge and ability. This is the point on which Jesus elaborates. Jesus gives examples of oaths that claim human control over God's business. There are few things I can know for sure, and there is little about the future I can control. Oaths convey certainty about things they should not (Jas 4:13–17).

It is far wiser to add qualifiers and exceptions to our words than oaths. We should recognize that our words might be wrong rather than employing oaths to guarantee correctness. It is better to say, "Yes, if the Lord wills, I will do my best to help you tomorrow," than "By heaven and earth and all that lies therein, I give you my oath and solemn pledge that I will be there to help you tomorrow." Why? Because flat tires happen. Storms happen. Illness happens. Death happens. Satan likes us to think we are in control.

Oaths add no power to your words but risk making you look foolish and deceptive. Even with an oath, you cannot control the future. Your words cannot even change the color of your hair (36). So, to the disciples of Jesus, oaths serve no practical or beneficial function, and they give Satan opportunities to destroy our integrity. So, let's leave oaths to him.

Consistency in Application

Jesus concludes by saying, "But let your statement be 'Yes, yes' or 'No, no'; anything beyond these is from the evil one" (Matt 6:37). Again, that's a radical application. I know oaths lack humility and can be used for manipulation, but can we really not say anything beyond "Yes" or "No"? I know of Christians who cannot in good conscience "swear to tell the truth" in a court of law. But what Jesus says goes even beyond that. This was repeated by His brother in James 5:12.

Perhaps this is another example of Jesus giving a hyperbolic extreme. Each statement of this sermon leaves us with hard questions. Do you really get taken to court for anger and saying, "Raca!"? Should we, in actuality, cut off limbs and gouge out eyes to avoid lust? Does divorcing a woman truly make her an adulteress? Is anything beyond "yes" or "no" literally "from the evil one" or "of evil"?

Be careful how you answer these questions. This is, admittedly, an interpretive struggle. We want to take Jesus seriously, but we don't want to bind as literal, what He obviously intends hyperbolically. We also don't want to say, "Ah, Jesus didn't mean it," and ignore His teaching. Hyperbole doesn't mean "not true." It may be an exaggerated truth, but it's not a falsehood. It is a valuable teaching strategy that we would be unwise to ignore.

We do not want to be guilty of picking and choosing which teachings to take seriously and which instructions to ignore. We must avoid interpreting Jesus based on our strengths, weaknesses, and situations in life. If we stop taking Jesus seriously about divorce when we want a divorce, we have become hypocrites. If we condemn and excommunicate divorced people but practice patience and grace and counseling for those who lust—or, more commonly, we do nothing, remain silent, and ignore the problem—we have also run into the issue of hypocrisy. If we approve of anger and insults aimed at our political enemies but reject anger and insults when hurled at us, again, we have stepped into hypocrisy.

I write all that because, in my experience, we apply some of what Jesus says with extreme strictness and rigidity, but other things Jesus says, we don't really know what to do with, so we do nothing. What Jesus says about oaths tends to fall into that second category. Christian speech concerning oaths and adding words to "yes" and "no" does not sound markedly different than the world. Everyone agrees we should be honest, but we still try to bolster that honesty with oaths and promises.

So, what should we do with this text? Like every passage in

this sermon, we should apply it. We should not so limit the scope of Jesus's teaching that we are unimpacted. Instead, we should try to transform our lives into conformity with His teachings in every way possible. Don't search for hyperbole to be evaded or metaphor to be ignored. Instead, search your heart for repentance and Jesus's words for guidance. Look for as many possible ways to obey rather than as few.

Rather than asking if Jesus is being hyperbolic or literal, we should ask ourselves whether we make promises about the future beyond our control. Do we lack humility when we speak? Do we add promises/oaths/vows/affirmations to manipulate others into believing us? Do I exaggerate the truth to impress people? Do I use deceptive strategies to hide the truth? Do I deceive people while convincing myself that I *technically* didn't lie? Does my life reflect trustworthiness and integrity? Will I sacrifice my desire or willingly accept punishment to keep my word? How dependable is my "yes"? How trustworthy is my "no"? What is the cost of my integrity? Will I lie if the burden is heavy enough? Will I lie to make my life easier? Will I tell the truth even if it embarrasses me? Will I speak the truth even if it harms me? Should people trust me? How can I become more honest than I am now? Would my neighbor trust me without an oath? How can I take fewer oaths? Can I live in such a way that I never again make an oath?

Reflection Questions

1. Why do oaths exist? What does the existence of oaths tell you about human nature? How can oaths be manipulative?? How can oaths be deceptive? Why is it better not to give oaths? Are any oaths acceptable?

2. Why is truth so important? How does "Truth" relate to God? What does honesty do for our relationships? How can we prove our integrity without oaths?

REFLECTION 25

"AN EYE FOR AN EYE": READ MATTHEW 5:38–48

Lex Talionis and the Human Condition

IN THIS NEXT SECTION, Jesus wants us to rethink the meaning of "An eye for an eye and a tooth for a tooth" (Exod 21:24, Lev 24:20, Deut 19:21). This idea of returning an equal amount of evil for evil is called *Lex Talionis,* and it's responsible for a tremendous amount of good in our world. It is accepted as a moral imperative by many governments and individuals. It is why you don't get locked away in prison for driving 7 miles an hour over the speed limit or get the death penalty for shoplifting. It rejects overzealous punishments for minor infractions. It rejects "cruel and unusual punishment." *Lex Talionis* keeps things just and fair. Even the rights of the perpetrator are remembered and honored.

It is a method of refusing to escalate a dangerous situation. It limits retaliation and justly structures retribution. If you knock out my eye, I will not knock out both of yours. We are limited to one eye for one eye. If you drop a bomb on us, we will not drop a thousand bombs on you. *Lex Talionis* requires the exercise of self-control and a commitment to repay evil in a measure no greater than what has been received. It curbs the natural human desire for disproportional vengeance.

While this wise and helpful practice moves people and societies in a better direction, Jesus doesn't embrace it. Instead, He calls His followers to something more drastic. Jesus does not say to carefully return only an equal and just amount of vengeance; He says to give up vengeance altogether. Jesus knows something about humanity. Something we like to ignore or pretend isn't true. Even when we try to practice *Lex Talionis* and limit our revenge to a just and proportional response, we tend to conceive just and proportional responses quite poorly. Wrongs inflicted on me always feel more severe than the wrongs I lay on you. Humans are not good at calculating revenge.

A Study of Escalation

The natural human tendency is toward escalation. In a creative study cleverly entitled "Two Eyes for an Eye: The Neuroscience of Force Escalation," a team of scientists performed an experiment that demonstrated "escalation is a natural by-product of neural processing."[22] Apparently, our brains are wired to seek revenge with compounding interest.

The experiment went something like this: twelve individual participants were grouped into six pairs. Everyone placed their left index finger into a fitted mold and their right index finger on a lever. Pushing the lever with one's right index finger would apply a corresponding amount of force to the left index finger of one's partner: the harder you push, the more pressure your partner receives. The participants were told to take turns pushing the lever so they would each receive and then apply pressure.

Now, this is where the experiment gets interesting. Unbeknownst to the partner, each participant was told to match the force felt on their finger when they pushed the lever. They were supposed to apply the exact equal amount of pressure they received. Theoretically, if both participants did this, a stable and equal level of force should be maintained throughout the experiment.

As you can imagine, a stable and equal level of force was not maintained. And it certainly did not decrease. Every time, the participants perceived feeling more pressure than they gave. Then, to "match" the pressure they felt, they would increase the pressure they gave. Feeling the pressure increase, their partner would also increase the pressure to "match" what they perceived. This cycle continued with each push of the lever, and the force increased for every team in the experiment.

The study notes, "In all cases, the forces escalated rapidly ... force escalation occurs rapidly even under instructions designed to achieve parity."[23] Even when the participants intentionally tried to match each other, they all, without realizing it, failed to do so. For all six pairs, each with over eight reciprocating turns, the pressure increased by an average force of 38% on each turn. *Lex Talionis* didn't work.

I'm sure that was a fun study to conduct. But the fun disappears when this human tendency plays out beyond the lab and in the real world. We underestimate how much force we give to others and overestimate how much we receive. Maybe it's obvious once you think about it, but we feel the pain we receive more acutely than the pain we cause. We can only assume what the pain of others feels like, but we intimately know the pain we feel. And we're pretty sure ours is worse.

Despite our best efforts, we stink at making things equal. That's true even when equality is our goal and no hatred or animosity exists. Once bad memories, hurt feelings, hate, anger, and rage are added to the situation, equality is thrown out the window, and revenge by any means necessary becomes the goal. This revenge does not exist to establish justice but to alleviate pain by inflicting it on others. This is the natural human tendency; it's why *lex talionis* so often fails, and it's what Jesus seeks to root out of our lives.

Living out His Truth

Jesus cuts through the theories of retributive justice to the one ideal that will ultimately let evil die. This idea led Jesus to the cross rather than the battlefield. Jesus tells us to completely give up revenge. He even says not to resist an evil person.

What in the world does it mean to not resist the evil person? What exactly counts as "resistance"? Does He mean all resistance is wrong? In any form? Or just lethal resistance? Or violent resistance? What about verbal resistance? Or financial resistance? Or peaceful resistance? Are there exceptions?

Also, what counts as "evil"? And who is this evil person? Is this only about personal relationships? Or does it apply to foreign evil? What about Hitler!? Do political enemies count? Is this teaching only for individual disciples? What about churches? Can churches have armed Christians who shoot and kill evil people? What about governments? Or nations? What if a Christian is in the government? Or the police? Or the military? Does he still have to live by this? Can he resist evil people? Can he kill his enemies? Can you love the person you are trying to kill? Can you kill to protect and defend others?

There are more intelligent people than me to answer those questions. But don't think those answers are easy or obvious. Don't assume your feelings are automatically right. Jesus is specifically correcting human intuitions and feelings. Are there exceptions? Maybe. I won't deny they probably exist. But my purpose in these reflections is not to focus on the possible exceptions. I think we do that enough. I want to see if we can focus on His words. It bothers me how often Christians teach the Sermon on the Mount just to explain away the Sermon on the Mount. Let's at least consider what it would be like to live it out. If you catch yourself thinking, "Oh, whew! The sermon doesn't apply here; I can do what I want," you're probably in dangerous territory.

Jesus helps us by following this statement with four examples of what "not resisting" means. These examples include violence, unlawful litigation, military oppression, and undeserved generosity. The problem is that His examples don't make it easier on us. Jesus gives a wide range of applications, from personal relationships to foreign enemies, and they each call us to resist using violence, and to submit, suffer, and sacrifice for others. There is no easy way to honestly obey these words. Obeying them would transform us.

Jesus mentions being slapped in the face, unjustly taken to court, forced by soldiers to march one mile, and giving to anyone who asks you. In response, we do not resist. In fact, we give even more than they took. Do we ever really think this way? These applications feel impossibly hard and unreasonable. But later in Matthew, Jesus does every one of them.

Jesus was slapped in the face (Matt 26:67) and was wrongfully taken to court (Matt 26:57–66). His clothes were even taken from Him (Matt 27:35). Jesus was forced by Roman soldiers to march to his own death (Matt 27:31). It's not an accident that Matthew records these events leading to the crucifixion. They each correspond to the words He spoke in this sermon. They each show His obedience.

Jesus did not resist evil, but He did overcome it. Through the cross, Jesus took the evil that was hurled at Him, and He swallowed it up in His death and emerged victorious over it in His resurrection. I like the words of Ed Gallagher in commenting on this passage. He writes, "We cannot achieve victory over evil except through the cross. The question should be not how we can resist this evil, but how we can overcome it, and the only way is through the cross."[24] We must pick up our crosses to follow after Jesus.

Jesus explicitly suffers through each example of evil, although He could have destroyed His enemies and saved Himself: "Do you think that I cannot appeal to My Father, and He will at once put at My disposal more than twelve legions of angels?" (Matt 26:53) The sermon's examples of non-retaliation correspond to the experiences Jesus faithfully endured. Jesus was no doubt capable and strong enough to resist His enemies. But it is not a matter of strength to fight evil, but faithfulness to overcome it.

Rather than repaying equally all those who rejected, betrayed, and crucified Him, Jesus took their evil, and all our evil, into Himself and let it die with Him. He acted in pursuit of redemption and salvation as an example for us to follow in our own suffering:

> When he was reviled, he did not revile in return; when he suffered, he did not threaten, but continued entrusting himself to him who judges justly. He himself bore our sins in his body on the tree, that we might die to sin and live to righteousness. By his wounds you have been healed" (1 Pet 2:23–24).

Jesus does not provide a recipe for an easy or happy life—although releasing the need for retaliation is a pathway to peace. He does not offer a foolproof method of bringing about repentance in others—although that certainly can and has happened. Many will continue to inflict suffering without remorse, and evil will remain (Matt 13:30). Instead, Jesus provides the challenge to cease being a source of that evil. He wants us to have no share in it. He challenges us to imitate the mercy of God rather than the evil of humanity. Jesus challenges us to let evil die.

Reflection Questions

1. What are the benefits of *Lex Talionis*? Why does it often go wrong? What does Jesus tell us to do instead? How does the cross embody this teaching of Jesus?
2. Why do we try to limit the application of Jesus's teachings? What would happen if Christians applied this to all areas of life? Is that possible? Is that wise?

Endnotes

[22] Sukhwinder S. Shergill, Paul M. Mays, Chris D. Frith, Daniel M. Wolpert, "Two Eyes for an Eye: The Neuroscience of Force Escalation," *Science* 301 [5630]: (2003): 187.

[23] Shergill, "Two Eyes for an Eye," 187.

[24] Gallagher, *Sermon on the Mount*, 84.

REFLECTION 26

GIVING UP VENGEANCE: READ MATTHEW 5:38–48

Does Retaliation Really Work?

HUMANS LIKE TO RETALIATE, and we often feel justified in doing so. Plus, we usually want the retaliation to be even more devastating than the initial wrong. Our rationale often goes like this: "If you harm me, I am morally justified in harming you even more severely. First of all, your harm was unprovoked, which makes it worse. So, your punishment should be harsher. Second, by responding more severely, I am teaching you a valuable lesson to never harm anyone again. Third, it will make me feel good and bring me closure." It is for justice that we seek revenge.

The problem with this thinking is that escalation generally leads to escalation. "If you knock out my eye, I'll knock out both of yours. That way, you'll never harm me again." But that's not how it works in the real world. What happens is the person you harm in retaliation comes back and retaliates even more severely. You'll lose another eye and your teeth and maybe receive a few broken ribs for good measure. Then, you get a group of friends to help you attack in response. Then, your enemy gets a group of friends. Hatred leads to an insult, which leads to violence, which leads to death. This isn't a rare story.

If retaliation really worked, then why hasn't it worked? We've been doing it for a long time. If violence and revenge brought peace, where is the peace? God knows we've tried this approach. Violence and retaliation have been humanity's standard approach throughout history. We've gotten really good at it.

We have majored in escalating violence in personal relationships and on a global scale. We've taken vengeance and bloodshed to cataclysmic levels. We can build bombs. In a flash, we can eviscerate cities and kill hundreds of thousands of men, women, and children. In fact, we have. We can make this world unlivable. So, obviously, with this much power, violence, and fear, we should have peace now, right? Since the threat of violence, warfare, and death constantly hangs over our heads, everyone acts kind, peaceably, and Christ-like, right?

When we doubt or evade the wisdom of Jesus out of fear it won't work, let's remember two things. First, this sermon is not about what works. It's about demonstrating the righteousness of God. It's about the inbreaking of the kingdom of heaven on earth. It's about living as light, salt, and a city on a hill, even if the only result is rejection and persecution. It's a call to live differently so that God's holiness can be seen and experienced amid chaos. Second, revenge and violence have certainly not worked any better!

Giving Jesus a Fair Try

Maybe Jesus isn't quite as foolish as He seems. Maybe Jesus isn't the One whose head is filled with unrealistic fantasies of the power of love. Perhaps we're the ones drunk on misconceptions of the power of retaliation. Maybe thinking that violence is superior to love in bringing peace doesn't make much sense.

Jesus's words have scarcely been practiced on a wide scale. We catch glimpses of it here and there. The first few hundred years of Christianity may supply our best case study of practicing these ideals. Year after year, though many Christians suffered, Jesus's message spread throughout the Roman Empire. It made a world-transforming impact. Maybe there is something to it.

Incredible good can be accomplished by taking Jesus's words about nonretaliation seriously. However, we can only live this way if we adopt the following challenge: "Love your enemies" (Matt 5:44). Jesus's command to give up retaliation is built on the ethic of love for all. Our love for all is rooted in God's love for all. They cannot be separated. By adopting God's love and giving up revenge, we show the love of God to a world that needs to see it.

The love of God is compelling, powerful, and transformative. I do not know how, when, or in exactly what ways the love of God will overwhelm the world, but I'm convinced it will. In the age to come, God's love will remain. There will come a glorious day when all wrongs are made right, hatred is eliminated, love wins, and God reigns supreme. On that day, those who are in the tombs will come forth.

The resurrection is central to ethical Christian behavior. Hope of eternal life is essential to understanding our call to love our enemies and endure persecution. Without the resurrection, there is no reason to rejoice in persecution or love our enemies. Instead, we should avoid persecution at all costs. Hate, harm, or even kill your enemies if you can get away with it. Live however you want! But with the resurrection, we are motivated to endure and lovingly persevere in obedience to Christ while trusting God's perfect judgment as we await that final day.

Until that day, the world may continue unchanged when you practice the love of God. But you will be changed. You will look at your church, family, friends, neighbors, and enemies differently. You'll see value in each person. You'll see the image of God in even the lowliest human, and remember that no matter who stands before you, you are seeing a person loved by God. You're seeing a person God loved enough to die for.

Giving up Vengeance

What happens when we give up the need for vengeance?

We actualize our faith in God. There is no way to give up vengeance without tremendous faith in God. We must trust that God handles injustice better than we do. We must trust that if we suffer in the present world, there will be victory in the world to come. Taking our own revenge betrays a lack of reliance on God as the perfect judge. God tells us, "Vengeance is Mine, I will repay" (Rom 12:19). Do we believe that? Can we leave vengeance to God? Vengeance is not inherently wrong, but it is not ours to give. Have faith in God and allow Him to make those decisions.

We imitate God rather than our enemies. Harming the one who hurt us does not give us control, nor does it give God control. Instead, we fumble control to the perpetrator. Because of them, we find ourselves engaging in a cruel act we otherwise never would have done. Christian ethics thrive in response to Jesus, not in reaction against our enemies. When we return evil for evil, we conform to the one who harmed us rather than the One who saved us.

We demonstrate God's goodness to the world. Jesus calls us to live differently than the rest of the world (Matt 5:13–16). If our justice comes from within ourselves and not from Jesus, others will never see Jesus in us. If we take revenge and act hatefully to others, "do not even the Gentiles do the same?" (Matt 5:47). Through suffering, you can demonstrate the way of

Christ. You have the opportunity to shine the light of the glory of God in a world of darkness.

We lessen the amount of evil in the world. By choosing revenge, we multiply sin in the world. We take one evil and make it two. Then, in all likelihood, that two becomes four, then eight, and so on. When we do not retaliate, we let evil die. We are to be the one community in which evil cannot spread. We become the cleansing agent that halts the world's evil and suffocates it within our midst. If all followers of Jesus took these words seriously, then evil, violence, and revenge would shrink as the church grew.

We uniquely share with Jesus. If we suffer unjustly and let that evil die unrepaid, then we share with Jesus in His suffering. We embody the message of the cross and carry it ourselves. Paul writes that he wants to know Christ "and the fellowship of His sufferings, being conformed to His death" (Phil 3:10). As soon as we take revenge, we have broken fellowship in the sufferings of Christ and chosen our own way. In retaliation, we suffer with the world, but through sacrificial love, we suffer with Jesus.

We overcome evil. The only way to overcome evil is with good: "Do not be overcome by evil, but overcome evil with good" (Rom 12:21). Fire cannot put out fire, and hatred does not extinguish hatred. Acts of kindness, motivated by love and rooted in the nature of God, can change hearts, save relationships, and put evil to death. Respond with kindness and generosity to your enemies and see what happens. It might change them. It might not. But Jesus will be seen, and you will be changed more fully into His image.

We experience the peace of letting go. Despite what the movies show us, revenge does not lead to peace. Any feelings of relief or satisfaction received by inflicting pain do not come from God. True peace is found when you forfeit the obligation to imitate your enemies and can confidently say, "The Lord is my helper, I will not be afraid. What will man do to me?" (Heb 13:6). Then you can look with compassion on those who wrong you. They are sheep without a shepherd. You can rejoice in your sufferings (Matt 5:11–12), "knowing that you have for yourselves a better possession and a lasting one" (Heb 10:34). Do not let the actions of others steal your goodness, hope, confidence, or peace.

Reflection Questions

1. How is forgiveness more powerful than revenge? How is love more powerful than hate? How is service to enemies more powerful than violence against them?
2. What are some benefits of giving up vengeance? What are the possible costs of giving up vengeance? How can it help our relationships with others? How can it strengthen our relationship with God?

REFLECTION 27

LOVING YOUR ENEMY: READ MATTHEW 5:38–48

God Is Known through Love

THESE FINAL TWO challenges from Jesus: "Do not resist the evil person" (Matt 5:39) and "Love your enemies" (Matt 5:43) cannot be separated. The "evil person" who slaps your face, takes you to court, or makes you go one mile is also the "enemy" Jesus calls you to love. That enemy may be a neighbor, business associate, or foreign soldier occupying your land. This is a revolutionary idea and one of Jesus's most unique teachings.

Historian John Dickson describes this teaching as

> Christ's special legacy in the world. He was *possessed*, we might say, with a sense of God's love for all, including enemies, and *that* is why he felt he had to die for them. This divine mercy must be the central ethic for his students, he taught, because it is *who God is*.[25]

Jesus not only taught His followers to love, but Jesus showed how to do it. It is one thing to say, "Love your enemies" and quite another to die on the cross for them. Jesus was no mere armchair theologian or high-minded philosopher; He was the living embodiment of the love of God. Christians love because God is love. The love we give both imitates God and is an experience of God. Apart from love, you cannot know God. The apostle John, having spent a lifetime being molded by the teachings of Jesus, beautifully presents this idea in these words:

> Beloved, let us love one another, for love is from God; and everyone who loves is born of God and knows God. The one who does not love does not know God, for God is love. By this the love of God was manifested in us, that God has sent His only begotten Son into the world so that we might live through Him. In this is love, not that we loved God, but that He loved us and sent His Son to be the propitiation for our sins. Beloved, if God so loved us, we also ought to love one another. No one has seen God at any time; if we love one another, God abides in us, and His love is perfected in us (1 John 4:7–12).

Let's take a brief break from Matthew to reflect on this passage in 1 John. John writes, "Everyone who loves is born of God and knows God." Think about the meaning of those words. By saying we are born of God when we love, John echoes the idea of Jesus in the sermon: "Love your enemies and pray for those who persecute you, *so that you may be sons of your Father who is in heaven*" (Matt 5:44–45). Spiritual birth is found in love. We are "born of God" and "sons of God" through the love we extend.

Not only are we born of God through love, but we know God through love. If you want to know God, then love others. When people ask how they can come to know God, we may tell them to read the Bible and pray. That's excellent advice. But what is John's answer? Love one another.

If God is love, then loving others is the most direct way to experience the presence and reality of God. No apologetic argument for the existence of God is greater than the practice of love. *The Brothers Karamazov* is among the greatest books ever written. (That's not just my opinion. It's objective fact!) Early in the book, when counseling a woman about her lack of faith, Father Zossima, the wise elder at the local monastery, discusses the relationship between doubt and love.

He is asked how we might prove our faith. How can we prove life after death? How can we prove there is more in this world than what we see? Zossima responds,

> There is no proving it, though you can be convinced of it ... By the experience of active love. Strive to love your neighbor actively and indefatigably. In as far as you advance in love you will grow surer of the reality of God and the immortality of your soul. If you attain to perfect self-forgetfulness in the love of your neighbor, then you will believe without doubt, and no doubt can possibly enter your soul. This has been tried. This is certain."

While some might debate whether it can be "proven," what Zossima says about active love is right in line with 1 John and the Sermon on the Mount. Love is the greatest answer to this world's problems. Later in *The Brother's Karamazov,* there is a gripping discussion between two brothers, Ivan, a brilliant atheist intellectual, and Alyosha, a believer who has given his life to the monastery and studies under Father Zossima. In the chapters called "Rebellion" and "The Grand Inquisitor," Ivan argues against the existence, or at least the character, of God based on the problem of evil (particularly the suffering of children). It is the strongest case against God I have ever read. (Dostoevsky is masterful.) Alyosha, the Christian, cannot produce an adequate response to it. However, as the book's story unfolds, we find out that Father Zossima's words at the beginning ring true. Ivan's worldview ultimately leads to violence, murder, and an unlivable reality. Trust in God is not found merely in reason and argument but through active love for one another. According to John, love is how we know God. According to Jesus, love is how we become "sons of our Father."

Love is God's abiding presence with us; anyone capable of love can know God. Thus, community is an essential part of experiencing God. We must have a "one another" to love for God to be known. Worship with others. Pray for others. Serve others and serve with others. Sacrifice for others. Reach out, give, forgive, and love. This is how we know God.

When John continues, "In this is love ... that He loved us and sent His Son to be the propitiation for our sins," he affirms that God did not wait for us to deserve love before He extended it. He loved us as sinners. He loved His enemies. If we strive to imitate the love of God, there can be no sinner, foreigner, or enemy unloved by His church.

Next, John writes, "No one has seen God at any time." Why bring up the invisibility of God in this context? Because while human eyes cannot behold the divine presence, we can experience and know that presence through love. We perceive God through love rather than eyesight. When we love one another, God abides with us. When our love is extended beyond ourselves, even to our enemies, the initiative of God through Jesus is reignited, and the church engages in God's mission on earth.

Loving Enemies is Hard

Miroslav Volf is a brilliant theologian and professor at Yale Divinity School. Back in 1984, in communist Yugoslavia, Volf was selected for compulsory military service. During his service, the government viewed him with extreme suspicion for several reasons. 1. His wife was an American citizen. 2. He studied theology at a Western school. 3. His father, as a Christian pastor, was nearly executed by the communists as an "enemy of the people."

The government surrounded Volf with spies. He could trust nobody. Even within his own military unit, his fellow soldiers casually gave him copies of Western magazines and spoke to him about religion and politics. This was done to catch him expressing thoughts considered to be dangerous. Anything suspicious that came from his mouth was reported. Volf was assigned a job in a small room, bugged with microphones, and they recorded every word he spoke.

Eventually, after quotations, photographs, and a foot-tall stack of papers containing "evidence" against him were collected, Volf was summoned for questioning and examination. A man known as "Captain G." was the primary examiner. He made Volf's life utterly dreadful. Captain G., along with other examiners, lied, pressured, insulted, accused, threatened, and psychologically tortured Volf for months. In his book *The End of Memory* (which you should now go purchase and read), Volf explains what it means to live as a Christian when you have been terribly wronged. He describes how disciples of Jesus ought to "love one's neighbors, even if they prove to be enemies."[26]

As Volf remembers his months of interrogation and abuse, he writes words that anyone who has been wronged yet desires to follow Jesus would do well to read:

> To triumph fully, evil needs two victories, not one. The first victory happens when an evil deed is perpetrated; the second victory, when evil is returned. After the first victory, evil would

> die if the second victory did not infuse it with new life. In my own situation, I could do nothing about the first victory of evil, but I could do something about the second. Captain G. would not mold me into his image. Instead of returning evil for evil, I would heed the Apostle Paul and try to overcome evil with good (Romans 12:21). After all, I myself had been redeemed by the God who in Christ died for the redemption of the ungodly.[27]

Be Perfect

Leviticus 19:18—and that whole chapter—was instrumental in forming Jesus's ethics of love. Jesus encountered a tendency of many to interpret the word "neighbor" in such a narrow way that it removed the burden of love. If my "neighbor" is only the person who lives near me, shares my nationality, looks like me, votes like me, believes and worships like me, and is kind, generous, trustworthy, hard-working, and upstanding, then I can certainly love my neighbor. It's easy. Jesus asks, "If you love those who love you, what reward do you have? Do not even the tax collectors do the same?" (Matt 5:46–47). If loving our neighbor is easy, it's time to expand our definition of neighbor.

For Christians, culture should not provide our definition or parameters of love. That's what Jesus does. If we listen to Him, we will be notably more loving, sacrificial, forgiving, and generous than others. Love should be our defining characteristic. Our love should excel way beyond normal cultural expectations. Jesus challenges us to broaden our interpretation of the word "neighbor" so that we see Jews and Gentiles, countrymen and foreigners, friends and enemies, as our neighbors.

God sends sunshine and rain on the just and the unjust, the good and the evil (Matt 5:39, 45). In this way, God's blessings fall on all people, and our love, prayers, and greetings should do the same (Matt 5:44, 46–47). We should "be perfect, as your heavenly Father is perfect" (Matt 5:48; see Luke 6:36; 1 Pet 1:16; Lev 19:2; 20:7, 26; 21:28). Through love and generosity (see Matt 19:21), we reflect the image of God.

God's love is perfect, whole, and universal. Therefore, do not only love your family, friends, or fellow citizens but also the pagan Romans occupying your country, the greedy swindler who sued you for your cloak, and the jerk who slapped your face. Love even the persecutor who stands against Jesus. This is how we become "perfect" like the heavenly Father.

This love overwhelms hatred, confronts evil with good, and meets persecution with prayer. We should be willing to pray that God's grace and mercy, which we need daily, are also extended to our enemies. Rather than adding hatred to hatred and evil to evil, let us extinguish the inferno of hate and the flames of hostility with the peaceful love of God. Do not resist evil; overcome it. If we seek to be a city set on a hill, a light in the darkness, and the salt of the earth, let's begin by taking love where only Christ has brought it before.

Reflection Questions

1. In your life, who is the hardest to love? Is it a person? Or a group of people you lump together? Do you desire to love them? What helps you love them? What makes it harder to love them? Can you find any good qualities in them?
2. How does love make us children of God? What two victories does evil need in order to survive? How does Jesus's death on the cross answer the problem of evil? How can we conquer evil in our lives today?

Endnotes

[25] John Dickson, *Bullies and Saints: An Honest Look at the Good and Evil of Christian History* (Grand Rapids: Zondervan, 2021), 29.

[26] Miroslav Volf, *The End of Memory: Remembering Rightly in a Violent World* (Grand Rapids: Eerdmans, 2006), 14.

[27] Volf, *Memory*, 14.

REFLECTION 28

SINCERE RIGHTEOUSNESS: READ MATTHEW 6:1–18

Checking for Pride

IN MATTHEW 6, Jesus shifts from discussing elevated righteousness to sincere righteousness. Righteousness is a keyword in this sermon and almost everything Jesus says centers around it. Followers of Jesus are challenged to be the most righteous people on earth. That's the only way we shine as a light to the world.

Attaining this elevated righteousness has a potential pitfall, though. I might notice if my life and actions become more righteous than everyone else. I might start to think that I'm a pretty awesome fella. Elevation in righteousness may lead to a plummet in humility. So, how do we guard against this? The next move Jesus makes in this sermon is to discuss practicing righteousness sincerely. We must obey God for the right reasons. We do not follow Christ to look great, outperform others, or reap the rewards from our peers. Instead, we obey out of humble love for God.

In Matthew 6:1–18, Jesus reminds His disciples that righteousness must never be practiced for glory, respect, or honor from people. Sincere, internal commitment to God should motivate us even if nobody sees it. One test of our sincerity is to ask whether our practices change depending on who is around us. Are we as generous "in secret" as we are in public? Do we tip the waiter more when our friends or date may see us? How and why are our public prayers different than our prayers at home? How much do the faces around us impact our righteousness?

Behind the Barn

When I played football in high school, we had to run. A lot. It was about working hard, getting in shape, persevering through fatigue, mental toughness, preparing for the 4th quarter, and all that sports jargon. Our practice facilities comprised several full-sized football fields, a weight room, and a turf barn. This was that old-fashioned hard, scratchy turf carpet laid on concrete. When you played on this, you always ended up covered in turf burns: those glistening, shiny, red patches where the skin was scrapped off. We'd practice in the turf barn when the weather outside was dangerous or sometimes if we were preparing for a game on a turf field.

While most of our running and conditioning was sprint work, we'd occasionally finish off practice or work out some soreness with a long run. We'd run laps around the property, including that big turf barn. You learned a lot about your teammates behind that big barn. Behind that barn, the coaches couldn't see you anymore. Behind that barn, you realized who you could trust. You saw who was committed. You saw who worked hard and who was lazy. You saw who had integrity and who didn't. You saw who stopped running, walked, rested, and caught their breath. But you also saw who would keep working just as hard even when the coaches couldn't see. You also saw the leaders on the team confront, challenge, and encourage everyone to keep going.

Jesus challenges His followers to practice righteousness

behind the barn. He wants our righteousness to be present even when nobody else sees it. Will we obey even "in secret" (Matt 6:4, 6, 18)? Matthew 6 is a motive diagnostic. We are always called to practice the same righteousness whether we are with people or alone and whether we are seen or not.

Sometimes, being seen can produce something good. Jesus said a few verses earlier: "Let your light shine before men in such a way that they may see your good works, and glorify your Father who is in heaven" (Matt 5:16). God can be glorified when people see our good works. But that's quite different from glorifying me because of my good works. Do you practice righteousness because of internal commitment, or is it an external show? Are you clean on the outside but rotten inside? Would you practice righteousness if only God saw? Would you practice righteousness if only God received the glory? These are the questions we must answer as disciples of Jesus.

Give, Pray, and Fast

Jesus provides three examples of acts of righteousness that people tend to perform for praise: generosity, prayer, and fasting. Each of these actions is righteous and should be performed by followers of Jesus. Yes, you should give to the poor, pray, and fast. These are crucial practices that improve the lives of others and connect you to God in profound and meaningful ways. You can grow closer to God through each of these disciplines. But, like anything else, the wrong motives and intentions can destroy good deeds.

Imagine a husband giving his wife thoughtful and generous gifts, having lengthy, deep conversations with her, and sacrificing his own enjoyment to prioritize her. He sounds like a fine chap and a quality husband. A man that any woman should be happy to have. Now imagine he recognizes that also. He does those things, shows them off on Facebook, and tells others about them. He even wants other women to see and know how great a husband He is. His service to his wife is also his bragging/flirting material. If he is a good husband only to impress other women, is he still a good husband?

If we give, pray, and fast, not out of devotion to God but to impress the people around us, are we still practicing righteousness? Or are we using God to benefit ourselves? Have we become servants of pride and selfishness? If these practices are supposed to cultivate deeper relationships with God, isn't it a slap in His face to use them to impress others? It's like using our wives to impress our girlfriends. With the wrong motives, we are using God to impress others. And God allows it. But that's it. That is our whole reward. God lets us enjoy that temporal satisfaction, but no further reward is given.

In the first-century Roman world, generosity was practiced and respected. For example, a wealthy freedman may donate a hefty sum to build a public bathhouse, temple, or theatre in his city. Great honor came with such philanthropy. The question Jesus wants us to grapple with is, would you still be generous if it came with no honor? Or if the honor was given to another?

Jesus teaches us how to practice righteousness in a way that protects us from pride. We should give to the poor as followers of Jesus. But don't put your name on a plaque or post it on Instagram. Do not sound a trumpet or do it in front of a crowd. Talk to God about it and no one else.

Why do you pray, and when do you pray? How does your Sunday morning church prayer compare to your prayer in bed at night? Jesus says to pray alone at home, and if only God hears you, that is enough. Jesus critiques the Jewish leaders who pray publicly to be seen and Gentiles who repeat lengthy, meaningless words. Since God already knows your life, wants, needs, and thoughts, you do not have to over-explain things to Him. Prayers should be short, simple, and sincere. If you find yourself praying in front of others, do not try to impress them. Just speak honestly, briefly, and lovingly.

You should fast, and now is a great time to start. I can't help but think a lot of good would come if more churches and Christians in our culture practiced regular fasting. Fasting is a beautiful reminder that man does not live by bread alone. Do you want more time to rest, study, pray, or reflect on God throughout your day? Fast! Think about how much time we spend on food: buying, planning, preparing, cooking, eating, and cleaning up, just to do it again. Perhaps we could periodically spend that time on something spiritual.

Experiencing the discomfort of an empty stomach could remind us of the men, women, and children forced to live with those pains daily. Fasting reminds us of others, encourages gratitude for what we have, and challenges us to practice generosity. Those stomach growls could serve as a spiritual alarm clock, reminding us to give thanks, send an encouraging message, study the Bible, hug our families, or pray. Have a big decision coming up? Have a loved one suffering health difficulties? Concerned about your children? Pray. Fast. Use those moments of hunger as a reminder to turn your anxieties over to God.

As you do this, remember that this is an act of righteousness between you and God. It's not a production about your self-control, holiness, or toughness. If only God knows, that is enough. He is why we are doing it. And He will reward you for doing it. That's right. Matthew 6 repeatedly emphasizes that those who give, pray, and fast are rewarded. And you get to decide who rewards you.

You can either be rewarded by God or those around you. If you do it for the praise of people, you might get it. People may think lovely things about you. They may even say nice things about you. You may develop a reputation as a godly person or spiritual guru. Congratulations. That would be your reward.

On the other hand, you also may lose credibility with the people who perceive your motives. That happens, too. You may just get eye-rolls. At the end of the day, you may or may not get that small reward among your peers. But either way, if you do it for them, you can be sure you will lose God's reward for you.

God is watching in secret. He sees the things you do in secret. He sees you behind the barn. He sees you in your inner room with your door closed. What will He find there? Is that where you conceal your sins? Is that where you cheat, lust, and scheme? Or will God find you praying? Will God find you generous? Will God see you fasting? Will God see sincere love and commitment to your relationship with Him? If that is what He finds, He not only appreciates it, but He also rewards it. Perhaps now and perhaps in the age to come. But I can guarantee whatever reward God has in store will far surpass a pat on the back from those around us.

Reflection Questions

1. How are righteousness and pride linked? How can righteousness destroy pride? How can pride destroy righteousness? How do you balance letting your light shine before men (which is good) and practicing righteousness to be noticed by men (which is bad)?
2. Are giving, prayer, and fasting still valuable ways to practice righteousness today? Do you give sacrificially? Do you pray fervently? Do you fast at all? How might dedication to these spiritual practices help you?

REFLECTION 29

THE MODEL PRAYER, PART 1: READ MATTHEW 6:9–13

Using Jesus's Prayer

IF YOU WANT to learn about prayer, listen to Jesus. There is no greater authority in heaven and earth. I love that in the middle of the most famous sermon ever recorded, as Jesus teaches about the sincere practice of righteousness, He provides the model of a simple, brief, ideal prayer. I just timed myself saying it. From beginning to end, trying not to go too fast, the prayer took about 20 seconds. In those 20 seconds, Jesus addresses humanity's most pressing theological and practical needs.

Though this prayer is often called "The Lord's Prayer" or "The Model Prayer," it doesn't sound like most prayers I hear (or, to be honest, say). It is also often called the "Our Father." Though some faith traditions recite this prayer daily, I grew up hearing that this prayer is only an example of how we should pray, not a verbatim prayer to be repeated. What's interesting is how rarely it serves even as our example.

Our prayers are generally much longer. We want to explain all our requests in lengthy detail. We often add much larger, more reverent, and theologically richer vocabulary. And we would never end our prayers the way Jesus does here. We didn't recite this prayer for fear it would become a vain repetition, but then we still had vain repetitions in our prayers. Certain words and phrases become standard prayer liturgy, and we fall into the very trap we're trying to avoid. Not only did we not say Jesus's prayer, but our prayers didn't often sound like it. Maybe it's time to rethink that.

Refusing to say this prayer will not resolve the pitfalls Jesus warns against. In fact, the less we say the prayer, the less we'll think about it. The less we think about Jesus's prayer, the more distant it will drift from us. Before you know it, we'll be giving lengthy, repetitive prayers for the purpose of sounding creative, intelligent, articulate, or holy, and Jesus, the masterful example we should seek to imitate in prayer, will be ignored. Perhaps we're fearful that we'll be unclear or leave something out, but Jesus wants us to trust in the omniscience of God while we pray (Matt 6:8).

I don't think this should become the only prayer we pray. We certainly never want it to become mundane or mindlessly repetitive. But I believe there is a great benefit to regularly praying this prayer. For one thing, Jesus tells us to pray it (Matt 6:9, Luke 11:2). Our response should not be, "Nah, I can pray pretty good on my own. You just leave it to me." Jesus gave us a powerful, true, divinely guided, specific prayer. It is a gift. Wouldn't it be crazy never to use it?

If nothing else, praying these words is an act of humility. It should remind us that Jesus is better at crafting prayers than we are. Spontaneity and self-sufficiency are not spiritual virtues. Rely on Jesus even in prayer. Join Jesus in this prayer. Follow Him through this prayer. Let Him lead you.

This prayer is also a reminder of what matters most in this life. What if we started off every day remembering the sacred name of God, the mission of the kingdom of God, the provisions of God, the essentiality of forgiveness, and God's deliverance from evil? I cannot help but think every follower of Jesus could benefit from that.

The Placement and Structure of the Prayer

The placement of this prayer at this part of the sermon, I believe, is important and intentional. This prayer is the center of the Sermon on the Mount. It is in the central chapter and is the middle example of sincere acts of righteousness—sandwiched between giving and fasting. Everything on both sides of this prayer hinges on the ideas within it.

The Lord's prayer is a list of imperatives that, taken together, define the ministry of Jesus, the mission of God, and our purpose on earth. In prayers, imperatives usually function as requests rather than commands. It's hard to see the grammatical structure of this prayer in our English Bibles, but a glance in a Greek text reveals seven consecutive imperatives.

1. Hallowed be Your name.
2. Your Kingdom come.
3. Your will be done on earth as it is in heaven.
4. Give us this day our daily bread.
5. Forgive us our debts as we also have forgiven our debtors.
6. Do not lead us into temptation.
7. Deliver us from evil.

The first three imperatives concern God acting for Himself: God's name, God's kingdom, and God's will. The final four imperatives are requests for God to act for us: our daily bread, our debts, our temptation, and our deliverance from evil. It is also crucial to note that this prayer does not ask for "my daily bread" or to "forgive me my debts." The personal pronouns are plural. This is a communal prayer that addresses God on behalf of the needs of all. This prayer is upward, inward, and outward-focused.

Clear and Confusing

In the next reflection, we will walk through the content of the prayer. There is no way to examine it comprehensively in this space, but this prayer is a wonderful mix of the clear teaching of Jesus and confusing uncertainties that have been and will be debated for centuries. This prayer is clear yet confusing, simple but challenging, straightforward and profound.

Regarding the unclear, several translational and interpretive issues have confounded Christians. One of these is the line, "Give us this day our daily bread." That sounds simple enough. But there is a confusing aspect of this verse. We don't know for sure what the Greek word ἐπιούσιον, traditionally translated as "daily," means. My *Reader's Greek New Testament* offers three possible translations for this word: "for today," "for tomorrow," or "necessary for existence."

If it means "for tomorrow," which is an ancient interpretation, it means to pray for tomorrow's bread instead of today's bread. Does that conflict with Matthew 6:34? One can certainly pray for tomorrow without worrying about tomorrow. There is no necessary conflict there. Jesus may be making the point that we should replace worry with prayer when considering tomorrow's needs.

Or the word may mean "necessary for existence" or "essential." This would be a way of praying for God to give us the needed food for each day rather than excess or unnecessary food. This is a focal point in the teachings of Jesus. He calls us to simplicity and contentment rather than excess and luxury (Matt 6:19–20).

Since this Greek word isn't used elsewhere (except in Luke's parallel), there is nothing to compare it to. We have to take our best guess based on etymology (which is often unreliable for defining words), context, and the parallel in Luke 11:3. Interestingly, Luke 11:3 adds a description of "each day" to the phrase. Luke says, "Give us each day our daily bread." That could be a clue that our mystery word means "daily" or "for today" (though, perhaps that is redundant). Luke could also be saying, "Give us each day our necessary bread" (which makes a lot of sense). Admittedly, saying, "Give us each day tomorrow's bread," sounds a bit odd (but could still work).

I wish I could give a more definitive definition. Even the early church struggled with this word. I'm going to stick with the idea of "daily" in my interpretation, mainly because it's traditional, and Luke nudges me in that direction. But it's uncertain.

Other uncertainties include how exactly God forgives us based on how we forgive others. Does that add elements of merit to our salvation? Or, consider whether God leads us into temptation or not. If God would never lead us into temptation, why is it necessary to pray for Him not to? If God does lead us into temptation, well, that raises a host of other questions. Why would He do this? Does He only lead us into certain kinds of temptations? Another uncertainty is whether the final imperative should be translated as "Deliver us from evil" or "Deliver us from the evil one." Is Jesus talking about evil in general? Or is He talking about Satan specifically?

Even the conclusion of the prayer raises questions. What is the last word? Does Jesus end the prayer after the word "evil"? That's how most modern translations conclude the prayer, and that's what my vote would be. But that's not the traditional conclusion. In our Greek manuscripts throughout history, the conclusion has changed often and grown substantially. The prayer concludes in different manuscripts in each of these ways: "deliver us from evil," "deliver us from evil. Amen," "deliver us from evil, for yours is the kingdom and the power and the glory into the ages. Amen," "deliver us from evil, for yours is the kingdom and the power and the glory of the Father and of the Son and of the Holy Spirit into the ages. Amen." We also have many combinations of those words in different orders. Some do not have "and the power," or "and the glory," but everything else is the same. It seems that everyone wanted to make the ending a little more pious, and it grew and grew over time. Ironically, this is what Jesus is telling us to avoid in prayer.

While there are mysteries about the prayer, some things are very clear. We should pray to God our Father with sincerity and humility. We should pray for His name, mission, and purposes in our world, as well as our needs and our role within His purposes.

Reflection Questions

1. Is this a prayer Christians would benefit from praying today? Is there anything wrong with repetition in prayer? How do we keep prayer from becoming a thoughtless habit?
2. What can we learn about prayer from Jesus? How can pride seep into our prayers? What does it mean to pray in secret? What are some mysteries about prayer?

REFLECTION 30

THE MODEL PRAYER, PART 2: READ MATTHEW 6:9–13

Our Father and His Name

"*Our Father who is in heaven ...*" Jesus invites us to address God as our own Father. God is called Father throughout this sermon (Matt 5:16, 45, 48; 6:1, 4, 6, 8, 9, 14, 25, 18, 26, 32; 7:11, 21). God relates to us as earthly fathers do. As children imitate their earthly fathers, we are called to imitate our heavenly Father (Matt 5:45, 48). As earthly fathers provide for their children, so our heavenly Father provides for us (Matt 6:32, 7:9–11). As our earthly fathers forgive our mistakes and disobedience, so our heavenly Father does (Matt 6:14). As earthly fathers are to be obeyed, so also is our heavenly Father (Matt 7:21). As our earthly fathers reward good behavior, so does our heavenly Father (Matt 6:1, 4, 6, 18).

Now, sadly, many earthly fathers are not like those mentioned above. The description "who is in heaven" differentiates our "heavenly" Father from our "earthly" fathers (Matt 23:9). Some fathers spend little or no time with their children. They do not provide, bless, forgive, or teach. One of the blessings of having a heavenly Father is that He is everything earthly fathers should be and more.

"Hallowed be Your name." This is the first imperative of the prayer, which beseeches God to consecrate and sanctify His name. God's name matters. God's name is His reputation. We are called to bear His name with obedience, loyalty, and honor. When Israel, who was called by God's name, rebelled, it harmed God's reputation among the nations. He was mocked because of their sins. Often, God acts in defense of His own name, which is dragged through the mud by His people (Isa 48:11, Ezek 36:22–23). The holiness of God's name should be seen in us by our conduct and actions. But when we fail, Jesus is praying for God to still make His name sacred.

God's Mission and Kingdom

"Your Kingdom Come." This line is crucial to the entire ministry of Jesus. This is what Jesus's life, teaching, and ministry are about. Every word that follows in this prayer portrays an aspect of God's kingdom. Jesus rejects Satan's offer of the kingdoms of this world in pursuit of God's kingdom (Matt 4:8–11). He begins His preaching, saying, "Repent, for the kingdom of heaven is at hand," and travels throughout Galilee "proclaiming the gospel of the kingdom" (Matt 4:17, 23). Jesus's teachings, healings, death, and resurrection are all bringing about God's kingdom. Here, He prays for the success of that mission.

"Your will be done, on earth as it is in heaven." This is a most helpful description of what the kingdom of heaven is all about. Jesus has authority in heaven and on earth to bring about God's will on earth as in heaven. This is our kingdom mission as followers of Jesus. This is one reason why this prayer is still of utmost importance to pray today. Wherever God's will is rejected on earth, we must keep praying for His kingdom to come.

Our Needs for Life and Holiness

"Give us this day our daily bread." These words are the fourth and central imperative in the prayer, which is the central example of sincerely practiced righteousness in Matthew 6, which is the central chapter and section in the Sermon on the Mount. These words remind us that God is concerned not only with our spiritual needs but also our physical. Accomplishing God's will on earth, as in heaven, will include food for all people to eat. God's physical blessings, however, should also teach us spiritual truths.

This God-given bread should remind every reader of the manna in the wilderness. That manna was given to meet the physical needs of Israel but also to teach important spiritual truths (Deut 8:3) and complete reliance upon God. God did not want them to grow their own food; He wanted them to receive miraculous sustenance from Him every single day. He wanted this bread to be a daily need met only by Him. This is why they could not hoard it or accumulate more than needed. Every night, parents put down their children with nothing to eat the next day, hoping, praying, trusting, and relying on God's provision. This was an essential lesson to learn before entering the Promised Land, where they would have an abundance. God is the ultimate provider of all we enjoy.

"And forgive us our debts, as we also have forgiven our debtors." Yikes. I like the request, but I hate the qualification. After reading the first half of the Sermon on the Mount, I'm confident I'll be asking God for forgiveness quite a bit. I certainly want to be forgiven, but I'd much rather ground it in God's mercy, grace, and steadfast love rather than how well I forgive others. But you read that right, and we should take it seriously.

We are to pray that God's forgiveness of us reflects our forgiveness of others. Two quick points come to mind. First, God wants to forgive us, but He wants that forgiveness to be contagious. One way to do that is to make giving forgiveness a requirement for receiving forgiveness. If we take this seriously, forgiveness should spread like wildfire. Collectively, we can only be God's church when we practice forgiveness. If the church does not forgive, we should not expect it to be forgiven (Matt 6:14–15).

Second, if we want to be forgiven quickly, graciously, and fully, then let's forgive others quickly, graciously, and fully. If someone has not yet earned my forgiveness, I don't want that to stop me because I know that I'll never earn God's forgiveness. We mustn't be stingy. If I want God to forgive undeserving me, then I should forgive undeserving them. If I offer forgiveness only for the worthy, God may just do the same.

"And do not lead us into temptation." This is a somewhat confusing and controversial phrase in this prayer. The main point isn't confusing: we want God to lead us away from temptation rather than into it. But that begs the question of whether God ever leads us into temptation. We should remember James 1:13–16, but we should also remember Matthew 4:1: Jesus was "led up by the Spirit into the wilderness to be tempted by the devil." If I'm Jesus, this seems like a prayer I want to offer.

Perhaps there's a distinction between being "led into temptation" by God and being "tempted" by God. Either way, we are called to pray for God to lead us elsewhere. As a community of God's people, we want to live holy and blameless lives. We don't want unnecessary temptations to hinder our obedience or mission. Jesus was led into temptation on our behalf, and He overcame it. Let's not dabble in temptation but flee from it with God's help and leadership.

"But deliver us from evil." Rather than leading us into temptation, we want God to deliver us from evil (or "the evil one"). Again, this is getting to the heart of the gospel of the kingdom. We can be rescued from evil because Jesus was not. Jesus confronted the evil one head-on. As the world turned to dark-

ness on that sinister day, Jesus took the brunt of all the hatred, malice, and violence the world could muster. He took it into Himself through death and conquered it through the resurrection. As Paul puts it, "He made Him who knew no sin to be sin on our behalf, so that we might become the righteousness of God in Him" (2 Cor 5:21). In Jesus, we see God's deliverance. We should remember and pray for that deliverance daily.

Reflection Questions

1. Why is it meaningful to call God "our Father?" How does the phrase "in heaven" distinguish God from our earthly fathers? What are the ramifications of all Christians having one Father? Why should we pray for the name of God?
2. How does this prayer help us understand the kingdom? How does this prayer demonstrate trust in God's reign and will? What human needs are addressed in this prayer? What responsibilities does this prayer place on those who pray it?

REFLECTION 31

WEALTH, ANXIETY, AND THE KINGDOM OF HEAVEN: READ MATTHEW 6:19–34

Storing Up Treasure

JESUS IS AT IT AGAIN. Jesus has no compunction about making my life hard. For example, Jesus commands, "Do not store up for yourselves treasures on earth ... But store up for yourselves treasures in heaven" (Matt 6:19–20). If I had my druthers, Jesus would have said, "Do not greedily store up treasures on earth ...." Or, I wish Jesus said, "Do not only store up treasure for yourselves on earth ... But also store up treasures in heaven."

Being a preacher is hard because I'm not allowed to create my own material. If Jesus would follow my advice, I'd have a much easier time preaching this text. I'd also have a much easier time living this text. I could stand behind the pulpit and condemn greed; everyone would say, "Amen," and then we could all go home to our treasure. We could think, "As long as I'm not greedy with it, it doesn't matter how much money I have." But that's not what Jesus says.

If Jesus would help me out a bit, I could condemn prioritizing money over the kingdom of God. That's easy. I could preach against being only committed to money and say we should also commit ourselves to God's kingdom. Then everyone could happily say, "Amen" again. We could think, "As long as I'm more fully seeking God's kingdom, I can store up my treasure on earth also." But Jesus does not give us those easy talking points.

Jesus does not condemn greed or misplaced priorities; He condemns storing up treasures on earth. Jesus is picking on our savings here. He does not denounce serving money instead of God; He rejects serving money and God (Matt 6:24). Jesus is not addressing a heart problem but a storage problem. Unfortunately, we tend to store our treasure in the wrong places.

While Jesus is definitely concerned about our hearts, He does not tell us where to place our hearts. Instead, He tells us where to place our treasure. Apparently, Jesus knows something about humanity. He knows our heart follows our treasure (Matt 6:21). He does not tell us to put our hearts in heaven so that our treasure may follow. He says it the other way around. He says it the worst way. We should stick our treasure in heaven instead of the earth to guarantee that our heart ends in the right place. Our heart is never far behind our treasure.

Jesus knows we will fail if we try to separate our hearts and our treasure. We'd love to place our hearts with God and our treasures on earth. We initially may begin to store up treasure on earth with a pure heart, but once that treasure grows, our hearts follow after it. So, if you want your heart to be with God, give your treasure to Him.

How Do We Do This?

Let's see if we can find an out here, shall we? What kind of treasure is Jesus talking about? Maybe He's being metaphorical, and I can still keep all my money. But the problem is that the treasure Jesus describes is pretty clearly money, possessions, and wealth. This wealth can be stolen, and while it is here today, it may be gone tomorrow. This is the treasure on which anxiety feeds.

Maybe it's the treasure in heaven that is metaphorical? After all, I can't place any literal dollars in heaven. I'd like this passage more if we could make this treasure something else. Then, we can say, "Well, I'll keep my money on earth, but I'll store my real treasure—my time, love, faith, hope, peace, goodness, obedience, and sincerity—in heaven. There is no treasure greater than that." That way, we don't lose any money.

The problem is that the treasure is probably wealth in both instances. If that's true, how do we store it in heaven? Jesus provides an interesting answer. As Jesus speaks with the rich young ruler, who has accumulated a massive treasure on earth, He tells him to "sell your possessions and give to the poor, and you will have treasure in heaven" (Matt 19:21; see also Luke 12:33). Jesus tells him how to transfer his funds from earth to heaven: Give to the poor.

God keeps track of what you have and what you give. Once your treasure, through giving to others, is stored in heaven, there is no longer any fear or concern about it rotting or being stolen. It isn't lost. It is safe and will always remain. There is no longer any reason to ever worry about that money. It is in the most secure and trusted bank imaginable. Our trust is what determines our actions here. Do we really believe in heaven? Do we really trust God with our wealth?

Matthew 6:22–23 presents a good illustration. When we singularly serve God, our eyes look to God. They are clear, and through them, our bodies are filled with God's light. However, our eyes become bad when we cloud them with materialism by gazing at money, wealth, and excess (see Matt 20:15). They snuff out the light and let darkness fill us. You cannot have one good eye filling you with light and one bad eye filling you with darkness. Even the light within you will be extinguished by the darkness! God brings clarity and brightness while materialism dims and darkens.

Jesus addresses our connection to wealth with three illustrations: storage, eyes, and masters. A follower of Jesus cannot store treasure on earth and in heaven (Matt 6:19–21). He cannot have an eye on God and another on wealth (Matt 6:22–23). And He cannot serve two masters (Matt 6:24).

When we have two masters, we inevitably compare them. Our loyalty belongs to the master we love, and our lip service belongs to the master we despise. Yet, tragically, for so many, our lip service is given to God while our decisions, pleasures, and futures are all about our money.

There is no avoiding money in this world. I don't think Jesus wants us to. We will have varying amounts of money and possessions, but what do we do with them? How much is too much? Is there a number? I don't know. Our treasures raise many questions. Do we serve them? Love them? Trust them? Hope in them? Hoard them? Store them up? Build bigger barns for a rainier day? Do we keep collecting and collecting and hoping for security?

Or do we use those goods? Do we enjoy them? Are we generous with them? Do we share them with others? Do we give them away? Do we make memories? Don't let your money rot in storage; use it for a valuable and meaningful purpose. You're allowed to enjoy it. You're allowed to use it in meaningful ways. But don't collect more than you need and let the excess sit and be wasted for fear of the future. Be thoughtful, wise, generous, and trusting.

Storing our wealth is a subtle way of replacing God. I don't know what the future holds, but I know it would be wiser to put our trust in God rather than our wealth. Be humble, kind, and willing to share. And remember, God sees what you give in secret and will reward you (Matt 6:4).

Anxiety and Kingdom-Focus

Worry and anxiety provide an excellent test to determine where our hearts reside. It's hard to get rid of anxiety. As in all other areas of life, perfect obedience will never fully be attained. It'll be a lifelong struggle.

Throughout this struggle, we should regularly ask ourselves, "What do we worry the most about? And what causes us the most anxiety?" The answer is telling. Usually, our heart belongs to the things that most often concern us. Is it our kids? That makes sense if we really love them. Is it the church? Paul often felt internal pressure and concern for the church (2 Cor 11:28). Paul even speaks positively of Timothy's "concern" (μεριμνήσει) for the Christians at Philippi (Phil 2:20). That is the same word used in Philippians 4:6 and here in Matthew 6:25, 27, 28, 31, 34.

Does our anxiety and worry stem from politics and the direction of our country? Is it vacations, possessions, wealth, and retirement? Is it the worry of this world? Jesus says when those become our concerns, our lives become unfruitful in God's kingdom (Matt 13:22).

Casting our anxieties on God, enjoying the moments He gives, and trusting Him for future provision is a freeing declaration of the care and love of God (Matt 6:26, 28–32). It is a recognition that anxiety will not solve our problems (Matt 6:27). It is a humble demonstration of our inability to control the world (Matt 6:33, 1 Pet 5:6–7), and it frees us up to focus on what truly matters in this life: "But seek first His kingdom and His righteousness, and all these things will be added to you" (Matt 6:33).

This promise can be troubling when we consider that, throughout the world, sometimes Christians are homeless and have no food. Before we blame the suffering by saying, "They must not be seeking God's kingdom first," maybe we should first look at ourselves. Perhaps this is a challenge for Christians with excess to meet the needs of those without. Perhaps God "adds these things" to others through the generosity of His people.

Matthew 6:33 makes a lot of sense in light of Acts 4:32–35. Perhaps God has supplied what was needed for everyone, but we hoarded it for ourselves. Going back to Matthew 6:19, one should not "store treasure on earth" because God intends for that treasure to feed and clothe others. When that happens, the treasure is stored in heaven and also enjoyed on earth by others. Nothing is lost. The treasure multiplies instead of rots. The church must be, at its heart, a loving, generous, and self-sacrificial community meeting the needs of others and serving as God's agents of justice in this world.

Reflection Questions

1. What are some myths we believe about money? What myths do we believe about anxiety? What should Christians do with their money? How do we store "treasure on earth"? How do we store "treasure in heaven"? What changes can you make financially to honor God and serve others?
2. Why would money be a competitor for God? How can we enjoy God? How does God provide for us? How do we seek first the kingdom and His righteousness? What responsibilities does this passage put on us?

REFLECTION 32

JUDGING OTHERS AND FEEDING PIGS: READ MATTHEW 7:1–6

Do not Judge

IN MATTHEW 6:14–15, Jesus promises that God will forgive us if we forgive others. But if we withhold forgiveness, God will do the same. Major takeaway? Forgive as much as possible because you're gonna need it.

The reverse of that is also true. You can expect a harsh, condemning Judge if you judge and condemn harshly. But, on the other hand, if I want a graceful and kind Judge, I should practice some kindness and grace. Major takeaway? Relax a bit when you look at others.

The more righteous person is the person who judges less. Remember that. We sometimes assume the opposite. Being critical, finding fault, noticing every misstep of a church, or catching all the errors in a Bible class does not make one righteous or a good Christian example. In fact, it may just make one a jerk. And if you act like this, you're setting yourself up for an exacting, merciless, and critical judgment.

These verses are regularly used as fodder in our arguments. Some Christians, determined to ignore Jesus about everything else, cling to Matthew 7:1 as tightly as humanly possible. They ignore His kingdom requirements and live any godless way they want, but when someone notices, they whip out these words faster than pistols in an old Western. These verses are always on the hip, ready to draw and excuse any selfish, unjust behavior.

Not to be outmaneuvered, the excessively judgmental among us have found comfortable ways of ignoring this verse. You'll often hear this verse met with, "No! We're supposed to judge with righteous judgment!" (John 7:24). What usually goes unnoticed is the context of John 7, which is about judging the actions and identity of Jesus to see whether He is the Messiah or has a demon (John 7:12–32). Jesus is not telling us how to judge each other; He's telling us how to judge Him.

Those convicted to defend their judgmentalism will note that Jesus's point here is about "hypocritical judgment." This is true. It's also about reciprocal judgment. God will judge you as you judge others. So, clearly, if you condemn someone for lying, but you are also a liar, then your own standard of judgment will condemn you. However, be careful not to define "hypocritical" so strategically that this passage becomes irrelevant.

Many people don't pause even for a moment before judging others because they've swept this passage away into obscurity. They think, "If I'm not committing the exact same sin right now, then I'm not being hypocritical." It may be more helpful to remember that if you have struggles with sin (which you do), you should be patient, kind, and graceful to the struggles of others. And don't assume the worst in them because they lack the fortune of being you. Like snowflakes, our sins and failures are never the exact same. Let's remember that we're all in this mess together, and Jesus is our hope out of it. Not a cruel word, condescending Facebook post, or scathing letter from a self-righteous Christian.

Seeing Clearly

When God, who knows all of our sins and failures, sees us condemning each other, He sees a person with a massive log in one eye reaching for a speck of dust in someone else's. He sees the person soaked from head to toe, criticizing another about the drip on their shirt. He sees the person on fire, mocking another for standing too close to the flame.

You and I cannot see this image as God does. We don't know everyone's sins and failures. We see some public sins, and those are the ones we usually attack. But God sees everything. The whole scene looks different to Him. We see the external sins in Matthew 5 (murder, adultery, etc.), while God sees the internal (anger, lust, etc.). We see the external displays of righteousness in Matthew 6 (giving, praying, fasting), where God sees the pride and selfishness that contaminate them. God also sees the secret righteousness (anonymous giving, praying in the closet, private fasting) where we perceive nothing at all. We see the innocent-looking sheep, but God sees the dangerous wolf (Matt 7:15). God and humans have distinctly different visions. So, let's practice quietness and restraint and allow God to be the perfect Judge.

Look inside yourself before looking at another (Matt 7:5). Jesus isn't saying you cannot help another person. If some speck is in their eye, help may be appreciated. But let love be the motivation. And don't look silly by ignoring your own failures to criticize theirs. If you look internally with a modicum of honesty, you'll find enough work to be done that you won't have the time or energy left over to condemn others. And that's quite all right.

Pearls Before Swine

Matthew 7:6 is confusing. It appears suddenly and without interpretation. Jesus doesn't explain this brief proverb. We're on our own here. So, let's dive into it and see if we can glimpse what Jesus's main point is.

To start, it's helpful to know that a pig just isn't going to do much with a pearl. Likewise, a dog probably won't appreciate a Bible or baptism. The value of a pearl is relative to the one who has it. Don't waste something precious on those for whom it has no value. The gift will be spoiled and rejected, and you may get harmed. However, if you have something holy or valuable, enjoy it, protect it, and share it with others who will do the same.

Interpretations of this passage abound in commentaries, pulpits, and throughout church history. Some of the earliest interpreters from church history used Matthew 7:6 to support "closed communion." Meaning non-Christians should not share in communion. The Didache, one of our earliest Christian writings outside the New Testament, says, "But let no one eat or drink of your Eucharist except those who have been baptized into the name of the Lord, for the Lord has also spoken concerning this: 'Do not give what is holy to dogs.'" [28] In this interpretation, which I think is misguided, the "holy" is the Eucharist, and the "dog" is the unbaptized.

Some say "dogs" and "pigs" represent Gentiles, and Jesus is temporarily prohibiting a Gentile mission (Matt 10:5).[29] Randy Harris argues that the pearl is our allegiance and loyalty, and the dogs and pigs are Roman occupying forces. This reading basically means, "Don't give your allegiance, don't give your support, don't give your assurance to the government."[30]

Some argue that it's about spending our money to support the kingdom of God rather than wasting it on frivolous pleasures. In this reading, the pearl is literal wealth, and the dogs and pigs are the wasteful ways of the world. As John Nolland writes, "When it comes to where we should expend our resources, compared to God everything and everyone else is a dog or a pig."[31]

Some say it basically means you should know your audience and give what is needed. A pig gains nothing from a pearl but may enjoy some nice slop. Give the dog a bone, not a sacrament. Instead, give the pearl to someone who appreciates and benefits from it. Dallas Willard writes, "The problem with pearls for pigs is not that the pigs are not worthy. It is not worthiness that is in question here at all, but helpfulness ... ."[32] Don't give a poor person a lecture; give him some bread. Meet the needs of the pig rather than push pearls on him.

I find a measure of practical value in most of these interpretations. Yet, I tend to lean towards the idea that we shouldn't give the gospel of the kingdom to those who don't want it. Not that they are unworthy, but, like Willard says, it will be useless to them. The kingdom must be sought and prioritized. It cannot be forced upon anyone. I would read this saying in line with those "shake the dust off your feet" passages (Matt 10:14). God gives people the freedom to walk away (John 6:66), and we should honor that decision.

Placing this aphorism in this context is a struggle for interpreters. These words could serve to clarify further what Jesus just said about judging others: while we shouldn't judge others, we should probably notice when they have zero interest in our pearls. So, don't judge them, but listen to them. If they reject and find no value in what we offer, then before they become aggressive, move on to someone else who may appreciate it. It is also a helpful introduction to what Jesus is about to say regarding "asking, seeking, and knocking." Like a good Father, God wants us to ask so that He can give. And because He does not view us as pigs and dogs, He will share His precious pearls and holy things with those who ask Him.

Reflection Questions

1. In what ways is God a better Judge than us? How does He see the world differently? When can our words be helpful? When do they cause more damage? What attitudes must we avoid when we see sin in others?
2. What does it mean to throw pearls before swine? How can this happen? Is the gospel valuable to everyone? What does this passage tell us about evangelism? What does it tell us about holiness?

Endnotes

[28] Didache 9:5

[29] NT Wright, *Matthew for Everyone: Part 1* (London: Westminster John Knox, 2004), 70-71.

[30] Randy Harris, *Living Jesus,* 119.

[31] John Nolland, *The Gospel of Matthew* The New International Greek Testament Commentary (Grand Rapids: Eerdmans, 2005), 324.

[32] Dallas Willard, *The Divine Conspiracy: Rediscovering Our Hidden Life in God* (HarperCollins e-books, 1998), 252.

REFLECTION 33

ASKING, SEEKING, KNOCKING: READ MATTHEW 7:6–12

Children of a Perfect Father

We ended the last reflection by talking about pigs and dogs. From those words, Jesus transitions to a discussion of asking, giving, and receiving (Matt 7:7–12). We should not give pearls and holy things to dogs and pigs, but thankfully, God does not view us as dogs and pigs. We are His children. He offers His pearls to us. In Jesus's world, dogs and pigs were dangerous and unclean animals who ravaged the streets and wallowed in the mire. They would not be allowed inside a home, but if we knock on God's door, He will open it for us. He welcomes us as His children.

Jesus illustrates that flawed and sinful fathers still tend to give their sons what is best. If a son asks for bread or fish, a father will not give him a stone or snake. It's natural to want your children to succeed. We just enjoyed Christmas morning as a family. My sons are five and seven. It is fun to give them gifts. I want to see that excited look on their face when they see the presents on Christmas morning. I want them to leap for joy. But more than that, I want to see them succeed in life. I want to help them faithfully navigate this challenging world. If a flawed and sinful human father, like me, desires this, how much more does God? If we love our children, how much more does God love His children? If we give good things, how much greater are God's gifts?

The Challenge of Prayer

Now, in all honesty, this is another passage that makes me uncomfortable. It's a frustrating passage because, while I know it is true in some way, I *feel* like it's not true. I'm not saying Jesus is wrong, but sometimes it *feels* like Jesus is wrong. I know I cannot rely on my feelings. I know my feelings are flawed and unreliable guides to truth, but many times in my life, I've asked, begged, pleaded, sought, and knocked. Yet, I heard nothing back. Nothing was given, and nothing was found. Instead, it felt like a divine door was slammed in my face. Then I read this passage.

Jesus says, "Everyone who asks, receives … ." Great! But what about me? What about so many others? How many have asked for healing, marital bliss, or career success, only to be fired, divorced, or grow weaker and sicker until they die? Are we swine asking for God's pearls? Does He hear? Does He care?

We're not alone in asking these questions. These questions are not unique or profound. They are common to the life of faith. Many godly and faithful prophets have noticed this problem: "I cry to You for help, but You do not answer me; I stand up, and You turn Your attention against me. You have become cruel to me" (Job 30:20–21). "How long, O Lord, will I call for help, and You will not hear? I cry out to You, 'Violence!' Yet You do not save" (Hab 1:2–4). Just read through some of these Psalms, and you'll see this is a common complaint: Ps 22:1–2, 35:22–23, 74:1, 88:13–18, 89:46.

We know that God is omnipotent and, with zero effort, He can do what we ask in the blink of an eye. We know Jesus said that God would give to those who ask. We know God is supposed to love us and be our Father. And it sure seems like we're asking for good things. Yet when we pray and hope in God for some resolution, we're trampled by the experience of God's silence. We comfort ourselves by saying, "God always answers. Sometimes, He says, 'Yes.' Sometimes, He says, 'No.' And sometimes He says, 'not yet.'" That may be true, but in the moment, it doesn't really help. A "Yes" would have helped.

As Mary and Martha say to Jesus, "Lord, if You had been here, my brother would not have died" (John 11:21, 32), we want to say, "God, if You had been here, if You had been present, if You cared, you would have helped." And through our pain and frustration, we ask, "Why?"

Why did God not answer? Why did I even waste my breath praying? This has been a faith killer for many, and avoiding the problem won't help. Many have wandered away from God because of this struggle. Consider all those who have suffered devastation and pain while constantly and faithfully hoping, trusting, and praying. No wonder many meet Jesus's words with an eye roll, a shout of anger, or silence and dejection as they turn and walk away.

Why does this happen? Well, I can't really answer that question. Prayer is as unpredictable as God. Placing blame is never simple. Sometimes, we blame God; sometimes, we blame ourselves. Maybe we need more faith (Jas 1:7). Maybe we've been bad husbands (1 Pet 3:7). Maybe we gave up too quickly (Luke 11:5–13, 18:1–8). Maybe we're selfish (Jas 4:3). Perhaps we're swine or dogs in God's eyes. Or maybe it's not us. Perhaps it's God. Maybe He has other plans (Isa 55:8–9, Rom 11:33), wants me to learn something (2 Cor 12:8–9), or really will answer in the next week, month, or year? I don't know.

Maybe we're being too negative. If we think about it, I bet we can remember times we've prayed and God has answered. This probably happens a lot. It's easy to forget the good things in times of pain and doubt. It's easy to forget about the daily gifts God gives us. It's easy to forget about the continual blessings we pray for simply out of habit or routine. Sometimes, we forget that clothing, shelter, and food are gifts (Matt 6:26, 30–34; 1 Tim 6:8). We like big, splashy answers with miraculous outcomes, and we tend to take those common, daily answers for granted. Sometimes, we even forget the big things. Prayer will always be a mystery. It raises so many questions. Will God really change the future because of my prayers? Didn't God already know I would pray? Was my prayer already factored into the future? Can my prayer change God's mind? What about 10,000 prayers? Is God persuaded by sheer numbers? Is the future open for change? Wouldn't God already know that change?

If I'm sick, pray, and recover, do I know God healed me? What if I hadn't prayed? Would I have remained sick or died? Could I prove that God heard or answered me? If I pray and get that job I want, is God the reason? Couldn't I have simply been qualified and met a need? What if I don't get the job I so badly wanted? Is that a punishment? Would more prayer have worked? Or am I simply unqualified, and God had nothing to do with it? What does God do when two faithful people pray for the same job? What about when one prays for sunshine while a neighbor prays for rain?

Prayer and Jesus

Prayer creates more questions than it answers and makes a poor apologetic argument. We can prove very little about prayer. But maybe we don't need to. Perhaps prayer shouldn't be an apologetic argument. Maybe it isn't supposed to prove anything about God. Prayer is about something else. Our best bet, rather than proving prayers' efficacy, answering every question, figuring out the precise mechanisms for prayer, or judging

God's love based on His answers, is to trust God and imitate Jesus. Pray because Jesus prayed and taught us to. Pray regularly and rely on God's response. Whatever that may look like.

We experience nothing in prayer that Jesus isn't perfectly aware of. He's not naïve. Jesus knows about this problem, too. He knows that praying for a Lamborghini will not magically produce a Lamborghini from the heavens, and 1000 prayers won't produce 1000 Lamborghinis. Jesus doesn't promise that. The examples Jesus gives are requests for bread and fish (Matt 7:9–10). Interestingly, Jesus provides these exact things to the crowds in Matthew 14:13–21 and Matthew 15:32–39.

We should not read Jesus's words without the Lord's Prayer in mind (Matt 6:9–13). Jesus already told us how to pray, and He didn't include much of what we often ask for. God is no magic Genie, and we are not His master. He also isn't some random slot machine. God is a free, personal, thinking, planning, eternal Being. We cannot read His mind and do not know what He will do. He factors infinitely more information into His decisions than we will ever have.

Jesus knows about those prayers that seem to go unanswered. He prayed them. He prayed them in Gethsemane (Matt 26:36–46). Three times, He asked for God's intervention before the cross. However, immediately after praying, Jesus says, "Behold, the hour is at hand and the Son of Man is being betrayed into the hands of sinners" (Matt 26:44–45). I think Jesus knew what was going to happen. He prayed anyway.

Jesus, in agony, uttered those heart-wrenching words of Psalm 22:1, "My God, My God, why have you forsaken Me?" (Matt 27:46). The following line in that Psalm is, "Far from my deliverance are the words of my groaning. O my God, I cry by day, but You do not answer; And by night, but I have no rest" (Ps 22:1–2). Jesus prayed for deliverance; when He wasn't delivered, He prayed about His forsakenness. Jesus prayed with honesty, the good and the bad.

Prayer isn't always about getting what we want. God's goodness isn't defined by how well He conforms to my will. Quite the contrary, in prayer, we rely on Him and trust in His will (Matt 26:39, 42). Good fathers give good gifts to their children; sometimes, those gifts are brushed teeth and no candy. To a kid (and to me), that sounds like a lousy gift, but a loving father gives it.

On the other hand, a good father will occasionally give his children cookies and let them stay up late for a special occasion. Sometimes the father understands the difference, and the children do not. We don't need to understand but to trust.

Loving God only so far as He does whatever we say is an unstable foundation that produces a poor relationship. Prayer is a means of giving God our time, honesty, trust, and hope. Prayer is the worship of pouring ourselves out to Him, regardless of what He does. In prayer, we give God our hearts. Prayer is about building the most important relationship we will ever have with the God who loves us, deserves our trust, and opens the door to His children.

Reflection Questions

1. How is prayer an act of trust? How does prayer strengthen our relationship with God? How does prayer change us over time? How can wrong expectations harm us in our prayer lives?
2. What can the cross teach us about prayer? What can you do today to grow in your prayer life? What can you thank God for right now? What struggles are you battling through? Beginning now, spend the next several minutes in completely honest and open prayer with God.

REFLECTION 34

WHAT YOU DO MATTERS: READ MATTHEW 7:12–28

The Golden Rule

Jesus has covered many topics and challenged us in many ways. But, if we boil it all down to one basic idea, it will sound a lot like this: "In everything, therefore, treat people the same way you want them to treat you, for this is the Law and the Prophets" (Matt 7:12). This passage links back to Matthew 5:17–18: "Do not think that I came to abolish the Law or the Prophets; I did not come to abolish but to fulfill." Everything in between is how to fulfill the Law and Prophets. This is further explained in Matthew 22:40, where we find out that the Law and the Prophets depend on loving God and loving our neighbors. The Law and Prophets are properly understood and fulfilled when we "treat others as we want to be treated." Do you want angry people insulting you? Do you want perverts objectifying you? Do you want your spouse to divorce you? Do you want to be lied to? Do you want people withholding forgiveness or seeking revenge and retribution? Do you want to be slapped in the face? Do you want church leaders to be insincere glory seekers? Do you want others to store the treasure, leaving you nothing? Do you want to be judged harshly? I assume you would answer "no" to those questions. So don't do those things.

These words are often called "The Golden Rule." It's an essential part of any philosophical discussion of ethics and well-being. It is sometimes contrasted with "The Silver Rule." The silver rule is that one should not harm others because one wouldn't want to be harmed. However, Jesus goes further. We should not only refuse to harm others but actively seek to do good for others.

I've recently heard several people criticize the Golden Rule and replace it with the higher "Platinum Rule." Instead of "Treat others the way you want to be treated," it says, "Treat others the way they want to be treated." While I like the idea of this Platinum Rule, it doesn't actually add anything to the Golden Rule. Jesus does not say, "If you like mayonnaise sandwiches, give them to people who don't." That would be an obvious misunderstanding. Instead, implied in this rule is that if you want your feelings and desires considered, then you should consider the feelings and desires of others. To follow the Golden Rule, ask, "What kind of sandwich do you like?" because that's the question you would want to hear.

This Golden Rule is an ethical summary of the Sermon on the Mount and the Law and the Prophets. It is a safe bet that if you adhere to this aphorism, what you do will be consistent with God's kingdom. But as we can see, this is a rare way of life.

The Great Divide

Jesus understands that His teachings throughout this sermon are difficult. While we should never read this sermon devoid of grace, we should remember that Jesus is serious about obedience. Despite how popular it is to suggest otherwise, our obedience to Jesus impacts our standing before God. Giving Jesus our faith includes our loyalty, actions, and whole lives.

Jesus closes His sermon with several pictures of division. Like Matthew 25:31–46, Jesus describes two categories of people. Those who do what He said and those who do not. This division is pictured as two roads (Matt 7:13–14), two kinds of fruit trees (Matt 7:17–19), two fates at the judgment (Matt 7:21–23), and two workers building a house (Matt 7:24–27).

The Two Roads: We should interpret the Sermon on the Mount with these two roads in mind. We should periodically test our interpretations by asking, "Do most people do this or not?" If we interpret the difficulties out of Jesus's words, we may be interpreting ourselves comfortably on that broad and easy path. If we find excuses to justify our anger, insults, lusts, divorce, dishonesty, or hatred, we may be walking with a culturally Christian crowd into destruction. Jesus says only "few" will find life. That's distressing. It's important to remember, however, that words like "many" and "few" are relative. For example, 20 people would be a terribly low number of fans at an NFL football game, but it would be a massive number of children to have.

Other passages speak of "a great multitude which no one could count, from every nation and all tribes and peoples and tongues" entering God's presence with worship and awe (Rev 7:9). The worldwide family of God, made up of disciples from every nation (Matt 28:19), will be a large number. Perhaps the largest in the garden (Matt 13:32). Those who obey the Sermon on the Mount will be few compared to those who do not. But, thinking globally, over time and history, many will be saved. And that number has no limit. There is room for multitudes on that narrow road. Anyone who chooses the narrow road can fit.

The Two Fruit Trees: Who should we listen to along the journey? How are we supposed to know true prophets from false prophets? The Sermon on the Mount provides a valuable test. We cannot tell by looking. On the outside, they look like sheep. They probably don't murder and commit adultery publicly

(Matt 5). We may even see them giving, praying, and fasting (Matt 6). Externally, they look the part. But internally, they have not been converted to Jesus. Internally, they are angry, lustful, and proud. Internally, they are ravenous wolves.

How can we ever distinguish between the true and the false? How can we see the inside? One thought is to open up our Bibles and scrutinize their doctrine. But a lot of false prophets can say the right things. We could utilize Deuteronomy 18:21–22 and wait and see if what the prophet says comes to pass. Jesus suggests a different approach. He says to look at their fruit production. Is it good or bad? What emerges from a person reveals what is inside (Matt 15:11–20, 12:33–37).

A prophet can teach true things and still be a false prophet. A "true" or "false" prophet is not distinguished solely by the content of their message but by their character. A false prophet teaches from false motives like greed, lust, pride, or vengeance. He has not internalized the words of Jesus and produces fruit like malice, division, greed, anger, insult, etc. (Matt 23:15; perhaps Gal 5:19–23 could be a helpful guide). He may look like a sheep and generate a following, but he leads them down that broad road.

The Two Fates at Judgment: Standing before the perfect Judge, we realize what separates the true prophets from the false ones. God sees the ravenous wolf underneath the sheep's clothing. We heard the wolf saying, "Lord, Lord," and listened to their prophecies in the name of Jesus (Matt 7:21–22). They were convincing. They could even exorcize demons and perform miracles! But according to Jesus, those are not the marks of a true prophet or follower.

Be careful when saying, "Miracles existed in the first century to confirm the truth of the prophet's message." Apparently, even false prophets could perform miracles. The church in Corinth had all kinds of prophets, tongue speakers, and miracle workers, but they were divisive and prideful and used their gifts to bolster their own egos rather than to further the work of God. Prophecy, miracles, and casting out demons are not the litmus test for sincerity or truth. Jesus wants us to look for something else.

This passage reminds me of 1 Corinthians 13:1–3. There, Paul hypothetically describes the greatest spiritual gifts imaginable. Imagine speaking not only in the tongues of men but also in the heavenly tongues of angels. Paul mentions not only prophecy but understanding all mysteries and knowledge. Paul writes about a faith that could remove mountains and a generosity that would give up everything for others. Yet even those great and impressive gifts are nothing if they do not come from love.

Similarly, Jesus mentions those who can prophesy, cast out demons, and perform many miracles, but if one does not do what Jesus says, those great acts mean nothing. Those great acts will not save. If you can speak in tongues, heal the sick, move mountains, prophesy flawlessly, and authoritatively cast out demons, but you hate your enemies, serve wealth alongside God, or do not forgive others, you are missing the kingdom.

Jesus wants us to look to the Sermon on the Mount. This sermon reveals the inside of men. This sermon separates the sheep from the ravenous wolf. Are we obeying Jesus or just using His name? This sermon is where we'll find our answer. Notice how each example Jesus gives (prophecy, casting out demons, and miracles) is a boast in religious performance. Each of those actions makes one look powerful, righteous, and impressive before men. Notice, also, how these are not the things Jesus commanded us to do in this sermon.

It's easy to do the things that make others respect you. Everyone wants to impress. But Jesus doesn't call us to perform great miracles. He calls us to turn the other cheek and pray in our closets. That may make us look weak. People may never know how long we fasted or how beautifully we prayed. We may never get recognition for our piety. And that is quite alright. That quiet, peaceful, faithful, obedient path is where we find life.

The Two Workers: Jesus concludes this most potent and enduring sermon with a dramatic call to actualize His words through obedience. Do not only hear, ponder, or appreciate them. Jesus does not call us to philosophize or analyze. Instead, Jesus wants us to obey. That is how we find wisdom and life. Wisdom is not gained by thinking but by doing.

We will not flawlessly adhere to the standard Jesus set. We cannot build the perfect house. But we can build on the perfect foundation (Matt 16:16–18), and that house can weather any storm. Those who stand firm and endure when everything around them crumbles are founded and built on obeying the words of Jesus. To build on anything else guarantees destruction. By themselves, Jesus's words will not make one wise, give strength, or ensure eternal life. The power of Jesus's words is realized when implemented into our daily lives.

Spend time with this amazing and authoritative sermon (Matt 7:28–29). Read it and apply it. Then, make daily strategic goals to better obey each specific section. This sermon reveals the heart of Jesus. It reveals God and His reign. It is one thing to say Jesus is Lord; it is quite another to demonstrate it through obedience to His words.

Reflection Questions

1. How are the Law and Prophets best summarized? How should the golden rule impact your reading of Scripture? How should it impact your relationship with others? Your spouse? Kids? Parents?

Coworkers? Do you really treat others the way you want to be treated by them?

2. What path are you on? What fruit are you producing? Will you stand with confidence before God on judgment? What is the foundation of the house you are building? How can we know whether we are pleasing to God? How can the Sermon on the Mount help us answer these questions?

REFLECTION 35

THE COMPASSIONATE PHYSICIAN: READ MATTHEW 8:1–17

Sickness and Sin in Isaiah 53

HAVING CONCLUDED the Sermon on the Mount, Jesus descends from the mountain, and large crowds follow Him. He immediately resumes His ministry of healing, which occurred before the sermon (Matt 4:23–25). Jesus could preach to large crowds (Matt 4:25, 5:1, 7:28, 8:1) because He healed as nobody else could.

Healing is an essential part of His kingdom work. The kingdom of heaven is realized when God's will is done on earth as in heaven (Matt 6:10). In heaven, the infirmities, pains, diseases, and disabilities of this life are cleansed, healed, and set right. Thus, Jesus's ministry actualizes God's reign on earth.

When Matthew reflects on the healing ministry of Jesus, he cannot help but find resonance with various Old Testament passages. Many healings are recorded in Matthew 8 and 9, and each of them—in fact, all of Jesus's healing miracles—should cause us to consider God's Servant in Isaiah 53. Matthew interprets Jesus's ministry of healing, saying, "This was to fulfill what was spoken through Isaiah the prophet: He Himself took our infirmities and carried away our diseases" (Matt 8:17, Isa 53:4).

Isaiah 53 is a familiar passage for many Christians. It's quoted several times in the New Testament, and Christians have always seen Jesus there (Acts 8:32–35). Interestingly, Matthew's citation focuses on the healing ministry of Jesus rather than His mission to forgive sins. Clearly, throughout Matthew, Jesus is doing both. In fact, the word "save" (σῴζω) is used to describe saving from sin (Matt 1:21), saving from storms and death (Matt 8:25, 14:30, 27:40–42), and saving from illness (Matt 9:21). Jesus came to save people from sin, death, and sickness. This is all kingdom work that Jesus participated in, and the church should carry on today.

The link between saving from illness and saving from sin exists throughout Matthew. Even Isaiah 53:4, Matthew's cited text, has a unique textual history connecting "disease" and "sin." Based on the Hebrew text, the Old Testament says, "Surely our griefs He Himself bore, and our sorrows He carried." The words "griefs" (חֳלִי), for example, is usually translated as "sickness" or "illness" in other passages (Deuteronomy 7:15; 28:59, 61; 1 Kings 17:17; 2 Kings 1:2; etc.). The Septuagint, however, translates that word with the Greek word "sins" (ἁμαρτίας). Those translators saw the "sickness" as a spiritual sickness.

Rather than sticking with the Septuagint reading that "He bore our sins," Matthew's citation corresponds more closely to the original Hebrew, using ἀσθένεια, which is usually translated as "weakness," "illness," or "infirmity" (Luke 5:15, John 11:4, Acts 28:9, etc.). Matthew could have stuck with the Septuagint and used Isaiah 53 to describe how Jesus bore our sins, but instead, Matthew wants us to see this as an allusion to the physical healing Jesus provides.

Ministry for Body and Soul

As disciples of Jesus, caring for the physical needs of our neighbors is an essential part of caring for their spiritual needs. I've heard it said that when we see people, we should see their souls. And we should. We should certainly see and care about souls. But we should also see bodies. We should see complete humans, both body and soul, as we carry on the ministry of Jesus.

We should never neglect one in preference to the other. Medical missions, efforts to provide pure drinking water in areas without it, offering education and support in inner cities, helping people rebuild and regroup after natural disasters, and offering food and shelter locally and abroad are crucial ways to live like Jesus in our world. To preach the gospel without concern for the physical well-being of our neighbors is not to preach the gospel at all. Or, at least, it is to preach a watered-down gospel that fails to represent the reality of the mission of Jesus. It neglects the kingdom of heaven.

Jesus links saving people from infirmities with saving them from sin because the two must be linked. Admittedly, I have not seen the church perform the types of miracles Jesus did. But maybe miracles aren't necessary for us to love, show concern, and help people. I know of medical mission trips where qualified and gifted church members freely cared for those who had been unable to receive medical care. I know of a lady in Guatemala who, after being rendered blind by cataracts, visited a medical missions campaign, had cataract surgery, and could soon see again. The church gave sight to the blind. That is a powerful example of the good news of the kingdom still impacting the world through Jesus.

In two passages in Matthew—Matthew 4:23 and Matthew 9:35—Jesus is said to be "proclaiming the gospel of the kingdom" (κηρύσσων τὸ εὐαγγέλιον τῆς βασιλείας). But in both passages, Jesus was not only preaching the kingdom's gospel, but He was also "healing every kind of disease and every kind of sickness" (Matt 4:23, 9:35). They are linked, and we shouldn't separate them.

When John the Baptist, in prison, sent disciples to see whether Jesus truly was the Expected One, Jesus described His ministry in this way: "The blind receive sight and the lame walk, the lepers are cleansed and the deaf hear, the dead are raised up, and the poor have the gospel preached to them" (Matt 11:5). The gospel is preached, to be sure, but it is not preached in isolation. It is preached to the poor because the kingdom of heaven seeks to help the impoverished (Acts 4:32–35). The gospel is preached as part of a holistic healing ministry. Jesus, the Suffering Servant of Isaiah 53, bears our diseases and carries away our sorrows. Jesus not only preached the good news, but He also demonstrated it.

The Compassion of Christ

Another passage that links physical and spiritual healing in the ministry of Jesus is Matthew 9:1–13. The two stories in this section describe Jesus healing a paralyzed man and sharing a meal with sinners and tax collectors. These two stories are placed back to back as Matthew intentionally melds the theology of healing and forgiveness.

When a paralyzed man was brought to Jesus, rather than immediately healing the man physically, Jesus shocked the crowds by saying, "Take courage, son; your sins are forgiven" (Matt 9:2). Perhaps by this point, people are used to Jesus healing the body, but when Jesus extends forgiveness of sins, the scribes reason, "This man blasphemes!" (Matt 9:3).

God is who forgives sins. Way back at the beginning of the book, Matthew introduces Jesus by two names: Immanuel, meaning "God with us," and Jesus, who "will save His people from their sins" (Matt 1:21–23). Jesus can forgive sins because He is the God who saves. In defense of His actions, Jesus demonstrates His authority to forgive sins by healing the paralyzed man. Jesus says, "'But so that you may know that the Son of Man has authority on earth to forgive sins'—then He said to the paralytic, 'Get up, pick up your bed and go home'" (Matt 9:6).

To prove the efficacy of His spiritual healing and forgiveness, which human eyes cannot see, Jesus offers physical healing, which can be seen. Jesus needed to care for people's physical well-being to prove that He could provide spiritual healing. Why would we think any differently? Why would we expect people to trust us with their invisible spiritual struggles when we have shown zero interest in their visible physical struggles?

Immediately following this story, Jesus calls Matthew, a tax collector and companion of sinners, to become a follower. This is a shocking and controversial move. Jesus unapologetically invites controversy repeatedly in His ministry, but it always has a purpose. He wants people to see that Matthew matters and that Matthew is a disciple. Jesus's kingdom is for all, even the sinners and tax collectors. Or, as Jesus will say, especially for them.

After calling Matthew, Jesus dines with other tax collectors and sinners. This raises the ire of the Pharisees, who find no good reason for a holy person, prophet, or teacher ever to spend time with such dreadful company. Jesus calls them out on their misapprehension of His actions.

Jesus is with the spiritually sick because He is the great physician. This designation is situated in the middle of a lengthy catalog of healing stories throughout Matthew 8 and 9. The healing stories support and verify that Jesus is the great physician. In addition, these healing stories prove "that the Son of Man has authority on earth to forgive sins" (Matt 9:6). Jesus forgives, heals, and dines with others because He understands the expression, "I desire compassion/mercy and not sacrifice" (Matt 9:13; see Hos 6:6 and Matt 12:7). Sacrifice is empty and meaningless when offered devoid of compassion. In Hosea 6, Israel wanted to receive God's mercy, love, and healing. They wanted God to heal, bandage, revive, and raise them on the third day (Hos 6:1–2). But their loyalty was fickle and short-lived at best (Hos 6:4). They wanted to receive mercy and compassion but refused to extend it.

Perhaps they thought God would be merciful to them if they offered sacrifice. But no, if you want to receive God's mercy, offer mercy to others (Matt 5:7). God desires us to be merciful rather than multiply sacrifices. Like forgiveness (Matt 6:14–15, 18:35) and judgment (Matt 7:2), this is another passage indicating that God will treat us in proportion to how we treat others.

Jesus has compassion and mercy. He extends it to the physically ill and the spiritually sick. Jesus is the great physician, full of compassion, calling sinners to a new way of life.

Reflection Questions

1. What does the healing ministry of Jesus reveal about Him? What does it reveal about the kingdom of heaven? What does it reveal about the ministry of the church today? How can we share in this ministry?
2. How are healing miracles and forgiveness of sins related? When have you received mercy? How can you extend mercy to others?

REFLECTION 36

HIS IMPACT SPREADS: READ MATTHEW 8:1–9:33

A Leper, Centurion, and Mother-in-Law

As noted in the last reflection, Jesus's healing ministry fulfills Isaiah 53. It links Jesus to the Suffering Servant who "took our infirmities and carried away our diseases" (Matt 8:17). These healings also prove that He can save and forgive sins (Matt 9:6). If the church wants to imitate Jesus and join His mission in the world, we must take on both sides of this healing ministry also. So, let's quickly stroll through Matthew's index of healing stories and see what else we can learn.

Jesus cleanses a leper in Matthew 8:2–4. This leper, who was supposed to stand at a distance, separated from humanity (Lev 14), was touched by Jesus. Yet, instead of Jesus becoming unclean, Jesus cleansed the leper. This story sets a precedent that we will notice throughout these two chapters. Jesus is not afraid to eat with tax collectors and sinners, nor is He afraid to touch the unclean. Jesus will constantly surround Himself with the unclean and emerge undefiled. What happens instead is that His purity spreads and cleanses all around Him. This is what the sacrifices of the Old Testament were supposed to do.

They cleansed the defiled. Jesus is the walking, talking, living, and breathing agent of cleansing in our world.

Next, a centurion comes to Jesus (Matt 8:5–13). This is an incredible scene. A Roman centurion with authority, respect, and power, a ruler of the Gentiles, comes to Jesus requesting that one of his servants be healed. Here is a man of high status who cares for his servants.

Though this man represents the violent, hostile, and pagan Roman empire and military, Jesus does not send him away. Though this man represents the kingdoms of this world, which are under the rule of Satan (Matt 4:8–10), he becomes the surprising hero of our story. It's not always a pretty sight when we encounter Roman officials in Matthew. Herod slaughtered the babies of Bethlehem, another Herod beheaded John the Baptist, and Pilate ordered Jesus to be nailed to a cross. Here, a Roman military man with rank and status appears. While we might be tempted to assume the worst, the kingdom of God is seen in the most unexpected places.

Interestingly, it's at the foot of the cross where another Roman centurion declares, "Truly this was the Son of God!" (Matt 26:54). In Acts, the first fully Gentile convert to the way of Christ is a centurion named Cornelius (Acts 10:1). Each of these centurion stories points to the surprising, transformative, worldwide reach of the kingdom of heaven.

This centurion so trusts the authority of Jesus (Matt 7:29) that he doesn't want to trouble the Lord with a trip to his house. Instead, he humbly tells Jesus to simply speak the word, and his servant would be healed. He is right, too. Jesus's power can travel time and space to heal a servant sight unseen. There is no limit to what Jesus can accomplish.

Jesus is astonished by this man's faith, which surpasses all those in Israel. To Jesus, this is a picture of the ultimate realization of the kingdom where Gentiles from the East and West will dine with Abraham, Isaac, and Jacob. Surprisingly, the "sons of the kingdom," perhaps unbelieving Israelites who first had the table reserved for them, will not be allowed inside for the feast. This centurion's faith is a pointer to a future grand day where all races and nationalities will dine together at the same table (compare with Gal 2:12–14).

Jesus then heals Peter's mother-in-law and a whole host of people who are demon-possessed and ill (Matt 8:14–16). Think about all Jesus has done. Jesus touches the unclean, heals a servant, commends the faith of a Gentile, and takes away the fever of Peter's mother-in-law. In these healing stories, Jesus heals Jew and Gentile, servant and free, and male and female, and "many" others (Matt 8:16). This sounds a little bit like Galatians 3:28. There is an important message here: Nobody outside the grasp of God's kingdom.

Crossing the Sea

Next, Jesus crosses over the Sea of Galilee in a boat to the country of the Gadarenes (Matt 8:23–34). We will see the kingdom's mission extend even further in this scene. Two crucial events happen next. First, a storm arises on the sea, sending the boat out of control. The chaotic waters rage and seek to destroy. As Jesus slumbers, the disciples fear the worst. Jesus then awakes and rebukes the sea, and the sea humbly and calmly obeys.

The disciples, in amazement, ask, "What kind of man is this, that even the winds and the sea obey Him?" (Matt 8:27). A read through the creation account in Genesis 1:6–10, the flood of Noah in Genesis 7–8, the dividing of the Red Sea in Exodus 14:13–31, and Psalms 65:7, 89:9, 104:6–7, 107:23–30, gives a clear answer to their question. Just like God is the One who can forgive sins (Matt 9:2), God is also the One who controls the winds and the sea. Jesus is "God with us."

Second, as Jesus brought calm to the chaos of the waters,

Jesus also brought calm to the demonic chaos in the lives of two sufferers. These men lived among the tombs, were extremely violent, and kept all others fearfully away. Jesus arrives on land to find Himself in a sea of uncleanness. He is on the side of the sea heavily populated by Gentiles, among the dead bodies of the tombs, within a short distance of a herd of pigs, and approached by men with unclean spirits. But remember, Jesus touches lepers, talks with a Roman centurion (even agreeing to potentially enter his house), and dines with tax collectors and sinners. Jesus isn't afraid of a little unclean. With unparalleled authority, Jesus casts the unclean spirits from the men into a herd of pigs who then run into the sea and perish.

Jesus is cleansing everything around Him. The leprosy is cleansed, sickness is cured, demons are gone, and pigs have perished. Jesus not only cleanses and heals in Israel, but His authority extends over storms amid the sea. His words have power over the spiritual forces of darkness in the unseen realms. His orders are obeyed even in strange lands on the other side of the sea. His kingdom has no borders.

More Cleansing and Healing

Matthew 9:18–26 describes two more healings performed by Jesus, the Compassionate Physician and Suffering Servant. While on His way to raise the daughter of a synagogue official back to life. (This official already believes Jesus can raise the dead. This is an even more incredible depiction of his faith than given in Mark 5:23.) As He walks, Jesus is touched by an unclean woman. This woman has had a menstrual flow of blood for 12 years. She is suffering from the exact malady described in Leviticus 15:25–33.

She is supposed to keep herself distant from others and not touch anyone, as she would spread her uncleanness to them. She is supposed to live like a leper. But her faith cannot allow her to sit still as Jesus walks away. Trying to be as sly as possible, hoping to be entirely unnoticed, she sneaks behind Jesus. Briefly, gently, she touches the back fringe of his cloak. While this is clearly outlawed, she believes He alone can heal her. She has no other options. So, she tries to hide it and get His healing without being noticed.

Jesus notices. Rather than rebuking this woman for ignoring Leviticus 15 or touching Him while unclean, Jesus cleanses her and compliments her faith (like the centurion in 8:10, but unlike the disciples in Matt 8:26). This is another passage where Jesus makes physical contact with the unclean, but rather than Him becoming contaminated, His purity and cleansing power spread to others.

When Jesus arrives at the synagogue official's house, he touches the hand of the little girl who has died (Matt 9:25). Again, rather than becoming unclean, Jesus healed her and gave her life again. Remember, according to Numbers 19:11, "The one who touches the corpse of any person shall be unclean for seven days." Jesus touches the corpse, but it does not remain a corpse for long. Jesus has authority over death itself. He commands demons to flee, storms to be calm, and death to become life. They all obey.

From there, Jesus heals two blind men (Matt 9:27–31) and a mute man possessed by a demon (Matt 9:32–33). Matthew 8 and 9 exemplify the identity and mission of Jesus.

Whew. That is a lot of healing in these two chapters. Taken together, He offers cleansing from impurity, leprosy, and demonic forces. He saves from sickness and sin. He gives sight to the blind and life to the dead. He heals men and women, young and old, Jew and Gentile, men of importance (like synagogue officials), servants (like the centurion's servant), and the outcasts (like lepers and the woman with the flow of blood). He dines with all. He exercises authority inside and outside the holy lands and even demonstrates His power in the seas that divide them. There is no limit or border to the authority of Jesus and His coming kingdom. Every story establishes the truth that will be fulfilled in Matthew 28:18.

Reflection Questions

1. What different "types" of people does Jesus heal? What does this tell us about His love? How does Jesus's "cleansing" relate to His "healing" and "forgiving"? What does this teach us about purity regulations? What does this teach us about how to view others?
2. If Jesus were on earth performing miracles today, would you go to Him? What would you ask for? How is this message still relevant today? How can the church overcome purity barriers? How can the church offer healing? How can the church offer forgiveness?

REFLECTION 37

THE DISCIPLES' MISSION: READ MATTHEW 10:1–11:1

Delegating His Authority

MATTHEW just brilliantly portrayed the unparalleled, unlimited, uncompromising authority of Jesus through His words and actions. His power resides above every element of life, nature, and the spiritual realm. Jesus's sovereignty has traveled across the sea and to the lands on the other side. He has demonstrated dominion over the clean and unclean, Jew and Gentile, male and female, and servants and free men.

As Jesus continues to heal and exercise His divine control over this world, even larger crowds from all around stampede toward Him. When He sees them, He cannot help but feel compassion. He sees their distress and troubles. He sees their desperation and need. He sees a massive harvest for God's kingdom that needs to be reaped. Rather than working alone, God's plans have always included partnering with humans to accomplish His mission in the world (Matt 9:35–38).

Jesus, the Lord of the harvest, will do precisely that. He chooses workers to send out into those fields. Matthew 10 begins with Jesus sharing His authority with His twelve disciples. His twelve disciples can now accomplish the healings and exorcisms we saw in Matthew 8–9: "Jesus summoned His twelve disciples and gave them authority over unclean spirits, to cast them out, and to heal every kind of disease and every kind of sickness" (Matt 10:1).

While listing the twelve disciples by name, Matthew expressly acknowledges the "tax collector," "zealot," and "betrayer" among them. The kingdom of heaven continues to make an impact among the unlikeliest people. After listing this group, Jesus gives them instructions for a mission they will take. This mission will imitate what Jesus has done since chapter 4 (healing and teaching). It will also prepare them for their future after Jesus ascends on high. These instructions are the second major speech in the Gospel of Matthew.

Major Speech #2

Jesus begins His instructions by telling them where to go and what to do. They should focus on the house of Israel rather than the Samaritans and the Gentiles. That day will come. Jesus has already alluded to it several times. The last mission Jesus sends these disciples on will be about "all the nations/Gentiles" (Matt 28:18–20). The Book of Acts depicts that day. However, this mission has a limited geographical focus.

While on this mission, the disciples are to do the things Jesus has been doing. They are to preach "the kingdom of heaven is at hand" (Matt 10:7), just like Jesus and John the Baptist (Matt 3:2, 4:17). They are to combine the message of the kingdom with demonstrations of the kingdom: "Heal the sick, raise the dead, cleanse the lepers, cast out demons" (Matt 10:8). As we've noted with the ministry of Jesus, the kingdom includes both physical and spiritual healing. Neither should be neglected.

Jesus prepares His disciples for the many hardships they will no doubt face. They will face poverty, rejection, arrest, betrayal, and persecution (Matt 10:9–23). But Jesus gives them practical tips, encouragement, and a crucial mindset to carry with them as they encounter these trials. He already said, "Blessed are those who have been persecuted for the sake of righteousness" (Matthew 5:10–12). Now, He is calling His disciples to be among that blessed group.

Jesus tells them not to carry more than is needed for the day (Matt 10:9–10), much like His instructions in the Sermon on the Mount (Matt 6:19, 33). Jesus wants them to focus on the day at hand rather than storing up assurances for tomorrow. Every day of this mission is a new day to rely on God alone.

One way God will bless them is through the generosity and hospitality of those who receive their message (Matt 10:11–15). Jesus does not tell them to go looking for persecution or hardship. He doesn't want them forcing a message down the throats of those who do not want it. Don't force pigs to appreciate pearls. Find a peaceful residence and give peace there. If you are rejected, that is fine. Take your peace with you and move on. Shake the dust from your feet and leave it all in the hands of God.

Jesus does not tell them to hate, curse, or retaliate against those who reject or persecute them. Instead, Jesus prepares them for a mission consistent with the Sermon on the Mount. Leave them when they want you to leave and shake the dust from your feet. Faithfully move along to more profitable, receptive soil. Shaking off the dust from one's foot likely symbolized leaving Gentile/pagan territory. Jesus says those who reject the kingdom, even within Israel, are regarded as Gentiles. And God will judge them on the final day (Matt 10:15).

Jesus sends the twelve disciples as sheep into a dangerous world of wolves (Matt 10:16). This "sheep" imagery occurs regularly in Matthew (Matt 7:15; 9:36; 10:6, 16; 15:24; 18:12–14; 25:32–33). Jesus saw the crowds as "sheep without a shepherd" (Matt 9:36). He saw Israel as lost sheep who needed to be found (Matt 10:6,

15:24, 18:12). Lost sheep are always in danger of wolves. The wolves are like those beasts from Daniel 7.

Those wolves will hand the disciples to courts, beat, and scourge them. They will stand before governors and kings—as you keep reading Matthew, you'll see John the Baptist killed by a king (Matt 14:9) and Jesus executed by a governor (Matt 27:11). This will allow them to make a testimony to Gentiles and their rulers. This happens explicitly in Acts. From this point forward, Jesus's words should be read both about His disciples' current mission and hinting towards the post-resurrection fate of Christian missionaries. Many of these words will apply to both settings and some more obviously to the latter.

The disciples, though not going to Gentile cities (Matt 10:5), will be arrested and stand before Gentile kings and rulers (Matt 10:18). Thankfully, rather than facing them alone, the Spirit of the Father will be with disciples and will give them the testimony they need (Matt 10:18–20). God will not abandon them in difficult moments.

Through betrayal, hatred, and persecution, Jesus calls them to endure with the hope of salvation (Matt 10:22). He also encourages them to flee when the persecution gets too intense (Matt 10:23). There is no shame in running. In the book of Acts, this is one way that the early church spread. They did not stay and die in each city; they spread to surrounding cities and took the gospel with them (Acts 8:1–4).

This difficult mission will be fraught with trials, threats, and persecutions. Therefore, disciples should stay in peaceful places (Matt 10:13), expect rejection (Matt 10:14), believe in God's judgment (Matt 10:15), trust God's Spirit (Matt 10:20), hope in salvation (Matt 10:22), and flee when the heat is too intense (Matt 10:23).

The Nature of Discipleship

As disciples of Jesus, the twelve will be transformed into His image (Matt 10:24–25). They will preach, cast out demons, and heal like Jesus (Matt 10:7–8), but they will also suffer and be maligned like Jesus (Matt 10:24–25). Jesus was accused of casting out demons by Beelzebul, the ruler of demons (Matt 9:34, 12:24), and His disciples should expect to share in that slander. Yet, they should not fear (Matt 10:26, 28, 31).

Fear keeps one silent. Fear stymies the mission of the church. Jesus wants them not to think about the present fleeting struggle but to adopt an eschatological mindset with God as the ultimate judge (Matt 7:21–23, 10:15). Men can be punished for a moment. They can harm or even kill the body. But God is the ultimate judge of all humanity who can destroy both body and soul in Gehenna (Matt 10:26–28).

God also loves you, cares for you, and sees your value and purpose. The God who cares for the sparrows cares decidedly more for you (Matt 10:30; 6:26, 30). So remember your gracious judge and act now in view of His final judgment. Shout the message of Jesus from the mountain tops, proclaim it before kings and governors, and do not deny Him before men.

If we want Christ to confess us before the Father, we must confess Him before men (Matt 10:32–33). This, by the way, is not an allusion to the pre-baptismal confession of Jesus as the Son of God. It is the sustained confession of the Lordship of Jesus throughout one's life. Confessing Christ is not simply a "Step of Salvation" but a daily demand of discipleship. This is what Peter famously failed to do on that fateful night Jesus was arrested (Matt 26:69–75).

Following Jesus in this manner will come with a cost. It will come with a sword and division. It may create enmity even among families and loved ones. Yet, our ties to this world should never be more robust than our ties to the Lord. Discipleship comes with a cross. It may cost you your life. But, according to Jesus, we find true life through the cross (Matt 10:38–39).

Jesus concludes this speech by again connecting Himself to His disciples. They will share in His authority and ministry (Matt 10:1, 7–8), in His suffering, persecution, and cross (Matt 10:24–25, 38), but they will also share in His reward (Matt 10:40–42). The way Christ's followers are received equals the way Christ is received. Therefore, how we honor His missionaries and disciples expresses how we honor Him. Jesus uses this same line of reasoning with his parable in Matthew 25:35–46.

In the context of Matthew, those preaching the gospel of the kingdom should be received willingly and hospitably, with kindness and a glass of cold water. In our context, we should demonstrate hospitality and extend generosity toward those doing the work of Christ. Receive the disciple of Christ as you would receive Christ.

Reflection Questions

1. Why would Jesus send His disciples instead of going Himself? Why does God share responsibilities with flawed humans? What are the disciples supposed to do on this mission? What does this teach us about our mission?
2. What are the costs of following Jesus? What costs have you paid? How does fear impact our mission? Did Jesus bring peace or a sword? How can we offer kindness to servants of God?

REFLECTION 38

JESUS QUESTIONED: READ MATTHEW 11:2–12:14

Jesus and John

So far in Matthew, Jesus has been in the spotlight. Matthew has made a compelling case that Jesus is the Expected One. From His incredible birth, baptism, victory over temptations, the beginning of His ministry, the Sermon on the Mount, the lengthy list of healings, exorcisms, and miracles, His sending of the disciples (Matt 10), the focus has been on the glorious and unparalleled ministry of King Jesus. Now, the time has come to see the response.

The responses in Matthew 11–12 come as doubts, questions, accusations, and condemnations. Jesus is slandered and persecuted. Whole cities reject Him. Religious leaders accuse and condemn Him. Even John the Baptist begins to doubt Him. John has already proclaimed the greatness of Christ (Matt 3), but now, even he begins to wonder if we should be searching for someone else. This may seem incredible to us, but suffering has a way of plaguing the mind with overwhelming frustration, sorrow, and doubt. John is a prisoner as this section begins (Matt 11:2).

Matthew 11:2–19 again compares John the Baptist and Jesus

(see Matt 3:4–17). John has heard of the great works of Jesus (the word "works" [ἔργα] bookends this pericope in 11:2 and 11:19). Yet, John sits alone, suffering and imprisoned. Why isn't Jesus doing something? This is a common question to ask while suffering. You may have felt it also. If Jesus is truly the "Expected One," why does He ignore us in our time of great need? Should we look for hope elsewhere?

John sends some of his own disciples to Jesus for answers. The answers do not come in the form of deliverance for John. In fact, John will ultimately be executed in prison (Matt 14:1–12). Jesus doesn't offer a simple "yes" or "no" answer either. Instead, Jesus reminds John to trust in the promises of God and the evidence of Jesus's deeds. Matthew 11:19 says, "Wisdom is vindicated by her deeds." Jesus answers this question, vindicating Himself, by listing the deeds He has been doing.

Compare this list of deeds in Matthew 11:4–6—the blind receive sight, the lame walk, the lepers are cleansed, the deaf hear, the dead are raised, and the poor have the gospel preached to them—to Isaiah 29:18–19, 35:5–6, and 61:1–2. Jesus is doing the deeds of the Expected One. These deeds represent the ushering in of a new age of hope, salvation, and the presence of God. Jesus does not do everything we want Him to. He may not relieve our suffering or free us from our literal bonds, but "blessed is he who does not take offense at Me" (Matt 11:6).

These verses present the key to interpreting the miraculous works of Jesus so far in Matthew. They have been vindicating Him as the Expected One. They fulfill Isaiah's promises. John the Baptist needed this reminder.

As John's disciples leave, Jesus talks about John a bit. He does not rebuke John for his doubts. In fact, He describes John as a prophesied prophet! John was spoken of hundreds of years earlier by Malachi (Mal 3:1). John does not come as royalty in soft clothing or as a sycophant blown about by the current political winds but as a great prophet in the spirit of Elijah.

Elijah stood up against the king! He was not blown by the wind, meaning his preaching didn't waft in whatever direction the presiding powers blew. He opposed wicked rulers, no matter the cost, as a true prophet of God. In prison for standing against the king, John the Baptist is participating in that story.

He is the greatest of all born of women (Matt 11:11). He is a powerful prophet of God. He has been persecuted for the sake of righteousness and suffered violence aimed at the kingdom of heaven. Yet, even the least of those in the kingdom of heaven is greater than John (Matt 11:12).

That's a surprising passage. John already said that Jesus was greater than himself (Matt 3:11), and Jesus's greatness is shared among those within the coming kingdom. John was looking forward to the kingdom and was essential in its preparation, but like Moses viewing the promised land from the mountaintop (Deut 34:1–5), he died before entering. This is not to discount the greatness of John the Baptist but to remind us to prioritize the kingdom of heaven above all. We are gifted to share in the glory of Christ in His kingdom.

Jesus and John Rejected

A comparison between John and Jesus is made to conclude this section. We've already seen Jesus as the expected Messiah and John as the expected Elijah. They were both rejected. John is in prison, and Jesus is heading toward the cross. While John and Jesus had remarkably different lifestyles and ministries, neither found acceptance. Those who rejected their message of the kingdom found creative ways to condemn them both. Like musicians rejected at both a wedding and a funeral, Jesus and John are rejected no matter what tune they play.

They condemned John as demon-possessed because he lived an ascetic life in the wilderness, fasting regularly and denying himself comfortable lodgings, nice clothing, good food, and enjoyable wine. Most folks don't want to live that way. They rejected him as some lunatic who took this religious stuff way too seriously.

Jesus comes along and, after living that ascetic life for 40 days (Matt 4:1–11), spends a lot of time in cities among the people. He dines with them (Matt 9:9–17), celebrates with wine (John 2), and enjoys the good of God's creation. When people see Him, they think He is not spiritual or religious enough. He is a drunk and a glutton (see Deut 21:20) who rejects a holy life and spends time with sinners.

No matter what they do, John and Jesus are interpreted in the least sympathetic light possible. There is no winning. A good look at their deeds would vindicate them (Matt 11:19), but their generation has no interest in that.

Examples of this biased negativity are the cities of Chorazin, Bethsaida, and Capernaum, which had miracles and great "deeds" performed among them, but they did not repent. If Tyre and Sidon had seen those deeds or even Sodom of all places, they would have repented and avoided judgment. And God is well aware of that. God considers opportunity and local/cultural privilege as He judges. Apparently, He will judge Chorazin, Bethsaida, and Capernaum more harshly than even the most wicked cities in the Hebrew imagination. When the kingdom presents itself to us, we must take advantage of it.

The Lord of Sabbath

As we continue reading into Matthew 12, we see that not only has Jesus been accused of being a drunk and a glutton, but He and His disciples are accused of breaking Sabbath (Matt 12:1–14). Because Jesus's disciples picked some heads of grain and ate on the Sabbath, the Pharisees condemned them. Jesus argues that, in their quest to find fault, they have ignored Scripture and condemned the innocent (Matt 12:7).

They ignored the example of what David did in 1 Samuel 21:1–6. In desperation, David and his men ate the sacred bread in the Tabernacle. In ordinary circumstances, this bread was not to be eaten by anyone but the priests. However, no priest should watch someone starve while holding bread in his hand. The bread was not consecrated intentionally to keep David (the Anointed one) and his men starving. That was not the theology behind the sacred bread. That would have been cruel and lacking in neighborly love (the most important command). David ate and was not condemned for His action, so why should Jesus, the Anointed One, be condemned? If the Pharisees excused David's unlawfulness but condemned Jesus's innocent disciples, they showed their hypocrisy.

Jesus wants them to think about the purpose of the Sabbath. Sabbath was not intended to halt temple services, so the priests still serve and are innocent (Matt 12:5). Jesus, the Lord of Sabbath, should be our guide on Sabbath observance (Matt 12:8). By the way, what mere human could possibly claim to be the Lord of Sabbath? That is a designation that only makes sense for God.

The Sabbath controversies continue when Jesus heals a man with a withered hand on the Sabbath (Matt 12:9–14). Sabbath was never intended to keep a man's hand withered. What passage would teach that? Sabbath should not keep us from helping others or loving our neighbor. Neither should going to church, by the way. Doing good and helping others matters. To put it bluntly, "it is lawful to do good on the Sabbath" (Matt 12:12). That should seem obvious. Still, we sometimes get so bogged down in rigid mechanical obedience to the narrowest interpretations of Scripture that we forget to zoom out and think about the purpose, meaning, and intention of those Scriptures (Matt 7:12, 22:37–40).

These Sabbath controversies are introduced as Jesus stands, calling and inviting us to rest (Matt 11:28). He does not condemn us for picking heads of grain or doing good on Sabbath. He calls us to enjoy true rest as God intended (Matt 11:28). As Jesus has transformed how to understand purity regulations, He also transformed how we should view the Sabbath. So many had made the Sabbath a burden. So many have made all of life a burden. Cares and anxieties about wealth, popularity, power, and spiritual superiority have put a heavy load on our shoulders. Jesus, the Lord of Sabbath, wants to replace that load with His light and easy yoke. To the Christian, the Sabbath is not a day but a lifestyle. We should enjoy the good things God made, do good for others, and spend time in community. We should not live a life consumed by earning another dollar and getting ahead of our neighbors. Jesus wants us to receive true and rejuvenating rest in His kingdom (Matt 11:28–30).

Reflection Questions

1. Where does doubt come from? Is it wrong to have doubts? What are some of your doubts? What can you do to work through them? How did Jesus alleviate John's doubts?
2. Why was Jesus called a drunkard and a glutton? Why was John said to have a demon? What do these responses tell you about the hearts of that generation? How is wisdom justified by her deeds?

REFLECTION 39

SOMETHING GREATER IS HERE: READ MATTHEW 12:15–50

Fulfilling Isaiah

THE BOOK of Isaiah plays a pivotal role for Matthew in telling the story of Jesus. Along with a myriad of allusions to Isaiah, Matthew explicitly cites Isaiah and says it is "fulfilled" four separate times. When Jesus is first introduced in Matthew 1, the first passage He fulfills is Isaiah 7:14 (Matt 1:22–23). We discussed this passage earlier in this book, but remember, Jesus is assigned an important name in this Scripture: "They shall call His name Immanuel" (Matt 1:23). Jesus is presented as "God with us" throughout the rest of Matthew.

The second passage from Isaiah fulfilled by Jesus is Isaiah 9:1–2. This occurs when Jesus moves from Nazareth to Capernaum (Matt 4:13–16). Since Capernaum is in Galilee, "in the region of Zebulun and Naphtali," Matthew cannot help but think about Isaiah's promised King who brought light in "Galilee of the Gentiles" to the people sitting in darkness and the "shadow of death." As you continue to read Isaiah 9, you discover a Son whose "name" is called "Wonderful Counselor, Mighty God, Eternal Father, Prince of Peace" (Isa 9:6). Jesus is the divine King who shines light in the darkness even among Gentiles.

The third passage from Isaiah fulfilled by Jesus is Isaiah 53:4, as Jesus heals many and casts out demons (Matt 8:16–17). Isaiah 53 famously describes the "Suffering Servant" who gives Himself for the people. This Servant not only carries away sickness and affliction, as Jesus does through His healing ministry but also, "My Servant will justify the many, as He will bear their iniquities" (Isa 53:11). Jesus is the Suffering Servant who heals and saves.

With these passages in mind, look at Matthew 12:15–21. Matthew cites Isaiah 42:1–4 which is the lengthiest Old Testament citation in Matthew. The major themes presented in those earlier Isaiah passages reappear in this citation. Jesus is presented as the "Servant" chosen by God, beloved, and given the Spirit. That description of "Servant" is very important.

Isaiah has several "Servant Songs" that appear after chapter 40 (Isa 42:1–4, 49:1–6, 50:4–11, and 52:13–53:12). Matthew again identifies Jesus with this Servant. An earlier clue to this identity was Jesus's baptism, where the voice from heaven declared, "This is My beloved Son, in whom I am well-pleased" (Matt 3:17). It was at that time that the Spirit descended as a dove and lighted upon Jesus (Matt 3:16). That is all language and imagery from Isaiah 42:1–4.

The theme of Gentile impact re-emerges in this passage as well. Jesus "shall proclaim justice to the Gentiles" and "in His name the Gentiles will hope." This is how He shines light among the Gentiles (Isa 9:1).

This is also the third reference to Christ's "name" from the context of the Isaiah citations. Jesus is introduced with the name "Immanuel" from Isaiah. There is also that list of names from Isaiah 9:6. So, perhaps the "name" in which the Gentiles will hope is Jesus. Still, from the quotes of Isaiah, certainly "Immanuel" and "Wonderful Counselor, Mighty

God, Eternal Father, Prince of Peace" should also be in our minds.

Matthew uses this citation after Jesus warns the crowds "not to tell who He was" (Matt 12:16). The Servant from Israel, who gives His life for many and is the hope of justice and salvation to the Gentiles, does not scream His identity from the mountain tops. Instead, He "will not quarrel, nor cry out; nor will anyone hear His voice in the streets" (Matt 12:19). Matthew cites this passage to describe the secrecy of the Messiah. However, by including the surrounding verses in the quotation, Matthew uses this text to summarize the Messianic identity and mission of Jesus.

Thinking about Demons

The accusations against Jesus keep coming in Matthew 12. Jesus casts a demon out of a man who had been blind and mute. Jesus healed him in the presence of the crowds. That deed should vindicate Him (Matt 11:19). But no. He is accused of casting out demons "by Beelzebul the ruler of the demons" (Matt 12:24).

Jesus responds to these outlandish accusations in several ways (Matt 12:25–32), but I think He ultimately wants His accusers to stop and think about the big picture (Matt 12:33–37). Simplify matters and ask whether this action is good or bad. Rejoice if it is good and reject whatever is bad. Sometimes, it is just that simple. If the fruit is good, then the tree producing it is good (Matt 12:33). Eat it, be happy, and stop trying to condemn the tree. You will be held accountable for who you condemn, how you judge, and what you say (Matt 12:33–37). So be careful.

Jesus has performed incredible signs but has been rejected by the religious leaders. They've even attributed His exorcisms to the ruler of demons, which is a perfect example of grasping at straws. Why would Beelzebul empower a man to destroy the work of Beelzebul? It makes no sense, but it is the only explanation they can concoct. They must admit His miracles but reject His identity.

Shortly after this, in Matthew 12:38, the scribes and Pharisees have the audacity to tell Jesus, "Teacher, we want to see a sign from You." Um, the last one you attributed to Satan. Jesus does not put up with their disingenuous request and tells them that only one sign truly matters. There is one sign they need to be aware of, and it is the "sign of Jonah the prophet; for just as Jonah was three days and three nights in the belly of the sea monster, so will the Son of Man be three days and three nights in the heart of the earth" (Matt 12:39–40).

They ask this again in Matthew 16:1–4. After a long series of signs, the Pharisees and Sadducees ask Jesus for another one. If they were sincere, they could accept the multitude of signs He has already performed. But this was all a test (Matt 16:1). Jesus knows they are not stupid. For example, He knows they can read and interpret the appearance (signs) of the heavens to discern the weather. That's because they want to know the weather, and that knowledge benefits them. They do not want to truly see what Jesus is doing. They perceive no benefit. They have eyes but do not see. So, again, Jesus gives them only the "sign of Jonah" (Matt 16:4).

The resurrection of Jesus is the sign by which men will be judged. It is the ultimate dividing marker between those who believe and those who do not. Paul speaks about the resurrection as essential for faith, life, and salvation (Rom 10:9–10, 1 Cor 15:12–19). That is the sign Jesus will give to the scribes and Pharisees.

As Jesus continues teaching, He goes back to the idea of demon possessions in Matthew 12:43–45. This difficult passage makes an important point about "this evil generation." Jesus condemned His generation as "evil and adulterous" (Matt 12:39) and said that even Nineveh and the Queen of the South will judge and condemn it. This final analogy about demon possession shows how a generation could go from bad to worse.

Imagine a demon-possessed man who is cleansed of the demon. The evil spirit is cast out and searches for rest and perhaps a new host. Interestingly, the spirit avoids places with water (compared with Matt 8:32). After finding no new home, he decides to return to his old residence. When he arrives, he sees that nothing has taken his place. It is empty, clean, and ready for guests. So not only does the spirit return, but he brings seven other evil spirits, even more evil than him, to crash with him. Then this man, who thought the evil spirits were gone for good, ends up in a much worse state than he was in initially.

What in the world does that mean? Well, perhaps Jesus sees within His generation a superficial thirst for momentary revival but not a commitment to sustained repentance. It is one thing for a spirit to depart, but if you don't fill that void with something valuable, that spirit might return. It is one thing to accept the word of God for a day, month, or year, but it is something else to be transformed for the long haul.

If Jesus performs another sign, the people may be dazzled for a day. They may applaud and tell their friends, but it likely won't produce the needed change. However, belief in the resurrection, the beginning of a new age, and the inauguration of the kingdom of God have more staying power. The resurrection wasn't just a cool miracle that happened once, long ago. It's the ushering in of a whole new world. If you get on board with that, certainly, relapse is still possible, but at least you have something eternal to grasp. They needed to fill the house with the kingdom of God so that the demon had no place to return. Jesus sees within His generation the need for transformation and revival that lasts through the ages.

The Temple, Jonah, and Solomon

Let's conclude with one final note about Matthew 12. Remember those wicked cities Jesus mentioned in Matthew 11:20–24? Not only are Tyre, Sidon, and Sodom better than those cities surrounding Jesus (His wicked generation), but so is Nineveh! Because Nineveh repented at Jonah's preaching, but Jesus was ignored and rejected by His generation. And the Queen of the South traveled vast distances, from the ends of the earth, to hear the wisdom of Solomon (1 Kgs 10:1–13), yet Jesus's wisdom was rejected by those right in front of Him.

In both examples, the superior response is from Gentiles. Jesus is the one in whom the Gentiles will hope (Matt 12:21). Even the most wicked Gentiles of previous generations would have accepted Jesus. I mean, if Nineveh listened to Jonah's pitiful sermon (Jonah 3:4), how much more would they have listened to Jesus with His profound wisdom and signs? His words are better than Jonah's, and His sign is far greater.

In Solomon, we find a royal King and "Son of David" who was renowned for His wisdom. Solomon's wisdom was a gift from God, but Jesus is the embodiment of that God and the source of that wisdom. Jesus is far wiser and more faithful than Solomon ever was. If the Gentiles think they'll find wisdom in Solomon or repentance in Jonah (two obviously flawed characters), how much more will they find it in Jesus? Tragically, while these Gentiles would accept Him, Jesus's own countrymen, hometown, and generation reject Him.

At the end of Matthew 12:41 and 42, there is an interesting phrase that says, "Behold, something greater (πλεῖον) than Jonah is here" and "Behold, something greater (πλεῖον) than Solomon is here." This is reminiscent of Matthew 12:6, which says, "I say to you that something greater than the temple is here." Solomon and his wisdom, Jonah and his prophetic message, and even the temple with its sacrifices and worship cannot compare with what is found in Jesus.

Reflection Questions

1. How is Jesus like the temple? How is Jesus like Jonah? How is Jesus like Solomon? How is He greater than all three? Why does Matthew keep comparing Jesus to Old Testament figures?
2. Why would Jesus only give the sign of Jonah? Why would He not give additional signs? What have they said about His signs so far? Why is Nineveh more righteous than Jesus's generation?

REFLECTION 40

THE KINGDOM IN PARABLES: READ MATTHEW 13:1–53

Major Speech #3

JESUS's third major speech is a series of parables that explain the mysteries, nature, and value of the kingdom of heaven. Throughout Matthew, Jesus describes life in the kingdom (Matt 5–7), demonstrates the power of the kingdom (Matt 8–9), commissions His disciples to proclaim the kingdom (Matt 10), defends the kingdom (Matt 11–12), and now He uses parables to address the mysteries of the kingdom.

For some, these parables provide helpful insights, but others will fail to understand. Some have eyes that see and ears that hear (Matt 13:16) but others, "while seeing they do not see, and while hearing they do not hear" (Matt 13:13). Human failure to understand fulfills a Scripture from Isaiah 6:9–10:

> You will keep on hearing, but will not understand; you will keep on seeing, but will not perceive; for the heart of this people has become dull, with their ears they scarcely hear, and they have closed their eyes, otherwise they would see with their eyes, hear with their ears, and understand with their hearts and return, and I would heal them (Matt 13:14–15).

Let's note two facts about this Scriptural "fulfillment." First, a Scripture being "fulfilled" does not mean it was a prediction. Originally, this passage was about Isaiah's audience. Isaiah was not directly predicting the future Messiah's audience. But this Scripture is "fulfilled" when Jesus, like Isaiah, speaks the truth of God to His nation, and that nation, like Israel over 700 years earlier, rejects it. That Scripture came to pass for Isaiah, but the same attitudes and hearts appear in Jesus's day.

Second, it's important to note that Matthew's quotation says, "They have closed their eyes, otherwise they would see with their eyes" (Matt 13:15). Matthew is blaming the listener for refusing to see. They have intentionally closed their eyes. God would heal them if they would open their eyes, hear with open ears, and receive with a soft heart. Jesus blesses those who accept His message with seeing eyes and hearing ears (Matt 13:16).

Jesus's kingdom message is a blessing that many prophets and righteous people longed to know but could not (Matt 13:17). What a tragedy that some have it right in front of them but have closed their eyes. The evil cities mentioned in Matthew 11:20–24 and 12:41–42 would have repented had they been given this message. Tragically, many cities in Jesus's day were given the message and signs and still rejected it (see Matt 13:53–58).

The first parable, the Parable of the Sower, describes how differently people hear Jesus's message. Some people hear it, but like Isaiah's prophecy, they refuse it, and Satan snatches it away. Some hear and receive it, but as persecution and affliction arise, they fall away quickly. Some hear and accept it but spend their lives concerned with earthly worries or wealth. While they never openly reject the word, it lies dormant within them and produces nothing for the kingdom. However, some receive it with seeing eyes and hearing ears and produce fruit for the kingdom. To begin the parables, we are called to be those good, receptive, and productive hearers.

The Problem of the Kingdom

One problem we face with the kingdom of heaven is that it often fails to meet expectations. It does not look how we think it should. I recently heard someone argue that God's kingdom has not yet come on earth. He reasoned, "The greatest evidence that Jesus has not established His kingdom is to simply look at the world around you. Does this really look like the kingdom of God?"

This person isn't alone in this view, and I get it. Still, I believe the Bible is pretty clear that the kingdom is currently on earth. And the Gospels are the story of how that happened. Yet, there are clearly mysteries about this kingdom. God's will certainly isn't always done on earth as it is in heaven. Many times, it feels like Satan is more king than God.

This is one mystery Jesus helps us work through in these parables. The Parable of the Wheat and the Tares is similar to the Parable of the Sower in many ways. The imagery of planting seeds and yielding a crop is central to both. Even structurally, they follow a similar pattern. In both, Jesus offers a parable (Matt 13:3–9 and Matt 13:24–30) and its interpretation (Matt 13:18–23 and Matt 13:36–43). But right in between them, Jesus offers additional teaching (Matt 13:10–13, 16–17 and Matt 13:31–34), and we're informed about a fulfilled Scripture (Matt 13:14–15 and Matt 13:35).

Considering Jesus's words: "Blessed are your eyes, because they see; and your ears, because they hear," I think we must remember that these parables are about "seeing" and "hearing." The Parable of the Sower describes how certain people hear the word of God. The Parable of the Wheat and the Tares describes how we see God's kingdom.

The kingdom may be visible, yet it looks like a poorly planted wheat field infested with weeds. Sometimes, it may look good in some patches, but other spots are a mess. This is how our world works.

As disciples, our challenge is to trust that the kingdom is here even through the weeds. And we are challenged to faithfully wait on the Lord until the weeds are removed. There is no quick fix and we cannot solve this problem on our own. Our job is not to remove the weeds but to be the wheat. This parable presents a problem that only God will solve. Until that day comes, we must be patient and produce where God planted us. In between this parable and its interpretation, Jesus offers two additional parables that further illustrate His point. In the Parable of the Mustard Seed and the Parable of the Leaven, the kingdom has far more potential than we might think. It looks smaller than we expected. It may appear insignificant, like a tiny seed or a small amount of leaven. It may be a field full of weeds and tares. But just wait and see what God can do.

The cross must be remembered as we read these parables. On the cross, Jesus looked like a failure. He looked weak, insignificant, entirely unimpressive, and shameful. It looked like nothing would be accomplished through Him. In fact, at that moment, one could see Jesus's movement failing while the violence, hatred, cruelty, injustice, and darkness (literally) of the world gained victory.

He looked as insignificant as the smallest of seeds. You could see this world's tares choking out His life as the evil and horror of humanity reached its devastating climax. But to the eyes that see, something else was happening. Through the weeds of sin, the immeasurable love of God was blooming. The kingdom was breaking forth through the thorns and thistles of this cursed world to light the pathway to something greater.

Trusting God's victory to unfold requires a little waiting. The story does not end with the cross, nor do the parables end with leaven, mustard seeds, or weed-riddled fields. The weeds are removed. The seed becomes a tree. The leaven permeates all. And Jesus's cross and resurrection provide humanity's only true hope. The kingdom may be hidden in the weeds, but for the one who searches, something of immeasurable value exists to be found.

The Immeasurable Value of the Kingdom

This kingdom is both valuable and hidden. It must be searched out. It is like a buried treasure or a rare pearl. To those unaware of the treasure, a man who sells all he owns to buy a field looks foolish. But to the man who did see the treasure, it was a wise and prudent investment. Like a rare and priceless pearl, the kingdom is far more valuable than anything else we might own (see Matt 19:16–26).

It's fascinating to consider the paradigm shift that occurs when finding the kingdom. At one point, all those possessions that were purchased and owned seemed worth purchasing and owning. But they did not bring ultimate fulfillment. Ultimate value and fulfillment were discovered in that hidden treasure and pearl of great price. Once the true treasure was found, nothing else that once mattered was worth keeping. Those became barriers to what must be sought above all else (Matt 6:33; see Phil 3:7–11).

As we've noted, waiting is part of the kingdom. We must wait for the tares to be removed, the leaven to spread, and the mustard seed to grow. The kingdom, while already present, is not yet fully experienced in all its glory. God will bring it to perfection. However, it still beckons for our immediate action. We cannot wait to buy the field or the pearl. We cannot risk missing it.

Those who act quickly and give their allegiance to the kingdom, abandoning every encumbrance and following Jesus, will receive far more than they left (see Matt 19:27–30). And they will be found among the wheat when that final day of separation arrives. Jesus's next parable is about this separation. It is similar in many ways to the Wheat and the Tares, especially as they conclude (compare Matt 13:49–50 and Matt 13:40–42).

He uses the image of separating good and bad fish on the beach. The phrase "on the beach"[ἐπὶ τὸν αἰγιαλὸν] (Matt 13:48) is critical to notice. It's the exact phrase that begins this entire series of parables. In Matthew 13:2, Jesus enters a boat while the crowd stands and listens "on the beach" [ἐπὶ τὸν αἰγιαλὸν].

While Jesus left the crowds in verse 36, the image should still be fresh in our minds. As those crowds stood on the beach listening to Jesus's words, they could either accept or ignore them. They could either be wheat or weeds. They could pursue the kingdom or reject it. They could be good or bad fish. The same is true for us as we read. And a day is coming when God will stand with us all "on the beach" and separate the good from the bad.

Jesus ends this speech section with one final parable (Matt 13:51–52). After the disciples claim to understand Him, Jesus says, "Every scribe who has become a disciple of the kingdom of heaven is like a head of a household, who brings out of his treasure things new and old."

That's a fascinating conclusion. It's consistent with all Jesus has been doing and teaching so far in Matthew. He is not rejecting the old (Old Testament Scriptures, Law, or Moses). Instead, He is fulfilling and infusing the old with new elements and interpretations. He provides a new lens from which to view the old. He brings the kingdom in new and unprecedented ways. And His disciples reap the rewards of the ancient treasure and the new.

Reflection Questions

1. How has Jesus been bringing the "old" and "new" treasure in His message and actions? How is the kingdom like a treasure? What do these parables teach us about wealth? What do these parables teach us about priorities?
2. What do these parables teach us about waiting? Why is it valuable to be patient as we wait on God? What are we waiting for? What is God doing now in His kingdom? What are God's future plans for His kingdom?

REFLECTION 41

STORIES ABOUT THE ROCK: READ MATTHEW 14:22–33, 16:13–20, 26:31–46, AND 26:69–75

Emphasis on Rock

PETER IS a prominent figure in the New Testament and early Christianity. While we usually call him “Peter,” his name is Simon (Matt 4:18, 10:2), and “Peter” is a nickname that means “Rock.” In our modern world, it’s not uncommon to meet someone named “Peter.” But when Simon received this name, it was unique. In fact, one commentator notes,

> There are no documented instances of anyone’s ever being named ‘rock’ in Aramaic or Greek prior to Simon. Thus, English translations should render the word ‘stone’ or ‘rock,’ not ‘Peter,’ which gives the false impression that the word represented a common name ...[33]

Throughout this reflection, I’ll exercise the practice of calling him “Rock.” If it seems weird to you, good. That’s the point. It’s just as strange to name someone “Rock” today as it was to call him “Peter” back then.

We’ve already been introduced to Rock. His call story is in

Matthew 4:18–20. In fact, of the twelve disciples, Matthew only gives the call story of 5 of them: Rock, Andrew, James, John, and Matthew. We know Jesus stayed at Rock's house in Matthew 8:14 and healed his mother-in-law.

In Matthew 10, when Jesus sends out his disciples, the first one mentioned is "Simon, called Rock" (Matt 10:2). Rock is among those who heal, cast out demons, preach, suffer, and speak in the Holy Spirit. From this point forward in Matthew, Rock plays an especially prominent role. Matthew includes several unique Rock stories not mentioned in the other Gospels.

For example, while Jesus walks on water in Mark 6:48 and John 6:19, only Matthew records Rock walking on water (Matt 14:28–32). While Rock confesses Christ in the other Gospels (Matt 16:16, Mark 8:29, Luke 8:29, John 6:68–69), only in Matthew is Rock reciprocally blessed and given the keys to the kingdom of heaven (Matt 16:17–19). Only in Matthew is Rock told to catch a coin-bearing fish (Matt 17:24–27). Only in Matthew does Rock ask Jesus how many times to forgive his neighbor (Matt 18:21–35).

Of course, Matthew records common important Rock stories also: Rock's call story (Matt 4:18–20, Mark 1:16–18, Luke 5:1–11, John 1:40–42), the healing of his mother-in-law (Matt 8:14–15, Mark 1:29–31, Luke 4:38–39), his dramatic confession of faith (Matt 16:16, Mark 8:29, Luke 9:18–20), his rebuke of Jesus and being called Satan (Matt 16:22–23, Mark 8:32–33), the Transfiguration (Matt 17:4, Mark 9:5–6, Luke 9:28–36), his declaration to have left everything for Jesus (Matt 19:27, Mark 10:28, Luke 18:28–29), his vow to never abandon or deny Jesus (Matt 26:33–35, Mark 14:29–31, Luke 22:31–34), his sleeping instead of praying (Matt 26:39–46, Mark 14:37–42), and his denials (Matt 26:69–75, Mark 14:54–72, Luke 22:54–62).

The Imperfect Disciple

I am far from the perfect disciple. I regularly fall short of the kingdom's ideals. I have a long way to go, and I'll never reach the standard set by Jesus. So, what do I do? Do I hopelessly give up in futility and frustration? Or do I imperfectly follow as best I can, relying on the forgiveness and grace of Jesus? To answer this question, I believe Rock provides a healthy model. Matthew presents Rock as an exemplar of the imperfect Christian and the imperfect church. For this reason, Jesus directly links him to the founding of the church in Matthew 16:17–19.

Rock was committed to the Lord. In his best moments, he believed, followed, trusted, sacrificed, and acted faithfully! But at his worst, he lacked faith and was weak, selfish, confused, and cowardly. Rock was not always steady, firm, or Rock-like. Every time Rock does something faithful and true, he follows it up with some failure that leads to rebuke and correction (especially in the second half of Matthew). At times, Rock looks more like Jell-O, yet Jesus keeps calling him Rock.

Rock's cycle of faith and failure begins with walking on water in Matthew 14. This is the perfect picture of Matthew's entire presentation of Rock. It's also a picture of the church and the individual Christian life. In a boat on the sea, amid a storm, Jesus walks on the water to meet His disciples. There are obvious "Exodus" motifs at play here (instead of walking on dry land through the water, Jesus, the greater Moses, walks on top of the water as though it were dry land).

The disciples, gripped by fear, looking through the darkness, fog, rain, waves, and the tossing of the ship, believe a ghost is walking toward them. Jesus responds to their fear, saying, "Take courage, it is I; do not be afraid" (Matt 14:27). This also echoes back to Exodus when God speaks to Moses from the burning bush. The phrase "It is I" is the exact expression for the name of God in Exodus 3:14: "I Am." Jesus is not only a greater Moses but also the "I Am." He is "God with us" (Matt 1:23).

In Mark and John, this is when Jesus gets on the boat. In Matthew, however, Rock takes a courageous step of faith by asking to meet Jesus on the water. I cannot help but assume Jesus is pleased with this. Jesus says, "Come," and Rock steps onto the water. Standing on the water, in the middle of the night, amid a storm, Rock found himself where no mere man had stood before.

His faith caused him to take that monumental step, but the world around him eventually caught up to him. As the wind whistled through the air and the water splashed against his skin, fear, doubt, and reality hit him. Faithfulness followed by failure is the model of Rock in Matthew. Rock began to sink.

From here, continue reading Matthew with an eye on Rock to see how these stories play out repeatedly. Sometimes, Rock is a fantastic disciple. His thought-provoking questions allow Jesus to expound on His teaching (Matt 15:15, 18:21, 19:27). He makes profound declarations about Jesus's identity (Matt 16:16). He shows boldness and understands the mandatory sacrifices of allegiance to Jesus (Matt 26:33–35). Rock correctly answers a controversial question on behalf of Jesus before a miracle is worked through him (Matt 17:24–27). Jesus takes Rock with Him to witness incredible events like the transfiguration (Matt 17:1–8) or to be with Him in quiet moments of prayer and distress like in Gethsemane (Matt 26:36–37). Rock has a particularly special connection with Jesus.

However, Rock is also the one who, shortly after being called "Rock," was called "Satan" (Matt 16:18, 23). Rock had the shortsighted idea of building three tabernacles for Moses, Elijah, and Jesus during the Transfiguration. Rock repeatedly sleeps after Jesus warns him to "keep watching and praying that you may not enter into temptation; the spirit is willing, but the flesh is weak" (Matt 26:41). And sure enough, when temptation came, he was unprepared and denied Jesus three times (Matt 26:69–75). Matthew 26:75 is the final specific mention of Rock by name in Matthew, which says, "he went out and wept bitterly." Like so many of us, his spirit was willing, but his flesh was far too weak.

Lord, Save Me

So, what should we think of Rock? Going back to the scene where Rock walks on the water with Jesus, that story does not end with him sinking. In each of those failures mentioned above, Rock was sinking. He was in over his head. He was too weak to save himself. So, when Rock began to sink, he cried, "Lord, save me!" (Matt 14:30).

What do we do when confronted by our failures, weaknesses, and imperfections? What do we do when we fail to live up to the Sermon on the Mount? What do we do when the storm consumes us and the waves overwhelm us? Our best option is to cry, "Lord, save me!" And as Jesus reached out His hand and saved Rock, He will also reach out to us.

Our moments of failure are when we need Jesus the most. So often, tragically, because of doubt or feelings of worthlessness, many walk away from Jesus. We can put distance between ourselves and His saving hand because of Satan's lie that we are no longer wanted. We lack trust in His unfailing forgiveness and all-consuming grace. So, we sink. Alone. When He is right there with us, ready to save.

In many ways, Rock was the failure who sank in the water. He abandoned and denied Jesus before the crucifixion (Matt 10:32–33, 26:69–75). Yet, after the resurrection, he was also one of those eleven, worshipping Jesus on the mountain (Matt 28:16–

17). Even then, some of the disciples doubted (Matt 28:17). Was Rock one of them?

Interestingly, Jesus does not rebuke their doubts in that passage. He does not separate His disciples between those who doubt and those with total assurance. We don't even know who the doubters were (maybe Thomas?). Jesus speaks to all of them. He assures them and commissions them equally. He responds to their doubt by assigning them a mission for the kingdom of heaven.

Sometimes, getting back to work is the best way to move beyond doubt or failure. We will have doubts occasionally, but the work doesn't stop. And seeing the mission of God in action is one of the best answers to our doubts. Rock was given a world-transforming challenge. Jesus pulled him from the water, forgave his denials, and challenged him to change the world.

Earlier in Matthew, Jesus told Rock to forgive "up to seventy times seven" (Matt 18:22). Why? Because people need forgiveness. Rock needed forgiveness. We need forgiveness. And God is always willing to forgive. Forgiveness is a crucial part of Jesus's model prayer and a fundamental reason for His going to the cross. As long as we are imperfect, we stand in daily need of the grace of God. Like Rock, we are imperfect disciples. Let's follow the One who loves us anyway. Let's follow the Savior who pulls us from the waters, forgives us of our deepest failures, and commissions us to change the world.

Reflection Questions

1. Why is Peter such a relatable character to so many? Why is "Rock" a meaningful name for Peter? What does Peter teach us about the lifelong journey of faith? Why would Jesus choose someone with so many ups and downs?

2. Why did Peter get out of the boat? Who kept Peter on the water? Why did Peter sink? Who got Peter out of the water? How can this be a metaphor for faith, doubt, and salvation?

Endnotes

[33] M. Eugene Boring, *Matthew* TNIBC (Nashville: Abingdon Press, 2015), 249.

REFLECTION 42

"I WILL BUILD MY CHURCH": READ MATTHEW 16:1–20

Taking the Next Step

JESUS HAS BEEN BUSY. Since the death of John the Baptist, He has performed numerous signs and engaged in several public disputes. He's fed 5000 and 4000, walked on water, and healed multitudes including Jews and Gentiles. He's been criticized for not following the traditions of the elders and has been insincerely judged by the Pharisees and Sadducees. These events reveal crucial details about His identity and mission,[34] but His disciples have been slow to recognize them.

However, in Matthew 16, the disciples take the next step in their understanding of Jesus. To bring this about, Jesus takes them on a journey to Caesarea Philippi. A major contrast is being set up. Caesarea Philippi, recently renamed by the Romans, was a famous site for the worship of both pagan idols and Roman emperors. Craig Keener, in his *IVP Bible Background Commentary*, calls this location a

> pagan territory, near a grotto devoted to the worship of the Greek woodland deity Pan; Herod had also dedicated a temple

> for the worship of Caesar there. Few Jewish people would have expected it as a site for a divine revelation.[35]

Jesus, surrounded by idolatry and the cult of emperor worship, asks His disciples who people say He is. The discussion around the marketplace is that Jesus is the return of some great prophet. When Jesus then asks directly who the disciples say He is, Peter emerges with a narrative-transforming response: "You are the Christ, the Son of the living God" (Matt 16:16). Matthew's story will shift dramatically from this point forward.

Unlike the lifeless idols and gods all around, Jesus is the Son of the living God. Unlike Julius, Augustus, or Tiberius, Jesus is God's true Anointed One and chosen king. After the posthumous deification of Julius Caesar, his son, Augustus, regularly referred to himself as a son of a god. Jesus, however, is the Son of the "living" God. The word "living" separates God from idols and dead deified human rulers. Unlike the rumors swirling among the crowds, Jesus is more than a great prophet. He's more than an idol, a pagan deity, or a Roman emperor. Jesus is the Son of the One true and living God. Peter could not have had a better answer!

Yet, Peter still has a lot to learn. In just a minute, Peter will rebuke Jesus after hearing about His death and resurrection (Matt 16:21–22). Peter doesn't want a crucified Messiah. He wants a wealthy, powerful, and victorious king! That story benefits Peter much more. Peter knows that Jesus is the Christ but rejects Jesus's notion of what that means.

Jesus challenges Peter to set his mind on the will of God, and not his own desires (Matt 16:23). Peter needs to learn self-denial, the cross, and discipleship (Matt 16:24). He needs to learn what really matters most in this world (Matt 16:26–27). Peter is emblematic of the life of discipleship. He does not know everything; that's why He's a disciple and not the teacher.

He is still learning. But at least, in contrast to the Pharisees and Sadducees, Peter is genuinely learning from Jesus. Albeit he is confused on some matters, he's still growing. None of us will ever reach the point of complete comprehension. Our job as disciples is to watch, learn, grow, and follow.

Authority to the Rock

In between the confession and rebuke, Jesus blesses Peter (For Jesus's other blessings, see Matt 5:3–11, 11:6, 13:16–17, and 24:46). This is a beautiful but shocking passage. Peter is given more responsibility and a higher calling than he ever dreamed possible. A Galilean fisherman is given a name and a vocation that will forever change the world.

Matthew 16:17–19 is one of the most hotly contested passages in the New Testament. Its interpretation has largely been split down Catholic and Protestant lines. In this passage, Jesus blesses Rock (Peter), declares to build His church on "this rock," gives Rock the keys to the kingdom, and grants him authority to bind and loose on earth.

Some of the ambiguities in this text have shaped religious traditions and become dogmatic markers of faithfulness in Christian history. In the passage, Jesus blesses Simon in response to Simon's declaration of faith. Simon calls Jesus "Christ," so Jesus calls Simon "Rock" (the names "Peter" and "Cephas" come from the respective Greek and Aramaic words meaning rock). Jesus then makes a wordplay on the meaning of this name to teach about the community of faith He is erecting, saying, "You are Rock (Πέτρος, nominative, masculine) and upon this rock (πέτρᾳ, dative, feminine) I will build my church." So, what does that mean?

Is Peter the rock upon which the church is built? This would be a common Catholic interpretation but less common among Protestants. After all, Ephesians 2:20 describes the church as the household of God "built on the foundation of the apostles and prophets." Revelation 21:14 refers to the apostles as the foundation stones for the wall of New Jerusalem. Some interpreters see this as a similar statement, only directed specifically to Peter.

Plus, Jesus is blessing Peter because of his confession. Therefore, it makes some sense that His words describe Peter. Everything else in verse 19 describes the authority given to Peter, including the keys of the kingdom and the authority to bind and loose on earth. So, throughout church history, many have seen this as a blessing wherein Peter is the rock upon which Christ builds His church, who receives the keys of the kingdom and authority to bind and loose on earth.

Even with that interpretation, however, nothing in this passage suggests that Peter's authority would be the beginning of a long line of successive church leaders who would also share this authority. This blessing says nothing about a transfer of this authority from Peter to others after him. There is also nothing about infallibility or a specific office at the head of the church.

Peter is not the builder or owner of the church. He is no rival to Jesus. Rather, if Peter is the "Rock" upon which the church is built, this passage simply suggests that he is foundational to the building of the community of God, which he clearly is. It's not altogether different from Peter receiving the keys of the kingdom. Keys open doors. Peter opens the doors of the kingdom to both Jews and Gentiles (contrast with Matt 23:13). His work as "Rock" of the church may be seen in Pentecost and with the conversion of Cornelius. God used Peter for foundational, door-opening kingdom work.

The Church Belongs to Christ

However, "this rock" may best be read not as Peter but as Peter's confession. This is how many Protestants have interpreted it. This suggests that the church is built on the unalterable truth that Jesus "is the Christ, the Son of the living God." This would make the foundation much sturdier, as Peter still has a lot to learn and many failures ahead. Any fear that Peter is elevated to pope-like status is removed with this reading.

Instead, this interpretation focuses on the contrast between "Peter" (petros) and "this rock" (petra). This contrast is Jesus's way of saying, "Simon, you are Rock, but I will build My church on a much greater rock!"[36] This is supported by Paul's words in 1 Corinthians 3:11: "For no man can lay a foundation other than the one which is laid, which is Jesus Christ."

Either way, Jesus says "I will build My church." This means Jesus is the builder and owner. Jesus is building a new community. This community is proclaimed by Peter on Pentecost (Acts 2) and consists of those who, like Peter, share his confession about Christ. I like how N. T. Wright describes this blessing, saying, "Peter, with his declaration of faith, will be the starting point of this community."[37] That seems to be the main point of Jesus's blessing to Peter.

The language of this blessing should remind readers of Jesus's words at the conclusion of the Sermon on the Mount. The wise man builds his house on the rock. When the proper foundation is in place, the church can weather any storms hurled its way. To build on any other foundation is folly.

Reflection Questions

1. How did Jesus bless Peter? Upon what "rock" does Jesus build His church? Who is the builder and

owner of the church? What does this tell us about authority in the church?

2. Why is Peter's confession so powerful? Why does it matter that they were in Caesarea Philippi? What does "Christ" mean? What does "Son of God" mean? Why did Peter call the Father the "living" God?

Endnotes

[34] For more discussion of these stories, see Travis Bookout, *Cruciform Christ* (Florence, AL; Cypress Publications, 2022). In this book, I'm primarily focusing on material unique to Matthew.

[35] Craig Keener, *The IVP Bible Background Commentary: New Testament* 2nd ed. (Downers Grove: IVP Academic, 2014), 86.

[36] Although this contrast could simply be a necessary way of adding a masculine ending to the feminine word "petra," since Peter is male. Catholic interpretations see no theological significance to the change in gender or word ending. It is just normal Greek grammar.

[37] Tom Wright, *Matthew for Everyone Part 2: Chapters 16–28* (Louisville: Westminster John Knox Press, 2004), 8.

REFLECTION 43

VICTORY AND AUTHORITY IN THE CHURCH: READ MATTHEW 16:13–20 AND MATTHEW 18:15–20

The "Gates of Hades"

THE "GATES OF HADES" or "gates of death" will not prevail over the church Jesus builds. While the King James Version and several others translate this phrase as "gates of hell," I would go with "hades." Usually, a footnote in your English Bible will say one or the other. "Hades" is a transliteration of the actual Greek word that is used (ᾅδου, "of hades"). The word "Hell" is usually a translation of γέεννα (gehenna), which is not used in this passage. Hades is best understood as the realm of the dead.

The phrase "gates of hades/sheol/death" (or similar phrases) is found elsewhere in the Bible (Job 38:17, Ps 9:13, 107:18). King Hezekiah said he was "consigned to the gates of Sheol for the rest of my years" (Isa 38:10), because of an illness from which he did not expect to recover. The gates of hades represent the entrance into the realm of death. "Death" and "Hades" are linked in Revelation, and both are cast into the eternal fire (Rev 20:14).

Some have seen in this phrase a reference to a particular mythological portal to the underworld in Caesarea Philippi, near the grotto for the worship of Pan. In pagan thought, this was a gate that stood between this world and Hades. If this is the case, Jesus has a pretty powerful object lesson for His declaration that death and the underworld would not conquer God's kingdom. God's reign will endure with Christ throughout the ages.

Gates will not protect the forces of evil. Their borders will not prevail over Jesus's church. Their gates will not expand or invade the kingdom of God. In fact, heaven's reign is stronger than the gates of hades. Through the cross and resurrection, both sin and death are overcome in the church. While the sting of both is felt now, they will not win, and a great eschatological day of overthrow is coming. There is nowhere for the forces of darkness to hide, and no gate can protect them. This is a wonderful, confidence-building assurance of victory and life to the people of God who share in Peter's confession.

Binding and Loosing

The final phrase of Jesus's blessing, "Whatever you bind on earth shall be bound in heaven, and whatever you loose on earth shall be loosed in heaven," raises a good number of questions. Does Peter really have authority from Jesus to bind and loose on earth? Can Peter create new rules for the church? Can Peter change the rules that God has made? Can Peter forgive the sins of whoever he wants? Or is Peter only binding and loosing what God has already bound and loosed in heaven? If so, what is the difference between what Peter and anyone else can do? How is this a blessing?

As we look at this verse, a couple of points are important to state at the beginning. First, many Bibles will have a footnote providing an alternate translation. It says something like, "Whatever you bind on earth *shall have been* bound in heaven, and whatever you loose on earth *shall have been* loosed in heaven." This translation would suggest that Peter is only to follow/announce the teachings of heaven rather than create teachings to which heaven must adhere. The translation one prefers probably relies on one's beliefs.

Secondly, the authority given to Peter in this statement is also given to the other disciples in Matthew 18:18–20 (these are the only two passages in the Gospels that use the word "church"). The other disciples are not given "The keys to the kingdom," but they are given authority to "bind/loose" or "tie/untie." In that context, the discussion centers around how to respond to a sinning Christian. After a series of attempts to bring about repentance and reconciliation, the church must make decisions about their future relationship with that person. Suppose the person refuses to repent and will not allow for peaceful reconciliation. In that case, the church must "let him be to you as a Gentile and a tax collector" (Matt 18:17). This means, basically, expulsion from the community into "outsider" status.

This is a difficult thing for the church to do. It is a major responsibility for anyone to bear. Christ encourages the church, saying they have the authority to make these decisions (they can bind and loose). And that when they agree about these matters on earth and bring them to God in heaven, He will accomplish it. So, through prayer, what they decide on earth will be granted by God in heaven (Matt 18:19). And, thankfully, as they gather in Christ's name to prayerfully work through these difficulties, Christ will be among them.

Matthew 18:18–20 is similar in several ways to Matthew 28:20. Jesus tells His followers to make disciples by "teaching them to observe all that I have commanded you. And behold, I am with you always, to the end of the age" (Matt 28:20). The apostles have authority to teach (including binding and loosing) all that Christ commanded. The content ultimately comes from Christ, who holds all true authority in heaven and on earth. As they do this, Christ will be with them even to the end of the age.

In Matthew 16:19 and Matthew 18:18, we shouldn't think that Peter, the other disciples, or the church are given *carte blanche* on the church's doctrines. Peter can't say, "Never mind, you don't have to listen to the Sermon on the Mount anymore," and heaven would have to follow suit. When Jesus gives a command, Peter cannot say, "No. I have the keys, and I'll determine the rules now." Apostles, prophets, and church leaders are still under Christ's authority. It is Jesus's church.

However, there are difficult decisions that must be made in the church. And sometimes, it is not altogether clear exactly what must be done. Sometimes, leaders in the church, while honoring Christ as much as possible, must decide on difficult topics like disfellowship, how to handle COVID, or how much patience/grace to exercise in a given situation. I think it is appropriate for passages like this to instill confidence and assurance in the church as we seek, with open Bibles and prayers for wisdom, to honor Christ as we gather in His name to make decisions. According to Jesus, what we agree upon on earth will be done in Heaven, and Jesus will be among us (Matt 18:19–20).

Peter as a Disciple

Back to Matthew 16:19, I think the primary meaning of this concluding statement is that Peter will declare heaven's teachings on earth. There will be continuity between God's will in heaven and Peter's teachings on earth. But it must stem first and foremost from the will of God. Jesus prays, "Your will be done on earth as it is in heaven" (Matt 6:10). Peter has the duty of announcing the will of heaven on earth. Jesus gives him divine sanction to make that proclamation.

Peter must learn from his Teacher and then share that

teaching with others (Matt 28:20). The kingdom/reign of heaven is not the kingdom/reign of Peter. Yet, Peter, holding the keys of the kingdom/reign of heaven, has the unique responsibility of detailing God's kingdom/reign to the world after the ascension of Christ. Jesus will use Peter as heaven's special mouthpiece, which includes "binding" and "loosing" on earth.

I like how Jerome, the early church commentator, describes the authority of Peter in this passage. Jerome sees and corrects a misuse of this passage among the religious leaders of his day.

> The bishops and priests do not understand this passage. They assume for themselves some of the superciliousness of the Pharisees when they either condemn the innocent or think that they can loose the guilty. Yet in the sight of God, it is not the verdict of the priests but the life of the accused that is examined. We read in Leviticus about lepers that they are commanded to show themselves to the priests and, if they have leprosy, then they are established as unclean by the priest. This does not mean that the priests make them leprous or unclean, but that they have knowledge of the leprous and the non-leprous, and they can discern who is clean and who is unclean.[38]

Jerome illustrates this passage by observing how the priests declare someone clean or unclean. They have the authority to make that declaration, but it is based on their knowledge of leprosy, Torah, and God's will. It is not an arbitrary decision based on their position or whims. Likewise, Peter has the authority to proclaim right and wrong in the kingdom, but he does not have the authority to invent right and wrong. Rather, he binds and looses based on revelation. This is the same logic as Matthew 6:10 and 28:20.

The fact that Peter's confession did not come from "flesh and blood" but was revealed by the Father in heaven (Matt

16:17), demonstrates Peter's trustworthiness to proclaim, bind, and loose the will of the Father. Verse 17 is key. Peter's reception and confession of divine revelation is the grounding of his authority to bind and loose. If his source was "flesh and blood," it would have been inadequate (see Gal 1:12, 16). When Peter's mind is on man's interests, he gets rebuked (Mat 16:23). It must come from God. Jesus trusts Peter to speak what God revealed. For this reason, Christ delegates authority to Peter as a teacher and leader who binds and looses in the church.

Reflection Questions

1. What does this passage tell us about the future of the church? What does "hades" mean? What is the foundation of the church's hope? How shall we prevail over the gates of Hades?
2. What does it mean to "bind" and "loose" on earth? How does that relate to God's will in heaven? How does this passage connect with Matthew 6:10? How does this passage connect to Matthew 18:18–20?

Endnotes

[38] Jerome, *Commentary on Matthew* The Fathers of the Church. Translated by Thomas P. Scheck. (Washington, DC: The Catholic University of America Press, 2008), 192–93.

REFLECTION 44

GREAT ONES AND LITTLE ONES: READ MATTHEW 17:24–18:14

Major Speech #4

MATTHEW 18 begins Jesus's fourth major speech. This speech concludes with Jesus making His way into Judea for Passover and His impending arrest and crucifixion: "When Jesus had finished these words, He departed from Galilee and came into the region of Judea beyond the Jordan" (Matt 19:1). The next two reflections will discuss this speech and how it connects particularly to two major themes throughout Matthew. Matthew 18 provides Jesus's answer to questions about "greatness" (Matt 18:1) and "forgiveness" (Matt 18:21).

Those two topics (Matt 18:2–11 and 18:15–35) are bridged by a story in verses 12–14, where a man has 100 sheep, and one wanders away. In response, he leaves the 99 behind to find the one who went astray. Upon finding the one lost sheep, there was much rejoicing. Jesus concludes the short story, saying, "So it is not the will of your Father who is in heaven that one of these little ones perish" (Matt 18:14).

That one sheep who went astray is a "little one" God wants to save from perishing. Joyfully welcoming him back into the fold is an act of forgiveness. This story holds the two topics of this speech together. Jesus then begins discussing how to approach and welcome back a brother or sister in sin (Matt 18:15), which leads to Peter's question about how many times we should forgive (Matt 18:21).

This speech is about strengthening, encouraging, and forgiving one another in Jesus's new community. Rather than an individualistic sermon, this is about shared life in a church family. This speech specifically mentions the word "church" in 18:17. As we've already mentioned, that is a rare word in the Gospels (only used in Matt 16:18 and 18:17). This is a speech for the church to remember.

In the church, as with pretty much everywhere else, some are considered "great," and some are considered "little ones." Usually, those markers come from society's views of occupation, wealth, education, abilities, attractiveness, or a thousand other qualities. Societies tend to make hierarchies and then judge your human value on where you rank.

What a terrible sin it is for someone to be considered a "nothing" in the church. That may well happen in society, work, school, or even tragically at home, but the church should see God's worth in everyone, especially the "nothings." What a tragedy when youth groups exclude or ridicule the one considered unpopular, unathletic, or unattractive as if those are what makes one valuable or acceptable. What a grave error when elders are selected because of social status, wealth, or nepotism rather than the characteristics described in the New Testament.

The church must have a different view of reality. Wealth, popularity, or beauty are not the markers of the blessed person (remember the beatitudes!). Within the reign of God, all, especially the "little ones," should experience love and acceptance. In our gatherings and relationships, everyone should know that they matter to God. They should also know they matter to us!

Jesus's church is to be different. His church is to consist of the "little ones." In this context, the "little one" represents a humble person without power or prominence. Suppose you are considered a great one in this world. In that case, it's time to be "converted and become like children" (Matt 18:3). This is done through humility and service. If you're viewed as a "little one," then congratulations, you're already near the kingdom. Greatness in heaven's reign is found in humility and lowering oneself (Matt 18:4). In that way, "the last shall be first, and the first last" (Matt 20:16).

While most appreciate this vision of the church, we usually tend to struggle with it. We are not always humble. We uphold the world's definitions of value and dignity. We forget to treat others with utmost kindness, respect, and generosity. We both give and receive this kind of treatment. People, including Christians, are sometimes rude, hurtful, and unChristlike. We sin. Thus, the second half of this speech focuses on forgiveness.

For the church to survive, we must continually receive and extend forgiveness. Rather than a community defined by perfection, which we will never attain, we must be a community of shared forgiveness. Jesus calls for radical, continual, and exponential forgiveness in His kingdom.

Jesus Became a Little One

Like everything else you read, this text has a context. Since Matthew 16:21, Jesus has been preparing His disciples for His death. By now, He has warned them multiple times about His fate (Matt 17:22–23). This concept will be a constant struggle for them. In fact, the final description of the disciples in Matthew is "doubtful." After the resurrection, they gathered on a mountain. They worshipped Jesus, "but some were doubtful" (Matt 28:17). All the brilliant teachings, miracles, and even the resurrection could not eradicate their doubts. The crucifixion makes doubt inevitable.

Peter rebuked Jesus for even talking about it (Matt 16:22). In doing so, Peter took on the role of the tempter in the wilderness ("Get behind Me, Satan!"). Peter became "a stumbling block" (Matt 16:23). Peter knew deep within his bones that Jesus was a great one! He was the long-anticipated Messiah! The King of kings, Lord of lords, and the only true Son of the living God! Peter could not accept the shameful rejection and murder of Jesus. There is no power, beauty, wisdom, or greatness in public execution. The cross is "foolishness" and a "stumbling block" to many (1 Cor 1:22–24). Jesus's life and death demonstrate that the "little ones" matter. He associates with the lowly, dines with tax collectors and sinners, fellowships with the poor and outcasts, and heals and teaches the disabled and neglected. He is the King whose crown is thorns and whose throne is a cross. He is the Son of Man who came not to be served, "but to serve, and to give His life a ransom for many" (Matt 20:28). He is the God who emptied Himself (Phil 2:5–8) and the King who made Himself a servant. Jesus, the "great one," became a "little one," and challenges us to do the same.

Redefining Greatness

Right before this fourth speech began, back in Matthew 17:24–27, Peter was asked whether or not Jesus paid the two-drachma tax. That tax went to the temple and had its roots in Nehemiah 10:32–33. It was a show of loyalty to the temple. Peter says that Jesus does pay the tax. He then went inside the house to find Jesus.

Jesus uses this opportunity to teach a bit about privilege in the kingdom. He asks His disciples whether kings collect taxes from their sons or strangers. The disciples paid enough taxes to know the answer. They weren't "fortunate sons" with silver spoons. Kings collect taxes from strangers. Sons of kings are privileged as "great ones," but strangers are the "little ones" of little value.

Jesus, however, is the ultimate and supreme Son. He's the greatest of the great ones. So, should He pay taxes? Surprisingly, yes! Jesus does not align Himself with the great ones of privilege. He renders to Caesar the things that are Caesar's. He does this, according to Matthew 17:27, "so that we do not offend them."

The word "offend" is the same as "stumbling block" that pops up throughout Matthew (Matt 5:29–30; 11:6; 13:21, 57; 15:12; 17:27; 24:10; 26:31, 33; for the noun, see Matt 16:23; 18:7). It is an important word in Jesus's discussion of "little ones" in Matthew 18:6–9. We should never become stumbling blocks (Matt 18:6). We should never be the ones through whom stumbling blocks come (Matt 18:7). And we should avoid stumbling blocks at all costs (Matt 18:8–9).

Matthew 17:24–27 sets up a contrast between important people of privilege and ordinary folks burdened with taxes. Jesus demonstrates His unparalleled greatness as God's Son when He miraculously sends Peter out to catch a fish with a coin in its mouth. This miracle uniquely combines greatness (divine knowledge and orchestration of a miracle) and humility (using the catch to pay taxes and give to others). Jesus is a Son whose greatness is manifest in the performance of a miracle. But rather than using His miracles to get rich or exercise privilege as the Son of God, He humbly gives the money away and pays taxes like a "stranger." Unlike the sons of kings, Jesus lives as a humble, obedient stranger. He's great enough to perform a money-making miracle yet humble and selfless enough to give it away and pay His taxes. In this way, He does not offend or become a stumbling block. This miracle is a valuable introduction to Matthew 18, where Jesus calls His disciples to become "little ones" who do not offend or become stumbling blocks.

After this miracle, the disciples ask, "Who then is the greatest in the kingdom of heaven?" (Matt 18:1). They may have missed the point. Perhaps they are wondering about the privileges of greatness in God's kingdom. Jesus's answer is to forget about greatness and become the child, the servant, the last of all.

Matthew 16:21–28 and 20:20–28 are very similar texts. In Matthew 20:17–19, the mother of James and John seeks political power for her boys (Matt 20:20–21). The other disciples turn against them in anger and jealousy (Matt 20:24). See how quickly a thirst for power can divide followers of Jesus. They must never become like worldly "rulers" and "great men" who lord their power and exercise authority over others (Matt 20:25–28; see 1 Pet 5:2–4). That is not how the kingdom works! We must never, as followers of Christ, allow a lust for power to define our lives. Let other people waste their lives fighting for power, and you become the child who humbly and innocently believes, follows, obeys, and loves.

Reflection Questions

1. How does Jesus critique His surrounding culture? In what ways does He redefine "greatness"? How is the "little one" a metaphor? How was Jesus a "little one"? How does our society look out for "little ones"? How does our society ignore or trample "little ones"? What can the church do to help?
2. Why does Jesus pay taxes? Regarding privilege, how do kingdoms of this earth differ from the kingdom of heaven? What is the point of Jesus's miracle with the fish and the coin?

REFLECTION 45

FORGIVENESS AND RECONCILIATION: READ MATTHEW 18:15–35

Bringing Others Back to the Fold

In Matthew 18:12–14, Jesus tells a story about a lost sheep, or a "little one" (Matt 18:12–14), who is found and brought back into the fold. This story is analogous to a Christian who turns to sin before being found and brought back home (Matt 18:15–20). Jesus calls the wandering sinner a "little one" and a "sheep." Jesus paints that person in a surprisingly innocent light.

How do we view people who have sinned and wandered from God? What illustrations would we create? Jesus, who desires compassion and mercy rather than sacrifice (Matt 9:13; 12:7), employs the image of a lost sheep needing a shepherd (see Matt 9:36). God does not want to lose a single sheep or little child (Matt 18:14). These images may reshape our view of those who've wandered from the faith. Instead of seeing a worthless reprobate sinner, perhaps we should see a lost sheep or child who needs compassion and love. These more positive images may help us reach out and bring that child home.

How shall we bring that person back? How do we demonstrate such love, compassion, and grace? In Matthew 18:15–20, Jesus gives a progression of steps to guide us through the process. Shockingly, Jesus nowhere includes gossip or blasting that person for their sins on Facebook. Nor does he suggest forming teams within the church to slander and harm. In fact, just like Joseph wanted to put Mary away quietly to protect her reputation, Jesus wants us to bring a person back as discretely, respectfully, and as peacefully as possible.

If it is possible to privately bring this person to repentance, with no one else knowing about the sin, that should be the first step. There is no need to embarrass or bring unnecessary shame to someone (again, remember what Joseph's righteousness led him to do in Matt 1:19). Jesus does not suggest sweeping sin under the rug or ignoring it. Jesus calls for difficult conversations. The offended person has the right to speak and lovingly address the sin with the offender.

If that attempt is unsuccessful, bring only one or two more people to witness a second conversation. These people are called "witnesses." They are not witnesses to the sin, per se, but witnesses to the second appeal for repentance. There may have been no witnesses to the sin. And trying to find some may only lead to more gossip and spreading rumors. Instead, this step suggests we bring a small number of trusted and faithful believers with us to have a second conversation. These witnesses encourage reconciliation, show concern for the sinner, and establish the credibility of the accusation. They should be peacemakers (Matt 5:9).

These witnesses are essential. Jesus specifically quotes Deuteronomy 19:15: "A single witness shall not rise up against a man on account of any iniquity or any sin which he has committed; on the evidence of two or three witnesses a matter shall be confirmed." This ancient legal procedure for Israel provides a wise and beneficial practice for the church.

This law in Deuteronomy was given to protect the accused. Jesus has been and will be, falsely accused of sin (Matt 12:10, 24; 26:59ff.). His disciples experienced this also

(Matt 12:2). Jesus spent a lot of time with people accused of sin. Rather than the church forming hostile public witch hunts, Jesus wants accusations to be confirmed and handled discretely. Jesus is not about destroying people's lives. He not only wants to save people from sin but also protect them from gossip and false accusations. Jesus, who spends time with tax collectors and sinners, knows how relevant this point is.

It's easy to condemn the powerless. A "great one" or prominent leader is much harder to accuse. Unhealthy power dynamics can create safe spaces for sin to thrive and the word of the powerless to be dismissed. Jesus does not want false accusations flying around or oppression taking place. Jesus wants every fact established and confirmed by witnesses. It was easy to believe the false accusation against Joseph because he was a foreigner and a slave (Gen 39:17). Potiphar's wife had power; Joseph did not. Power, wealth, and connections determined his fate. Not truth. No witnesses confirmed her accusations, yet Joseph was thrown in prison.

The witnesses must confirm the charges. If these witnesses cannot establish the facts, then the accusation must be dropped. We cannot move to the next step on flimsy, unestablished, and baseless accusations. Remember, Jesus cares about the accused.

As a third step, the entire church family reaches out. Jesus does not give up on people easily. He does not want us to shrug our shoulders and move on when we lose a family member. As you love your sons or daughters, siblings, or parents, love also your family in Christ (Matt 12:46–50).

We cannot coerce or force people to stay. We should honor the wishes of the person who chooses to leave and remain in sin. If that is their choice, they shall be to us as the tax collector or Gentile. By the way, we should still love and be kind to Gentiles and tax collectors. This is not a call for animosity or hatred. We are simply giving them what they have chosen. But do not let them leave without an outpouring of love.

Each step should proceed from a sincere love for the person who has sinned. We are peacemakers seeking to restore fellowship (bringing the lost sheep home). We should approach others humbly and never from a position of superiority or self-righteousness. With godly motives and in the name of Christ, we reach out. When done correctly, Jesus assures us that He is with us (Matt 18:20).

A Word of Caution

We must now make a few additional points of clarification. First, this pattern is for when a person "sins." Not when a person irritates you, disagrees with you, or does something you deem unwise. Not everything you dislike is a sin. Jesus gives no license to become a judgmental watchdog who condemns everyone every time they don't act like you. Relax a bit and let people live their lives.

Secondly, if you are unwilling to have that first uncomfortable conversation, then the process ends right there. If you will not talk to the one who sinned, then you should not talk to anyone else. Let it go. It's hard to have that conversation. That difficulty can be useful. It can encourage us to keep small and frivolous disputes to a minimum. It is so easy to complain, write anonymous letters, gossip, or slander. Jesus rejects all that nonsense and says, if it really matters, then go have a difficult conversation.

Thirdly, and the importance of this warning cannot be overstated, this passage must be read with wisdom, compassion, and a thirst for justice; otherwise, it can be (and has been) used to ignore sins that should never be ignored. It has protected people who should have faced the consequences. Please don't read it that way. This happens more than we'd like to admit.

Some, to "protect the reputation of the church" or "save a leader from embarrassment," have used this passage to hide the sins of sexual predators and abusers. In so doing, they have made the church a convenient hiding place for sexual deviants and power-hungry narcissists.

This passage should never be used to break the law or hide abuse or crimes. If we hunger and thirst for righteousness and justice, we must never acquiesce to the harm of a victim while providing safety to an abuser. Contextually, this passage is about protecting the "little ones" and not catering to the "great ones."

If a crime is committed, no matter what the backlash may be, it must be reported. If someone in charge has abused their power, we must act no matter the fallout. Transparency and honesty will protect the church far more than secrecy and deception. Plus, even if it doesn't "protect the church," it's the godly thing to do.

Protecting Mary from shame (Matt 1:19) is not the same as hiding King Herod's sin (Matt 14:3–4). And we should know this. Reporting abuse and taking a strong stand against perpetrators will discourage further injustices and save potential victims. A victim should not be forced to privately face an abuser before the church will listen or help. That is a foolish recipe for manipulation and harm, and it is clearly not what Jesus was talking about. We should pay close attention to what dangerous power dynamics are at play. Do not forget Matthew 18:5–10; we must receive and protect the "little ones."

Our churches should be the safest places in the world for the abused. We should care, protect, support, comfort, love, and stand for the "little ones," that is, those without voice, power, or position of authority. Our care and concern for sinners should not come at the cost of silencing or ignoring those they've sinned against. Otherwise, we have become complicit in their abuse, and it would be better for a millstone to be hung around our necks as we sink to the bottom of the sea.

Radical Forgiveness

In Matthew 18:21–35, Jesus finishes this discussion with a story about forgiveness. Peter asks how many times we should forgive. Jesus wants us to be forgiving, but let's not be ridiculous, right? There must be a cut-off point somewhere. Jesus's answer goes back to the Sermon on the Mount, where we are challenged to imitate God's love (Matt 5:44–48). Wouldn't it be tragic if God had a cut-off point with forgiveness?

Jesus reminds us to forgive others because our heavenly Father is overwhelmingly forgiving to us. We have been forgiven more than we can ever forgive. God's forgiveness should motivate us to forgive. Forgiving others offers a glimpse and foretaste of the forgiveness God offers.

The principle in Matthew 5:7, 6:14–15, and 7:1–2 is detailed more fully in Matthew 18:23–35. If we judge and condemn others, we will be judged and condemned. However, if we extend mercy and forgive others, God, the ultimate source of mercy and forgiveness, will extend it to us. In fact, God extends it to us first. In the parable, the King forgave first. He extended forgiveness before He required it, and the King forgave an astronomical amount (some estimate about 200,000 years of labor). He forgave a debt that could never have been paid. But when his servant was unwilling to forgive, the King withdrew His forgiveness.

In this story, remaining forgiven is conditioned on forgiving others. Thus, God ensures that forgiveness does not stay with us but spreads to others around us. Everyone who is forgiven should then forgive. No relationship can endure without forgiveness. Forgiving others is an essential part of the Christian life. Treat others as God treats you. Be merciful, judge gracefully, and forgive quickly.

Reflection Questions

1. Why is it so hard to forgive? What does it mean to forgive? Who does forgiveness benefit? What is the relationship between forgiveness and guilt? Can you forgive while still hurt or angry? How can you start the process of forgiveness?
2. Why is it important that the church is forgiving? Can forgiveness enable predators and oppressors? How can forgiving one another be a sign of the kingdom? How does forgiving others teach us to be more like God? What does the cross teach us about forgiveness?

REFLECTION 46

THREE PARABLES ABOUT SONS: MATTHEW 21:23–22:14

The Temple, the Leaders, and Two Sons

UPON FINISHING HIS FOURTH SPEECH, Jesus travels a final time to Judea (Mat 19:1). Along the way, He addresses controversies and questions regarding divorce (Matt 19:1–12) and wealth (Matt 20:16–30). These further elaborate on what was introduced in the Sermon on the Mount (see Reflections #21–23 and #31). He also predicts His death and resurrection one last time (Matt 20:17–19) before arriving as the Son of David who gives sight to the blind (Matt 20:29–34).

Jesus fulfills Zechariah 9:9ff upon His royal entry into Jerusalem (Matt 21:1–11). Zechariah promised a coming King who would cut off the bow of war and "speak peace to the nations; And His dominion will be from sea to sea ..." (Zech 9:10; see Matt 28:18). This King is humble, mighty, and peaceful. He will have all dominion and authority and will rule Jews and Gentiles alike. They will find peace in Him.

In these scenes, Jesus is repeatedly hailed as the Son of David (Matt 20:30; 21:9, 15). David was unable to build a temple because of his violence (1 Chron 22:6–8). Jesus, however, will chastise the leaders of the temple, establish in Himself a new and greater temple, and instead of shedding His enemies' blood, He will be a peaceful King who sheds His own. Remember, Jesus is better described as "Lord of David" than "Son of David" (Matt 22:43–46).

Upon arrival, this humble, peaceful King enters the temple, flips the tables, spills the money all over the floor, and drives out those who are buying and selling. As He does this, Jesus references two Old Testament passages. He says, "My house shall be called a house of prayer," from Isaiah 56:11, and, "but you are making it a robber's den," alluding to Jeremiah 7:11. These passages help us interpret Jesus's prophetic sign in the temple.

Isaiah 56:1–7 is a beautiful description of God's temple welcoming all kinds of people into it, including the Gentile and the eunuch (contrast with Deut 23:1–8). Jeremiah 7 begins a famous sermon preached at the temple. This sermon announces the coming destruction of the temple (by the Babylonians) because of the sins of Israel, who shed innocent blood and oppressed the alien, the orphan, and the widow (Jer 7:1–7). Destruction is coming because they made God's house a "den of robbers" (Jer 7:11).

Jesus, the peaceful King, sees these same sins and consequences in His own day. Just as the Babylonians destroyed the temple, so will the Romans (Matt 24:1–2). The flipping of the tables is a prophetic demonstration, a warning, and a precursor to these dreadful events, which Jesus will detail clearly in the coming chapters (Matt 24:1–2). Jesus does not flip tables because He lost His temper and threw a fit. Jesus, as a prophet of Israel, provided a small prophetic picture of what was coming from the Romans.

Jesus then turned God's house back into a place of healing and acceptance (Matt 21:14–16). Jesus welcomed the blind and lame to the temple for healing (Matt 21:14). The children (Matt

18:2–6, 19:13–15, 21:16–17) are also welcomed in the temple, and they sing and shout praises to Jesus, the Son of David (Matt 21:16). This is what the temple should be. A great reversal is taking place. The blind and lame enter while the money changers are driven out. The children, to whom belongs the kingdom of heaven, get it right, while the prominent rulers get it all wrong.

The morning after transforming God's house from a robber's den to a place of healing and praise, Jesus curses a fig tree (21:18). This tree had leaves and looked healthy but produced no fruit. Appearances can be deceiving. This tree represents the temple, which looks so glamorous on the outside yet does not produce fruit for God. As many passages have made clear, Jesus cares more about the inside than the appearance on the outside (Matt 6:1–18, 15:15–20, 23:25–33).

The withering of the leafy fig tree is another picture of the coming destruction of the temple. It is another prophetic sign that looks back to Jeremiah's prophetic condemnation: "There will be no grapes on the vine and no figs on the fig tree, and the leaf will wither; and what I have given them will pass away" (Jer 8:13). Jesus is preparing the people for Jeremiah's words to play out again in their own day.

Angered by these actions, the rulers of the temple challenge Jesus on His authority to do and teach such deeds (Matt 21:23). Jesus responds with a question about John's baptism, followed by three parables about "sons" (Matt 21:24–22:14). Jesus's question about John's baptism gets to the heart of the temple controversy.

The chief priests and elders see Jesus as a challenge to their authority. The same is true with John's baptism. John's baptism offered forgiveness and a right relationship with God apart from the temple. People would go to John to repent and receive forgiveness instead of the temple and priests.

John's Baptism and Two Sons

Jesus asks whether John's baptism comes from heaven or men. If the leaders say it is from heaven, then they admit that God is working apart from the temple. Also, that answer will contradict their rejection of John. People would ask them, "If it's from heaven, why did you not accept it?" They didn't accept it because it challenged their status and power as temple leaders, but obviously, they cannot say that. Yet, they also cannot say it was from men because they fear the crowds who regard John as a prophet (Matt 21:25–26). They are stuck because either answer will discredit them before the crowds.

Their search for an answer is not based on truth at all. It's based on self-preservation. They want an answer, not that is true, but that will make them look good to the masses. It is about appearances. They seek a safe, politically correct answer that doesn't exist. So, they remain silent.

All these stories are related. The leaders wear the right clothes and say the right words, but their hearts are far from God (Matt 15:8). Just like the temple's beauty or the fig tree's leaves, they look good and healthy, but on further inspection, the temple is a den of robbers, the fig tree has no fruit, and the leaders are disobedient sons. Therefore, the temple is doomed, the fig tree withers and the rulers will be cast out.

Jesus responds to them with a parable about two sons. The first was told to work in the vineyard, and he said, "I will not," but soon regretted it and went. When you listen to his words, this son sounds disobedient, but his actions reveal an honest and sincere heart. He did not look the part at first but was ultimately pleasing to His father.

The second son was also told to work in the vineyard. He said, "Absolutely, father! Yes sir! You can count on me!" He sounds so good, loyal, and obedient. But this second son did not go. He looked and sounded obedient, but He rejected his father's will.

After telling this parable, Jesus says those shocking words: "Truly I say to you that the tax collectors and prostitutes will get into the kingdom of God before you" (Matt 21:31). There is no way the rulers of the temple will like hearing this. Tax collectors and prostitutes are the most detested sinners on earth, yet Jesus places them in the kingdom before the temple leaders.

Other than being sinners, tax collectors and prostitutes don't share much else in common. It's interesting that Jesus joins them together here. Prostitutes would generally be female, poor, oppressed, and abused by others. Tax collectors would generally be male, rich, oppressors, who abuse others. By linking these two, Jesus suggests that all sinners, from the top to the bottom, are welcomed into the kingdom before the "righteous" chief priests and elders.

Tax collectors and prostitutes are like the first son in the parable. They appeared to give God a "no," but when John the Baptist came, they heard, believed, and obeyed. Their appearance said "no," but their actions said "yes." The chief priests, however, look like they say "yes" to God. They work at the temple and wear beautiful robes and tithe and know the Torah, but when God spoke through John, their actions spoke a resounding "no." Remember, appearances can mislead (see Matt 7:15).

The Tenants and the Marriage Feast

The next "son" parable is Matthew 21:33–44, in which a man builds a vineyard and hires tenants to care for it while he is away. The description of building the vineyard mirrors the language and imagery of Isaiah 5:1–7. In both passages, God is the builder and owner, and Israel is the vineyard.

However, Matthew diverges from Isaiah's parable in several key ways. For example, in Isaiah 5, Israel does not produce good fruit, but in Matthew 21, Israel does. The problem in Matthew 21 is not the vineyard or the fruit production but the tenants who keep the fruit for themselves instead of giving it back to the owner. This "son" parable, like the ones before and after, is a critique of the temple leadership in Israel (see Matt 5:12 and 23:34–36).

The history of Israel's rejection of prophets is outlined in this parable (Matt 21:34–36). The landowner sends servants to gather fruit, but the tenants refuse them. They reject, beat, and even kill them. You can see this happen to the Old Testament prophets, and Jesus comments on this tragic history several times (Matt 5:12, 23:29–39).

Finally, the landowner sends His own Son, and the unimaginable happens. His Son is rejected, cast out, and murdered. When Jesus sees Israel, He sees fields white for harvest (Matt 9:37–38) and a vineyard producing good fruit, but the workers are few, and the tenants are wicked. The temple leaders kept the fruit for themselves and refused God's pleadings. This rebellion culminates in the killing of the Son (see Matt 16:21, 17:22–23, 20:17–19). Yet, with a concluding citation from Psalm 118:22–23, Jesus offers hope that God will use their rejection as a cornerstone to build something marvelous. The kingdom will instead be given to those who produce fruit (Matt 21:43, Matt 7:16, 21:18–19).

The final parable also has a father and son as the key characters and continues critiquing Israel's leadership. The father, a king, invites certain people to a wedding feast for his son, but they refuse to come. Then, like the previous parable, some even persecute and kill the king's servants. The king exacts vengeance upon them (Matt 22:7, another reference to the destruction of Jerusalem; see Matt 21:41 also) and then finds others who will come to the wedding.

This second group is a mixture of good and bad (Matt 22:10), but at least they come. The "good" and "bad" remind us of the "wheat" and "tares" that grow up together. It is a realistic portrayal that not all who enter are truly obedient. This second group probably includes the "tax collectors and prostitute" types mentioned in the first "son" parable (Matt 21:31–32). It may also hint toward Gentile inclusion (Matt 28:18–20).

There's an odd additional note at the end about a man who was removed from the party. He came to the feast but was not wearing proper attire. When asked about this, he offers no justifiable reason. He doesn't say that he is poor and cannot afford clothes. He gives no reason. Some have suggested that traditionally, a king would provide wedding garments for the attendants, but this man refused. Putting on new clothes is a common symbol in Christianity for demonstrating a truly transformed life: Romans 13:12, 14; Colossians 3:12; Galatians 3:27.

This improperly dressed man wants to be at the party but refuses to be changed. Perhaps like those in Matthew 7:21 who cry "Lord, Lord," but do not do the will of the Father, this man wants the benefits of the kingdom without conforming to the message of the kingdom. On that great Judgment Day, described in Matthew 25:31–46, all who appear before the King will be exposed before His eyes.

Reflection Questions

1. What do these three parables have in common? How can appearances be deceptive? In the first parable, how do the two sons relate to the religious leaders and rebellious sinners? How do they relate to John the Baptist?

2. In the second parable, why did the tenants refuse to give the vineyard owner His fruit? What history is this parable recounting? Who is the parable ultimately about? In the third parable, why were the guests unwilling to come to the wedding feast? Why did one man come but refuse to wear a wedding garment?

REFLECTION 47

WOE TO THE HYPOCRITES: READ MATTHEW 23:1–39

Major Speech #5

JESUS's final major speech is found in Matthew 23:1–25:46. This speech, like the Sermon on the Mount, is three chapters. It addresses many of the controversies that have arisen since Jesus entered Jerusalem and prepares us for what will happen next. In this speech, Jesus gives His final and ultimate prophetic words against the rulers of Jerusalem, predicts and describes the coming destruction of Jerusalem, and prepares His disciples for the inevitability of a lengthy delay in the ultimate return of the Son of Man.

Things have been heating up in the chapters leading to Matthew 23. After cleansing the temple and condemning its leaders (Matt 21:1–22:14), Jesus has been in constant controversy. The Pharisees and Herodians conspired to trap Jesus in a political argument about taxes (Matt 22:15–22). The Sadducees challenged Jesus about the resurrection (Matt 22:23–34). A lawyer tested Jesus concerning the "great commandment" in the Law (Matt 22:35–40). Finally, Jesus challenges their notions of the Messiah. He shows the inadequacy of the title "Son of David" ("Lord of David" would be most appropriate), and He silences

His critics (Matt 22:46). Matthew 23 is where He gives His full-scale, unambiguous, prophetic rebuke of the "blind guides" in Jerusalem.

One word of caution before we examine this chapter. There are parts of the Bible that have been used to fuel sinful attitudes and hateful discrimination. Christianity does not have a great track record in its dealings with Jews throughout history, and passages like Matthew 23 and John 8 have been used to justify anti-Semitic attitudes and actions. As you read this chapter, remember this is a prophetic critique of those contemporary rulers who abused their power and led people astray.

This is not an attack on a race or religion. This is not a statement about how Jews act or how they will act in the future. Jesus already described Israel as a vineyard that produces good fruit (Matt 21:33ff), but their leaders were halting it. Jesus is a Jew who loves Jews. This chapter is about the misuse of power and the quest for greatness, not a diatribe against Jews. This is a critique that every one of us needs to receive at times, especially those who lead others.

Remember, Jesus and His earliest followers were Jews. This is not a Christian vs Jewish debate but an intra-Jewish critique of certain leaders and power structures. In Matthew, Jesus also criticizes the way Gentiles exercise their power (Matt 20:25–26). And notably, this rebuke leads to lamentation (Matt 23:37–39) because the God who rebukes is also the God who loves.

Introducing the Speech

This passage is famous for its seven woes against the Pharisees. These include some of the harshest words in the New Testament. But before those woes, Jesus sets the tone for the sermon by describing the scribes and Pharisees as the opposite of Sermon-on-the-Mount-folk (Matt 23:2–12). In this final speech, so much of what Jesus says links back to His first. He sees the teachers of Israel as the opposite of everything He has been teaching: compare Matthew 23:5 with 6:1; Matthew 23:7 with 5:47; Matthew 23:15, 31 with 5:45; Matthew 23:16–22 with Matthew 5:33–37, etc. They have "seated themselves in the chair of Moses." If you remember Reflection #6, that seat belongs to Jesus. But these leaders have elevated themselves to prominent positions, and they love all the pageantry and formality that goes with it. They wear gaudy religious clothing, sit in the places of honor at banquets and in the synagogue, partake in respectful greetings, and wear titles of high esteem. What they fail to recognize is that each of these acts separates them from the people they are called to lead. Jesus wants them to remember that "you are all brothers" (Matt 23:8) and that "whoever exalts himself shall be humbled; and whoever humbles himself shall be exalted" (Matt 23:12).

The major problems are arrogance, hypocrisy, and abuse of power. God's word had become an unreasonable burden for many. Following Christ is definitely a challenge, but it is one that should remove the burdens of this world rather than increase their weight. Jesus calls His followers to a high standard of righteousness (Matt 5:10). But the cross-bearing call of Jesus is not the same as the "heavy burdens" placed on peoples' shoulders by the scribes and Pharisees (Matt 23:4). In fact, while following Jesus requires sacrifice, obedience, and even suffering, Jesus describes it as an easy yoke and a light burden where one finds rest (Matt 11:28–30). Jesus offered a true restful Sabbath while they even made the Sabbath a burden.

Strict obedience to God is not our major problem in this life. In fact, obedience to Jesus, while certainly having its own challenges, frees us from the relational, financial, and social pressures we grapple with daily. If we gave up the need for excess, praise, and superiority, we would find many of life's burdens gently fluttering away. Life could become simple, joyful, and meaningful if we stopped critically condemning others and let go of hatred or compulsion for revenge. It's hard to do, but it lightens our load as humans.

When Jesus looks at the Pharisees, He does not see people suffering for being too obedient. He doesn't even see their teaching as the main problem (Matt 23:2). Rather, He sees men exalting themselves over others based on a superficial and deceptive outward show of obedience. They care more about looking obedient than being obedient. They want applause for righteousness rather than the constraints of righteousness. This is what brings the woes upon them.

Seven Woes

Woe #1 — Matthew 23:13 — They fail to enter the kingdom (see Matt 5:20), but even worse, they shut it off to prevent others from entering (Matt 23:13). This is the opposite of what Peter was called to do (Matt 16:18–19). Peter was given the keys to open the kingdom to people. Jesus calls people to repent for the kingdom is coming (Matt 4:17). He preached the "good news of the kingdom" (Matt 4:23, 9:35). While Jesus and His movement prepare and open the kingdom to the world, the Pharisees are actively working to close it.

Woe #2 — Matthew 23:14, 15 — There is a textual variant here in the text, so some Bibles will have a verse 14 (which would make an eighth woe), and some do not. Verse 14, if you have it, references devouring widows' houses and offering long prayers. This seems to be taken from ideas in Mark 12:40 and Luke 20:47. This would also connect back to Matthew 6:5–8. But it is almost certainly a later addition to the text and was not originally in Matthew.

The original second woe is found in verse 15, where the scribes and Pharisees are condemned for searching far and wide for proselytes, only to make them "twice as much a son of hell." This happens when a new disciple looks more like a particular teacher/preacher/evangelist/missionary than Jesus. This happens all the time. You can see it when an influential teacher garners a following. His followers tend to share all his particular hobby horses, grudges, and attitudes.

That is a clear indication of misusing authority and influence to make miniature disciples of oneself while neglecting Jesus. When this happens, the negative qualities of the teacher are often highlighted in the actions of the student. Remember what Jesus said in the Sermon on the Mount: "You will know them by their fruits" (Matt 7:20). You can tell a lot about a teacher by looking at the disciples.

Woe #3 — Matthew 23:16–22 — This woe (Matt 23:16–22) further elaborates on the problem of manipulation and dishonest oaths. Back in the Sermon on the Mount, Jesus rejects oath-making outright (Matth 5:33–37), and this is one of the reasons why. Oaths are not intended to create loopholes in honesty.

Woe #4 — Matthew 23:23–34 — It is so easy to emphasize the wrong things. There was nothing wrong with tithing or precision (though this seems to be more than the Law required). But to put so much effort into a minute aspect of the tithe, yet ignore justice, mercy (Matt 9:13, 12:7), and faithfulness is as ludicrous as straining a gnat out of your drink before swallowing a camel. (Matt 7:3 is a similar illustration.) The gnat and the camel were generally considered the smallest and the largest unclean animals in the area. To emphasize the minuscule and neglect what matters infinitely more is a problem with many roots, including fear and pride, which lead to legalism and hypocrisy. It warps your whole view of God and humanity and is fuel for division and strife.

Woe # 5 and # 6 — Matthew 23:25–28 — These two woes share a similar critique, and we can all learn from it. We often focus on outward appearances and neglect the heart. We emphasize what men see rather than what God sees. This is what Matthew 6:1–18 and 15:10–20 are about. It's a major part of Jesus's controversy with the temple leaders in Matthew 21:23–32. In Israel, as a courtesy, tombs were whitewashed to be easily recognized and avoided (since touching the tomb would render one unclean—Num 19:14–19). Jesus sees this as an illustration of what His antagonists have become.

We care too much about appearances. Some Christians work so hard to look "sound" and "conservative" or "new-age" and "enlightened" that their desired reputation becomes their guiding light while large swaths of Scripture are ignored. When people dress up piously and perform outward signs of obedience but neglect love and generosity, they have become that beautiful tomb filled with rotting corpses. In the Sermon on the Mount, Jesus wants us to internalize the Law to let it purify us from the inside out. Murder and adultery are outward expressions of a heart rotted away by anger and lust. Jesus wants us to purify the inside rather than wash the outside.

Woe #7 — Matthew 23:29–36 — This woe describes the tombs of great prophets who were rejected, persecuted, and killed. These tombs have been decorated and memorialized, but the prophets were hated and despised. Sure, it's nice to honor a prophet's tomb, but it is better to listen while the prophet still lives. The scribes and Pharisees justified themselves by claiming they were better than their forefathers and would have listened!

Jesus, the greatest prophet, gives them the chance to prove this claim. How they respond to Him indicates how they would have responded to those prophets of old. Jesus will also send more prophets, wise men, and scribes to them (a reference to Christian evangelism). They will have many opportunities to listen to the prophets. But tragically, the scribes and Pharisees will do no better than those who came before (Matt 10:16–23). Thus, the contemporary leadership will share in the bloodshed of their forefathers (See Matt 21:35–39).

Reflection Questions

1. Why did Jesus have confrontations with the scribes and Pharisees? What did Jesus think about their teachings? What did Jesus think about their actions? Compare Matthew 23:4 to Matthew 11:28–30.
2. What does this chapter teach about hypocrisy? What are some examples of hypocrisy described in this chapter? Where do you see hypocrisy today? Why is hypocrisy such a damaging charge against the church? Where do you see hypocrisy in your own life?

REFLECTION 48

DESTRUCTION OF JERUSALEM:
READ MATTHEW 24:1–35

Setting the Context

IN MATTHEW 23:36, Jesus declares those fateful words, "Truly, I say to you, all these things will come upon this generation." This statement begins an inclusio that ends in Matthew 24:34, "Truly, I say to you, this generation will not pass away until all these things take place." The context in between these verses concerns "this generation."

Going back to the cleansing of the temple (Matt 21:12–13), Jesus has prophetically demonstrated and predicted the destruction of the temple. He flipped tables and drove everyone out as a small picture of what would be coming. He called the temple a "den of robbers," and He cursed a fig tree, causing the leaves to wither. Those words and actions come from Jeremiah when he stood long ago at the temple entrance and predicted its destruction (Jer 7:2, 11; 8:13).

In His parables and teachings, Jesus has alluded to the destruction of Jerusalem and the temple (Matt 21:41–45, 22:7). Now, again at the temple, as the disciples show Jesus the impressive beauty of that great structure (Matt 24:1), He says,

"Truly, I say to you, there will not be left here one stone upon another that will not be thrown down" (Matt 24:2). Again, as Jeremiah before Him, Jesus predicts, in devastating fashion, the destruction of the temple and the miserable fate Jerusalem will suffer. Historically, we know this happened in AD 70. Just as Jesus predicted, these events took place in the days of "this generation."

When Jesus sees His beloved Jerusalem facing destruction, He cannot help but lament over her:

> Oh Jerusalem, Jerusalem, the city that kills the prophets and stones those who are sent to it! How often I would have gathered your children together as a hen gathers her brood under her wings, and you were not willing! See, your house is left to you desolate (Matt 23:37–38).

Jesus repeatedly rebuked the leaders of Jerusalem and the temple in Matthew 21–23. But Jesus did not do this from vindictiveness or malice. He loves them and wants something better for them. He offers wings of protection. Remember, if you are going to rebuke someone, be sure it is combined with prayer, lamentation, love, and an offer to help.

The language Jesus uses of a hen gathering her brood under her wings shows that His love for Jerusalem is akin to a mother's protective and nurturing love for her children. In the Old Testament, God is portrayed as spreading His protective wings over Israel (Deut 32:10–12, Ps 91:1–4). Regarding this lamentation, Richard Hays describes

> two remarkable features of His sorrowful words. First, even though Jesus is facing impending violence and death, he does not appeal to God to grant the protection of sheltering wings; instead, he casts himself, at least metaphorically, in the role of

> the God whose wings seek to shelter Israel. Second, his lament portrays Jerusalem as rejecting the protection he has repeatedly sought to give ... These daring words ... are nothing other than a cry from the heart of Israel's God. [39]

Rather than Jesus requesting God's protective wings, Jesus offers His own. Jesus is the God whose protection is rejected by the leaders of Jerusalem. Therefore, with tears, Jesus says, "Your house is left to you desolate" (Matt 23:38). That word "desolate" is translated as "wilderness" or "desert" in other passages (Matt 3:1, 4:1, 14:15, etc.). The great temple will become a barren wasteland.

Three Questions

The disciples were undoubtedly shocked to hear His words about the temple's doom. Privately, they ask Him, "Tell us, when will these things be, and what will be the sign of your coming and of the end of the age?" (Matt 24:3) How we divide and interpret the meaning of these questions will shape how we understand Jesus's answers.

Some read Matthew 24 and immediately forget the context of the destruction of Jerusalem. This chapter is the climax of themes that have been building since Jesus cleansed the temple in Matthew 21:1–19. Jesus entered Jerusalem as King and briefly transformed the temple from a den of robbers to a home of healing (Matt 21:12–14). That is what Jesus will be doing writ large in the coming days and years. Essential to Jesus's Messianic mission is His enthronement as King and renewal of the temple. This will happen in the days of "this generation" (Matt 23:36, 24:34).

Many interpretations of Matthew 24 ignore this crucial temple setting and timeline. They fast forward a few thousand years and make the whole discussion about the end of the world. To do this, some teach that the word "generation" should be translated as "race." Meaning that "these things" will not happen in the lifetime of this "generation" but at some point, while the "race" of Jews remains.

I'd suggest looking back at every use of the word "generation" in Matthew (Matt 1:17; 11:16; 12:39, 41–42, 45; 16:4; 17:17, etc.). Jesus's genealogy is not divided into three sets of fourteen races but generations. Jesus does not call Israel a "faithless and twisted race" or an "evil and adulterous race." He condemned the attitudes of some in His current generation, not the race of a group of people. Contextually and grammatically, Matthew 23:36–24:34 should be read about the destruction of Jerusalem during Jesus's contemporary generation.

Matthew 24 uses a lot of apocalyptic language that sounds like total cosmic destruction. However, it is a mistake to interpret all apocalyptic language to describe the end of the world literally. I would encourage you to be skeptical of anyone who comes along interpreting news articles, natural disasters, or movements in the heavens as signs of the second coming. This is a common strategy for selling products, inducing fear, and controlling others. Not everyone who interprets this way has these impure motives, but we should at least be cautious when we hear it.

However, on the other hand, some read everything said by Jesus in Matthew 24 and 25 to be about Jerusalem's destruction. They see nothing in these chapters at all about the final coming of Jesus. I believe this is a more responsible approach, and a strong case can be made for it. If this is your view, it should not lead you to believe that there is no final coming of the Lord at the end of time or that Jesus has already come in this ultimate sense, but only that Matthew 24–25 does not discuss that final coming. There are a few clues in the text that lead me to take it in another direction. The details in this chapter, regardless of the position you hold, should be interpreted with humility and recognition that there is much still to learn.

So, in short, some interpret these chapters to be entirely about the end of the world. Some do this insincerely for manipulative political and financial reasons that we should outright reject. Some, in all sincerity and integrity, interpret these chapters to be about the end of time, and while I disagree, I recognize that the language is difficult and it's an easy mistake to make.

In the opposite direction, some interpret these chapters to be only about the destruction of Jerusalem, and they see nothing at all about the end of time. On this view, some say that there is no return of Jesus in our future and that he already came in AD 70 and will never come again.

This is dangerously misguided. Some believe that there is still a return of Jesus in our future, but we learn about it from verses other than Matthew 24–25. This view is the strongest of those just mentioned, but I still think it misses some important details. The view I take is that Matthew 24–25 addresses both the destruction of Jerusalem and the ultimate end of the age and the final coming of Jesus.

Interpretive Framework

I see Matthew 24 and 25 as an answer to those three questions asked in 24:2:

1. Tell us, when will these things be?
2. And what will be the sign of your coming?
3. And of the end of the age?"

The disciples probably thought they were asking only one question. Those three events, the destruction of the temple, the coming of the Son of Man, and the end of the age were expected to occur at the same time. The disciples want to know when it will happen and what signs will reveal it. Jesus, as His answers always do, adjusts their expectations. Looking at the words "these things" throughout this chapter will help you keep Jesus's answers organized in your mind (Matt 23:36; 24:2, 3, 8, 33, 34). After Jesus tells them that not one stone of the temple will be left upon another, they ask, "When will these things be?" (Matt 24:2–3) Jesus's answer, after a good number of details, is ultimately, "this generation will not pass away until all these things take place" (Matt 24:24). So, "these things" refers to the destruction of the temple that will occur during "this generation." Getting to that answer, Jesus warns them not to fall for false signs or false prophets (24:4–14) but instead to look for what was spoken by Daniel (Matt 24:15–21).

The second question, concerning His coming, is answered in two different ways. There is a sense in which the destruction of Jerusalem, along with Jesus's ascent and enthronement in heaven, is a coming of the Son of Man (Matt 24:27–31). But that is not the final and ultimate coming of the Son of Man, which Jesus addresses more fully after verse 36. We will discuss this more specifically in the next reflection.

The third question, concerning the end of the age, is answered in 24:36–25:46. While the destruction of Jerusalem and the enthronement of Christ at the right hand of the Father is the end of an age, it is not the final and ultimate end. Jesus expands His disciples' minds to consider the "end" in two ways.

"The end of the age" is an essential topic for Jesus to address. We'll see this more in Reflection #50, but Matthew emphasizes something here that is absent in Mark's parallel section. Mark has no parables or discussion about a long wait. It's easy to read Mark and expect these things to happen immediately. In fact, unlike Matthew, Mark never has a clear jump from the destruction of Jerusalem to the end of this present world. In Matthew, however, Jesus prepares His disciples for a long wait, aka, a delayed *parousia*.

According to Matthew, the final coming of the Lord will not happen quickly. The details concerning the destruction of Jerusalem, described from Matthew 23:36 to 24:34, are book-ended with the timeframe of "this generation." These events will happen quickly, and there are signs to watch for. But there are no signs after verse 36. There is also no more mention of "these things" after verse 36. Plus, at verse 36, the text switches from speaking about "those days" (24:19, 22, 29) to "that day" (24:36, 42, 50; 25:13).

Quite a few shifts happen once we get to verse 36. Jesus, after giving signs and warnings about the destruction of the temple in "this generation," switches to talk about a future day: "But concerning that day and hour no one knows, not even the angels of heaven nor the Son ..." (Matt 24:36). There are no signs. There is only the expectation of a lengthy wait.

In the parable in Matthew 24:48, the servant says, "My master is delayed." The following parable says, "the bride-groom was delayed" (Matt 25:5). The parable after that, again describing a lengthy wait, says, "Now after a long time the master of those servants came ..." (Matt 25:19). Matthew includes a theme about a delayed return that takes a long time. The temple's destruction will occur relatively quickly, but another day is coming that will be "delayed" and will not occur for a "long time."

Discussion Questions

1. What was the meaning and significance of the temple in Jerusalem? Why was its destruction so shocking? Why would the disciples connect it to the

coming of the Son of Man and the end of the age? How can people be misled about this topic?

2. What do you think Jesus is talking about in these texts? Is Jesus mostly concerned with the destruction of Jerusalem or the end of the world? How does the language between those two topics overlap?

Endnotes

[39] Hays, *Echoes*, 261.

REFLECTION 49

THE COMING OF THE SON OF MAN:
READ MATTHEW 24:1–35

The Need for Clarity

THE DISTINCTION between the destruction of the temple and the final coming of the Lord is important because if one were expecting all these events to take place simultaneously, then great confusion would result when the temple was destroyed, but the world continues with Jesus in the heavens. Jesus wants His disciples to know that even after the destruction of Jerusalem and the inauguration of a new age and reign, the old age of sin and death will continue. The two ages will continue together, much like a field with both wheat and tares.

This recalibration of Messianic expectations has been consistent throughout Matthew. The hope that the present world would be destroyed and a new perfect world would begin with the Messiah must be adjusted. Jesus wants His disciples to know that, while it is true, there will not be a sudden end to one age and the immediate beginning of a completely new age. Rather, there will be a lengthy time in which the old age and the new age exist concurrently. This is where we find ourselves. We live where these ages meet. Or as Paul words it, we are those "upon whom the ends of the ages have come" (1 Cor 10:11).

During this time, the wheat and tares will grow together in the field (Matt 13:36–43). Remember, in the parable of the wedding feast, it is after the destruction and burning of the city (Matt 22:7) that many, both good and bad, enter into the feast (Matt 22:10). The world will continue after the destruction of Jerusalem. It will be a world mixed with wheat and tares, good and bad, wise and foolish, sheep and goats. However, consistent in all of these images is an ultimate day of division when they will be separated by the great King (Matt 24:40–41, 25:31–46).

Walking Through the Text

Let's now walk through the text and see how these ideas play out. Verses 1–3 explicitly declare the temple's destruction. In verses 4–14, Jesus describes some of the things that will lead up to the destruction of the temple by Rome. While those things will happen before the destruction, they are not the ultimate sign of the end. In fact, those things always happen in every generation for all people. Nothing unique to the first century is found there.

There are always false prophets who lead astray. There are always wars and rumors of wars (certainly when Rome's armies are on the move), famines, and earthquakes. But these are not the end; they are merely "the beginning of the birth pangs" (Matt 24:6, 8). Christian missionaries will face tribulation and persecution during this time also (roughly AD 33 through 70). Matthew discussed this previously (Matt 10:16–22). But the gospel will spread to the nations before that fateful day (see Matt 28:18–20, Col 1:23).

Verses 15–28 discuss what to do when you see the end coming. This is the "abomination of desolation" standing in the "holy place" (temple) about which Daniel spoke (Dan 9:27, 11:31,

12:11). Unlike the many false prophets who will arise, Daniel is the true prophet we should heed. He will guide us in our understanding of the coming war against Jerusalem.

Daniel, who lived in exile at the time of Babylon's destruction of the temple in Jerusalem, uses "abomination of desolation" to discuss future attacks on the temple (Antiochus IV Epiphanes and Rome). Jesus uses Daniel's language to address the coming destruction of the temple. Jesus already warned that the temple will be "left to you desolate" (Matt 23:38). An "abomination" is coming that will make it "desolate." That "abomination" is the Roman pagan armies surrounding Jerusalem and entering the holy place (see Luke 21:20–24).

When this abomination begins, flee as fast as you can out of the city! Pray that nothing, like pregnancy, snow, or Sabbath, can slow you down! Get out fast because this may be the worst thing that has happened in human history, and only by God's grace will it be "cut short." Many will offer false hope in the wilderness or in false christs, but do not listen to them. When this day comes, there will be no doubt (Matt 24:27–28). Like lightning seen in the sky or vultures seen circling a carcass, so will be the sign of the Son of Man (Matt 24:30).

Riding the Clouds

Apocalyptic language floods verses 29–31. The language of verse 29 is borrowed from Isaiah 13:10, which describes the fall of Babylon. While the language sounds a lot like the end of the world, it is instead about the fall of a nation. The fall of Babylon was not the ultimate end, and neither will the fall of Jerusalem be. But it will feel like it. This language depicts that feeling of hopelessness and dread. The events will be so catastrophic that it will seem like all creation is falling apart. Just as we describe catastrophic events, like 9/11, as a "dark day," so ancient Israel had picture language to describe cataclysmic events. A "dark day" may literally be bright and sunny yet bring darkness to our souls.

Verse 30 describes the Son of Man riding on the clouds. Daniel 7:13 describes a scene where beasts (nations) come from the sea, while one like a Son of a Man, rides on the clouds to the throne of the Ancient of Days. The Son of Man then receives a kingdom and homage from all the nations (Dan 7:14). In the context of Matthew 24, where nations (beasts) fight and kill each other, Jesus again uses the language of Daniel. He borrows Daniel's image of the Son of Man riding on the clouds as an image of hope in a divine King who rules from the heavens while the nations wage war and destroy on earth.

In Daniel 7, the journey to the throne room is upward. The "coming of the Son of Man" is from earth to the heavens. Many assume the reverse is described in Matthew 24:30. But there is good reason to believe that this passage speaks of Jesus in the same upward trajectory that Daniel speaks of the Son of Man. He is riding the clouds toward the heavenly throne rather than to earth away from it. As N. T. Wright argues,

> The son of man 'comes' from the point of view of the heavenly world, that is, he comes from earth to heaven. His 'coming' in this sense, in other words, is not his 'return' to earth after a sojourn in heaven. It is his ascension, his vindication, the thing which demonstrates that his suffering has not been in vain.[40]

If this is correct, it certainly distinguishes this "coming" from His final coming. It also keeps with the imagery and context of Daniel 7. Plus, it makes sense of what Jesus says to Caiaphas in a few chapters: "From now on you will see the Son of Man seated at the right hand of Power and coming with the clouds of heaven" (Matt 26:64). Jesus says this will be seen "from now on ...." While it may not be seen with physical human eyes, it is a reality for our world. Jesus is the enthroned king. The "coming" of the Son of Man is also mentioned in Matthew 10:23 and 16:28. None of these other passages seem to have the final coming at the end of time in mind, so we should be careful not to force it into Matthew 24:30.

This language implies that the "coming on the clouds of the sky with power and glory" is the idea of enthronement when Jesus comes to heaven and takes His seat to reign. That's how Daniel, the primary source, uses the language. The destruction of the temple is a sign of Jesus's enthronement because Jesus, the true walking, talking, breathing, and living temple, has replaced the brick-and-mortar temple destroyed by Rome. Jesus is our true access to the Father. The removal of the old temple suggests the legitimacy of the new one.

Verse 31 relies on language and imagery from Isaiah 27:13 (see also Deut 30:4 and Zech 2:6). This imagery of sending angels with a trumpet to gather from the four winds envisions a day where the exiles, whom foreign oppressors have dominated, are gathered together safely again. As Jesus prepares His disciples for the destruction of Jerusalem, He employs this imagery. He seeks to protect His elect from the ravages of the beasts and Roman military. He offers safety and refuge.

It's easy to read these passages and lose sight of the topic, but remembering the context of Matthew 24 and examining the allusions to the Old Testament help us keep Jesus's words properly focused on the destruction of Jerusalem. I like how R. T. France summarizes these verses:

> Thus when the significance of the Old Testament imagery is appreciated, vv. 29–31 may be recognized, as the context virtually demanded, as a highly symbolic description of the theological significance of the coming destruction of the temple and its consequences.[41]

If we cannot view this language as anything other than the end of the whole cosmos, perhaps we need to recalibrate our understanding of how cataclysmic the destruction of the temple was in Jewish thought. And we need to attune our ears more precisely to the symbolic language of national collapse in the Hebrew Scriptures.

Verses 32–35 conclude the discussion of the destruction of the temple by reminding us of the fig tree (Matt 24:32, 21:18–19, Jer 8:13). A fig tree with leaves has already served as an image of the temple when Jesus cursed it and it withered. Now, again, a fig tree serves a similar image. By putting out its leaves, it becomes an example of how to read the signs and know the times. Just as a fig tree can tell you when summer is coming, so Jesus's warnings will prepare you for the destruction of the temple.

The signs will show that "these things" are "near," "at the very gates," and will occur before "this generation" passes away. The words of Jesus are truer and more enduring than even heaven and earth, so trust them and be prepared. Beginning in verse 36, however, Jesus discusses something that is not "near" but a mysterious day in the distant future that no one knows and will only come after a "long delay." Let's find out what it is.

Reflection Questions

1. Why is it important for Jesus to address the destruction of the temple? What does this mean about the identity of Jesus? What does this mean about the function and purpose of the temple?
2. Why do so many read this passage to be about the end of the world? How is the destruction of the temple the end of an age? Why is apocalyptic language so difficult to understand? How can the

Old Testament help us understand apocalyptic language?

Endnotes

[40] N. T. Wright, *Matthew: Part Two*, 122.

[41] R. T. France, *Matthew: An Introduction and Commentary, Vol. 1* Tyndale New Testament Commentaries (Downers Grove, IL: IVP Academic, 1985), 390.

REFLECTION 50

PREPARING FOR THE DELAY: READ MATTHEW 24:36–25:46

The Great Unknown

In Matthew 24:36, Jesus begins discussing what can be known about the final coming of the Lord. I take the expression "but of that day" to initiate a transition from "those days" of the destruction of Jerusalem to "that day" of the ultimate return of the Lord. The primary emphasis will be to prepare the church for a lengthy delay. We know that the Son of Man will return, but we do not know when it will happen, so we must live prepared. In the series of parables that follow verse 36, Matthew continually hints that the delay will be lengthy.

This is an important topic for the early church. Jesus has died, been resurrected, and has ascended to the Father while the church awaits His return. Yet that return has not happened. Years pass, and life remains the same. The gospel has spread even to Rome and throughout the known world. Yet, the return has not occurred. Even catastrophic events like the destruction of Jerusalem and the dismantling of the temple have come and gone, but the world goes on as it had. The earliest followers of Jesus, His disciples, and apostles, have died or been killed, yet Jesus is not here.

We know some in the early church began to ask, "Where is the promise of His coming? For since the fathers fell asleep, all things are continuing as they were from the beginning of creation" (2 Pet 3:4). One major difference between Matthew and Mark is that, while Mark says very little about a lengthy delay, Matthew makes it a major theme. Matthew includes parables, not in Mark, which help the reader maintain confidence and righteousness during that time between the destruction of Jerusalem and the ultimate and final coming of the Son of Man.

The presence of Jesus in the life of the church is promised throughout Matthew. From the very beginning, we learn that Jesus is "God with us." In Matthew 18:20, Jesus states, "Where two or three are gathered in my name, there am I among them." Matthew ends with the promise that He will be with us "always, to the end of the age" (Matt 28:20). While the delay may be long, we need to know that we are not alone. Matthew gives confidence to the church that, even if we do not see Him, Christ has not abandoned us. If the church will survive on earth, and the gates of Hades will not prevail against us, then we must maintain confident assurance that Christ is with us always.

The Long Delay

There will be a day, however, when His invisible presence will become visible. This ultimate coming of the Lord, however, will be at a time we do not know. Jesus likens it to the days of Noah when people lived their lives, made no preparation for coming judgment, and then were swept away in the flood. They were unaware and were taken away by the waters of judgment. That is how it will be when the Son of Man returns. People will be unaware, unready, and unprepared for the coming judgment.

Jesus makes an interesting distinction between the judgment of the flood and the judgment of the Son of Man (Matt

24:37–41). With the flood, if two men were in the field or two women grinding at the mill, they would both be swept/taken away. Judgment was universal (except for those on the ark). However, when the Son of Man returns, there will be a careful separation of the righteous from the wicked. One will be taken away to judgment while the other remains safe and secure to welcome the Son of Man's return.

This idea of separation is detailed more fully in the following parables, culminating with the sheep and the goats being separated on that final day (Matt 25:34, 46). By the way, there is no hint in this passage of the famous "Rapture" doctrine developed in the 19th century. This passage does not say some are taken to heaven while others remain on earth for tribulation. Nothing like that is stated. In fact, in context, the ones "taken" are akin to those "swept away" in the flood. This is the opposite picture of the rapture. Being "taken" means going to judgment. You don't want to be taken away; you want to remain and be "left behind" for the return of the Lord. You want to be ready, awake, and prepared for that day (Matt 24:42–44).

Jesus tells three parables to describe how to live during the delay (Matt 24:48; 25:5, 19). The first (Matt 24:45–51) tells us how to be a "faithful and wise servant" while the Master is away. That good servant is just as faithful and obedient when the Master is near as when the Master is on a journey. Those who let their morals and obedience slip away with the passage of time will be unprepared when the Master unexpectedly returns. Instead, we should live faithfully, honoring and obeying our Master at all times (read the Sermon on the Mount and Matt 25:35–36 to see what this obedience entails) so that when He returns, He finds us pleasing.

The second parable describes ten virgins preparing to welcome the bridegroom for the wedding (Matt 25:1–13). This passage teaches us how to wait with wisdom and faithfulness during the delay. Ten virgins all go to wait for the return of the bridegroom (see Matt 9:15). They all have lamps, are dressed properly, and are excited about the occasion. What separates them, what makes five wise and five foolish, is that five brought extra oil for the lamps to remain lit even after a delay, and five did not. Then, upon running out of oil, the five foolish virgins had to run at midnight to find dealers and buy more. While they were gone, the bridegroom returned, entered the celebration, and the door was shut. They missed the celebration because they were unprepared for the delay.

The third parable (Matt 25:14–30) is the famous parable of the talents. A talent is a massive amount of money. Estimates vary, but scholars suggest a talent is equivalent to approximately 15–20 years of paid labor. As a master prepares for a journey, he gives his incredible wealth to three servants for them to try to increase. He gives this wealth according to the ability of the servants.

Since the English word "talent" usually means "skill" or "ability," we often interpret this passage to be about skills that God has given us that he wants us to use. (Actually, this mistaken interpretation is why our English word talent means what it does.) However, in the parable, the talents are not the servants' abilities. Instead, the talents are distributed based on the abilities of the servants (25:15). That makes me think the talents might better be understood as "kingdom opportunities" rather than skills or abilities. God gives us opportunities in relation to our abilities or skills, and we are challenged to make the most out of each opportunity while the Master is away.

In the parable, the servant given the most opportunity (5 talents) was highly productive and produced five more talents. The servant given two talents produced two more, and the Master was equally pleased (25:21, 23). In the kingdom, it is expected that varying amounts will be produced, and our faithfulness is not measured in relation to one another. There is no competition in the kingdom (remember Matt 13:23). But it is also expected that we will take advantage of the opportunities given to us by our Master.

The third servant was given a talent, and he did nothing with it. A talent, in today's world, would likely be over $1,000,000. Being entrusted with a talent is no small matter. He disrespected his Master, acted out of fear rather than faithfulness, and produced nothing for the kingdom (Matt 13:22). Maybe, instead of being grateful for what he was given, he compared himself to the others and failed to see the value in his talent. Maybe this filled him with bitterness toward his master and others. He took a good thing (being given a talent), saw it as a bad thing, and made it a worse thing, which ended in his punishment (Matt 25:26–30).

The Separation

Each of these parables contains a separation between those who do what is right and those who do not (much like Matt 7:13–27 and Matt 13:41–43, 47–50). This separation is a further elaboration on Matt 24:40–41. The ones taken away and cast out are those who failed to act wisely and faithfully during the delay. In Matthew 25:31–46, we are given one more parable. This one is set after the long delay has ended, and "the Son of Man comes in his glory" (Matt 25:31). All the nations will appear before the one true King of all the earth on that day. The sheep, the faithful servants of the King, will be separated to the right, while the goats, who rejected the King, will be separated to the left. This separation will occur based on how those among the nations responded to the King.

Some lived out the true intentions of the Sermon on the Mount. They loved their neighbors as themselves (Matt 22:37–40), which included giving food, drink, acceptance, clothing, hospitality, and visitation. They met the needs of the King whenever He was suffering from hunger, thirst, cold, being a stranger, being sick, or being in prison. Now, you may ask, when was the King ever in any of those situations? What kind of King has no food or clothing? What kind of a King is a stranger or a prisoner? This is exactly what the sheep ask (Matt 25:37–39).

Jesus's answer is crucial. It reminds us that even though invisible, Jesus is absolutely still with us. In each of the parables leading up to this one, the Master or Bridegroom has been gone. The Son of Man has been away. Yet, somehow, in this parable, He is still present and able to be served. Jesus will soon promise to "be with you always, to the end of the age," and this parable tells us how. Even though Jesus will be at the right hand of the Father, at least one way He will continue to be with us is through His brethren (Matt 25:40, 18:20, 28:20). The way we treat the brethren is how we treat Jesus because Jesus remains with us through the brethren.

While we certainly should care for all people and serve all humanity, this particular parable is specifically about how we treat the family of Jesus (Matt 25:40, 45; see 12:48–49). Those who are separated to the left and cast into the eternal fire are those who neglected, ignored, and refused to help the brothers of Jesus. In so doing, they neglected, ignored, and refused to help Jesus. The early church took this idea very seriously. The "body of Christ" is still present on earth in the church. Those who persecute the church are persecuting Jesus (Acts 9:4–6). The way you treat, serve, and love the church while the Master, Bridegroom, and King is away will have eternal consequences to be meted out when He returns.

Reflection Questions

1. What are the signs of the final coming of Jesus? How are we to be prepared for it? Why has the wait been so long?
2. What will be the basis of the great separation at the end? Why does it matter how we treat each other? What acts of service can you render today in honor of Jesus?

REFLECTION 51

ARRESTED, TRIED, AND CRUCIFIED: READ MATTHEW 26:47–27:56

Discipleship Unraveled

THE NEXT TWO CHAPTERS, Matthew 26 and 27, are lengthy and bring about the conclusion that has been long foreboding over the story. From the beginning, we've known Jesus was the son of David (Matt 1:1) who would "save His people from their sins" (Matt 1:21). We've seen kings try to kill Him (Matt 2:1–18). He's been accused of blasphemy (Matt 9:3) and cohorting with Satan (Matt 9:34, 12:24). Conspiracies to kill Jesus have already been planned (Matt 12:14). This hatred and these plans are about to come to a head.

After Jesus's final speech, He announces to His disciples what happens next: "You know that after two days the Passover is coming, and the Son of Man will be delivered up to be crucified" (Matt 26:2). Similar warnings have been issued before (Matt 16:21, 17:22–23, 20:17–19) and His fate has been suggested in various parables (Matt 21:37–39). He has recounted Jerusalem's poor history with prophets (Matt 21:34–46, 22:3–6, 23:34–38; see also 5:10–12, 10:16–18, 24:9–14). He has told His disciples to pick up their own crosses and follow Him (Matt 10:38, 16:24–27). This story has been headed toward rejection, persecution, and crucifixion for some time now. Now is the time for Jesus to follow that long prophetic tradition of suffering in obedience to God, to blaze the trail of the cross for His disciples to follow, and to faithfully endure to save His people from their sins.

The conspirators now include the leaders of the temple and Jerusalem (Matt 26:3–4). They want a quiet and inconspicuous way to seize Jesus, but He is always among the crowds. Judas, who we've had our eye on since Matthew 10:4, knows where Jesus stays in private and cuts a deal with those leaders. For thirty pieces of silver, He betrays the Lord (Matt 26:14–16).

Sandwiched in between the quest to kill Jesus (Matt 26:3–5) and Judas' betrayal (Matt 26:14–16) is a story about a woman who anoints Jesus's head with expensive perfume (Matt 26:6–13). While the disciples (Judas; see John 12:4–8) only think about the wasted money, Jesus reminds them that a beautiful thing was done for Him. She treated Jesus as the true King and, in stark contrast to Judas, sacrificed her wealth to honor and bless Him. Judas and this woman are serving different masters (Matt 6:19–24). We should remember her as we proclaim the gospel throughout the world (Matt 26:13).

After these things, Jesus enters a home and predicts Judas's betrayal (Matt 26:20–25). He shares the Lord's Supper with His disciples (Matt 26:26–29) and then goes to the Mount of Olives (Matt 26:26–29). Then Jesus predicts Peter's denials (Matt 26:30–35). The Lord's Supper, in a tragic irony, is sandwiched between predictions about Judas' betrayal and Peter's denials. Soon, each disciple will abandon Him. We are reminded here that Jesus, by His compassion, shares meals with the unworthy (see Matt 9:10–13).

During this meal, Jesus, as the greater Moses leading the greater Exodus, redefines the symbols of the Passover. He does not abolish Passover but infuses it with new significance (see 1 Cor 5:7–8). We continue to rejoice in our escape from slavery, but the means and meaning of this escape have been transformed. The bread is now His body. Jesus calls the wine, "My blood of the covenant, which is poured out for many for forgiveness of sins" (Matt 26:28; see Exod 24:8, Jer 31:31–34, Heb 9:11–28). Instead of Israel's enemies being killed and overthrown, Jesus sheds His own blood for the forgiveness of His enemies. Through His blood, He freed us from bondage and welcomes us to dine with Him in His Father's kingdom (Matt 26:29; see Col 1:13–14).

Jesus then arrived at Gethsemane to spend intimate time in prayer with His Father. He prays honestly, sincerely, and reverently, asking for any other way. But ultimately, through faithful prayer, He chooses obedience no matter the cost. In contrast, the disciples, who should have been prayerful and obedient, slept in the weakness of their flesh (Matt 26:36–46). This foreshadows their response in the coming hours.

In the darkness, Judas leads the great crowd of soldiers, along with the leaders of Jerusalem, to Jesus. Judas uses a kiss, an act of trust, friendship, and love, as the painful marker of his betrayal. Seeing the crowds, Jesus's disciple (Peter; John 18:10–11) attacks and chooses the way of the sword. Jesus responds with a message we should all take to heart: "Put your sword back into its place. For all who take the sword will perish by the sword" (Matt 26:52). The sword is not the way of Jesus! Echoing back to the temptation in the wilderness, Jesus mentions that He could save Himself with twelve legions of angels, but instead, will fulfill Scripture and honor His Father (Matt 26:53–56).

Peter, at the height of his confusion and bewilderment, is then called upon to confess Jesus before men (Matt 26:69–75; see 10:28–33). His moment of greatest weakness and fear was when he had to make his biggest stand. He could not do it. Perhaps he should have stayed awake in prayer (Matt 26:40–41).

On Trial Before Men

Jesus stands before the high priest and the Sanhedrin court in a sham of a trial. False witnesses tell lies and contradictory testimony. What proves to be the most convincing testimony against Him is a misrepresentation of Jesus's words against the temple (Matt 26:61). In Matthew, while Jesus has warned about the destruction of the temple, Jesus has said nothing about personally tearing it down. In response and to align with Isaiah's Suffering Servant, Jesus chooses silence: "He was oppressed and afflicted, yet he opened not his mouth; like a lamb that is led to the slaughter, and like a sheep before its shearers is silent, so he opened not his mouth" (Isa 53:7, Matt 26:63). He offers no defense to the false charges.

After the high priest demands that Jesus state whether He is the Christ, the Son of God (compare Matt 26:63 and Matt 16:16), Jesus finally answers, "You have said so. But I tell you the truth, from now on you will see the Son of Man seated at the right hand of Power and coming with the clouds of heaven" (Matt 26:64). Jesus self-identifies as the divine Son of Man from Daniel 7, who, among the beasts of the earth, rides the clouds of heaven to the Father and is given "dominion and glory and a kingdom, that all peoples, nations, and languages should serve him; his dominion is an everlasting dominion, which shall not pass away, and his kingdom one that shall not be destroyed" (Dan 7:14). By referencing this passage in His answer, Jesus declares Himself to be the ultimate authoritative King who rules all the nations (see Matt 28:18–20).

Jesus is then accused of blasphemy and sentenced to death. He is beaten, spat upon, and mocked. Immediately after Jesus declares His identity, Peter, who made the same confession earlier (Matt 16:16), now denies Him three times.

Once morning arrives, Jesus is led to Pilate (Matt 27:1). While the Sanhedrin condemned Jesus to death, they did not have authority under Roman Law to exercise capital punishment. They needed the Romans to accomplish this. So, Jesus is brought to the Roman governor (Matt 27:2).

As Jesus is brought before Pilate to face His fate, we are given the details about the fate of Judas (Matt 27:3–10). Matthew is the only Gospel writer to tell us this part of the story. Being plagued by guilt at the charges brought against Jesus, Judas changed his mind and threw the money back. This blood money was unacceptable for the temple treasury, so it was used to purchase a field to bury foreigners. This is said to fulfill a passage from Jeremiah (Matt 27:7–10), and it seems to mingle together details from Jeremiah 32:6–8 with Zechariah 11:12–14.

Judas's sorrow led to suicide by hanging. As Jesus, the representative of the kingdom of heaven, prepares to meet with Pilate, the representative of the kingdoms of this world, Matthew tells a story of betrayal that ends in suicide by hanging. This side story about Judas uses language and imagery from an interesting account in the Old Testament.

Second Samuel 17:1–23 tells of David's kingdom clashing with the kingdom of his son, Absalom. Ahithophel, who had once been a counselor for King David, betrayed him and joined forces with Absalom. In 2 Samuel 17, Ahithophel devises a plan to have David killed. That plan is ultimately rejected, and David escapes. Then Ahithophel responds by "hanging himself" (2 Sam 17:23). Interestingly, Matthew 27:5 and the Septuagint translation of 2 Samuel 17:23 are the only verses in the Bible that use the word "hanged" (ἀπήγξατο).[42] These stories notably share clashing kingdoms, conflict among rulers, betrayal, murderous plots, and suicide by hanging.

Psalm 22 and the Crucifixion

On trial before Pilate, Jesus is silent other than the statement, "It is as you say" (Matt 27:11; see 26:25, 64). But other than that,

He remains silent from this point until He finally cries out, "Eli, Eli, lema sabachthani" (Matt 27:46) in the moments before His death. Pilate, who believes Jesus is innocent, unsuccessfully tried to get Jesus released (Matt 27:15–26). Pilate's wife, who apparently had a dream the night before, also tries to get Jesus released. However, Pilate, in the weakness of his flesh, plays the part of the coward and the unjust ruler and delivers Jesus to be beaten and crucified.

Pilate washes his hands to demonstrate his innocence of Jesus's blood, while the crowds cry out, "His blood shall be on us and on our children!" (Matt 27:25) While at some level, this may be a reference to the judgment meted out in AD 70, this also should remind us of Matthew 26:28, where His blood brings forgiveness of sins. This passage should certainly never cause prejudice against Jews (as it has been used before).

Jesus is then taken to be mocked, beaten, and crucified. He is abandoned, betrayed, and denied by His disciples. He is falsely accused and condemned by His countrymen. Pilate sentences him. Soldiers beat him. He is mocked by those crucified alongside Him. He is ridiculed by all who see Him. Yet, it is not these painful realities that break His silence. The sensed absence of God's presence plagues Him: "My God, My God, Why have You forsaken Me?" (Matt 27:46).

In Jesus's dying moments, He feels alone, abandoned, and forsaken. He reaches back to Psalm 22 and cries a prayer of lament to His Father. Psalm 22 is a crucial text for understanding the death of Jesus. Jesus directly cites Psalm 22:1–2. Psalm 22:7–8 describes mocking and sneering at the Lord's faithful servant. Psalm 22:8 is quoted by the bystanders who ridicule Jesus (Matt 27:43). Psalm 22:14–18 mentions being laid "in the dust of death" where "they pierced my hands and feet"[43] and "they divide my garments among them, and for my clothing they cast lots." Psalm 22 is a cry of anguish and lament which Jesus borrows to describe His experience of the cross. In doing so, Jesus taps into a deep reservoir of biblical imagery depicting the pain of those experiencing God's absence (Job 30:19–23, 26–28; Ps 44:17–26; 88:13–18; Hab 1:1–4, etc.). However, Psalm 22, much like the Gospel of Matthew, does not end with abandonment or forsakenness. Trust becomes the primary focus of this Psalm.

We find out that God "has not despised or abhorred the afflicted; Nor has He hidden His face from him; But when he cried to Him for help, He heard" (Ps 22:24). The Psalm proclaims not only will God be near and hear the cry of the distressed, but there will be a glorious day with peoples of all nations coming to the kingdom of God: "All the ends of the earth will remember and turn to the Lord, and all the families of the nations will worship before You. For the kingdom is the Lord's and He rules over the nations" (Ps 22:27–28). This Psalm, used repeatedly in Matthew's crucifixion narrative (Matt 27:35, 43, 46), moves with the flow of the Gospel of Matthew through the anguish of crucifixion and the glory of resurrection to the great commission of the risen Lord.

Reflection Questions

1. How does Judas relate to the theme of contrasting service to God and service to money throughout Matthew (Matt 6:19–24, 13:44–45, 19:16–30, etc.)? Why did Peter deny Jesus three times? Why did the disciples abandon Him? Did even God forsake Jesus?
2. Why is Psalm 22 so important for understanding righteous suffering? Why does Jesus quote this passage on the cross? Did the Father turn His face away from Jesus (Ps 22:24)?

Endnotes

[42] M. Eugene Boring, *The Gospel of Matthew: Introduction, Commentary, and Reflections* in *NIBC* (Nashville: Abingdon Press, 2015), 360.

[43] The Hebrew text is confusing here. It means something like, "like a lion my hands and feet." But since that seemingly makes no sense, an emendation was made so the text reads "bound" or "pierced" instead of "lion." But that wording is not in the Hebrew manuscripts or early translations. For a brief explanation see Robert Alter, *The Hebrew Bible: A Translation and Commentary, Vol. 3, The Writings* (New York: W.W. Norton and Company, 2019), 68. Other animals mentioned in the text include bulls (22:12), lions (22:13, 16, 21), dogs (16, 20), wild oxen (21), etc.) It may mean something like: "For dogs have surrounded me, a band of evildoers has encompassed me, and lions are at my hands and feet."

REFELCTION 52

THE RISEN KING: READ MATTHEW 28:16–20

Fulfilling the Law

MATTHEW CONCLUDES with the resurrected Jesus on a mountain, surrounded by His followers, issuing a challenge to take His kingdom to the nations/Gentiles. Matthew has been building to this conclusion from the opening chapter. Throughout Matthew, Jesus has redefined clean and unclean regulations. He has touched lepers, menstruous women, and dead bodies (Matt 8:3; 9:20, 25), and rather than Jesus becoming unclean, His purity and healing spread to them.

He changed common perceptions about clean and unclean foods (Matt 15:16–19), removing barriers of fellowship based on diet. He brought the cleansing power of the kingdom of heaven to the most defiled places imaginable, regions overflowing with unclean spirits, tombs, and pigs (Matt 8:28–34). Jesus Himself died, becoming a corpse, and entered the realm of the dead, only to victoriously push through to the glory of resurrection life on the other side. Jesus brought cleansing to death itself.

Jesus offered "sabbath" or "rest" in a universal and freeing way (Matt 11:28–30), unlike those who used God's gift of Sabbath as a burden to weigh others down (Matt 12:1–14). Jesus transformed the blood of the covenant, remembered during Passover, from the blood of a lamb (Exod 12:5–7) or a bull (Exod 24:8) to His blood shed for all men for their forgiveness (Matt 26:28). Jesus transformed the temple from a "den of robbers" to a "house of prayer for all the nations" and brought healing to the afflicted.

Jesus openly received, healed, and complimented Gentiles, lifting their faith as an example for Israel to follow (Matt 8:10–12, 15:21–28). He fulfilled Scripture about shining light on the Gentiles (Matt 4:15–16), proclaiming justice to the Gentiles, and being the hope of the Gentiles (Matt 12:18–21). Gentile women are listed in His genealogy. From His birth, Gentiles traveled great distances to worship Him as the heavens declared His glory (Matt 2:1–12). At His death, it was a Gentile who declared His Sonship (Matt 27:54). In these, and so many other ways, Jesus has been preparing the world for this mission to go unto the nations (Gentiles) and make disciples for the one true King of the cosmos, who possesses all authority over every nation and ruler, in heaven and on earth.

This mission is the fulfillment of the purpose and vocation of Israel since the call of Abraham. After the tower of Babel incident, which dispersed sinful man among the nations (Gen 11:1–9), Abraham was called so that through His seed, God might bring about blessing to the families and nations of the earth (Gen 12:2–3, 22:18, 28:14). God blessed Abraham so that the rest of the world would also be blessed (Gen 12:2).

The Law and covenant were given to Israel so they might become a "kingdom of priests and a holy nation" (Exod 19:5–6) to show others who God is. Israel carried/bore God's name (Exod 20:7) to demonstrate how to know and love God. Obedience to God was necessary so that the nations could see God's unique goodness. Idolatry and polytheism absolutely had to be forbidden; otherwise, the nations would learn of the wrong god. Faithfulness to the one God was essential for Israel to represent Him well to the surrounding world. Israel's purpose was always about the whole world.

Blessing the Nations

This mission to bless the nations included all Gentiles joining together in worship and obedience under the rule of God. This image is throughout the Old Testament: Isaiah 2:2–4, Micah 4:1–3, Zechariah 2:10–11, Daniel 7:13–14. Paul, after spending 15 chapters in Romans arguing for unity among Jews and Gentiles, concludes with a symphony of Scriptures—pulled from the Law (Deut 32:43), the Prophets (2 Sam 22:50, Isa 11:10), and the Psalms (Ps 18:49, 117:1)—that demonstrates that the entire Old Testament, each section, calls for the ultimate unity of all the nations into one family under God. The church, as renewed and expanded Israel, is God's divine instrument to accomplish this.

Early Christian baptismal statements include this element of all peoples being united: Galatians 3:26–28, 1 Corinthians 12:12–13, Colossians 3:9–11. This mission is the mystery of the Gospel revealed in Christ (Eph 3:1–10) and is essential to Christian life. When Peter refused to eat with Gentiles, he was not condemned for being rude or having bad manners, but because he was "not in step with the truth of the gospel" (Gal 2:14). We must never create two tables when Jesus gave His life to create one.

Going back to Abraham, God's mission in this world was unity among the nations, and the Gospel is His plan to make it happen. This mission is experienced when the church, made of followers of Christ from all the nations, worships God in unity. Its full realization will happen in the age to come (Rev 7:9–10 and 21:22–22:5). This mission means that divisive and sinful attitudes of racism, xenophobia, and nationalism are antithetical to the Gospel.

The politics of the Christian are found in Christ Himself, and our government is His kingdom. All humans, regardless of their nationality, color, or language, are welcomed fully into God's embrace through the good news of the victory of Christ. Jesus did not pave the way to this unity by destroying a nation, like Rome (as many would have wanted), but by conquering sin, death, and Satan (See Heb 2:14–15). These universal forces lie behind the localized nations, infusing them with glory, power, and authority. These are the forces that held us in captivity and exile. We escape from these forces in Christ's Exodus when He ends our exile. We now have freedom and life in the kingdom of heaven.

This mission also means that Jesus has not belittled, destroyed, or abolished the Law. And God has not rejected His people. Instead, He has honored, refreshed, and fulfilled the Law so that the ultimate purpose of the Law is realized in Him. Jesus has accomplished and expanded the vocation of Israel. Jesus provides what the Law always intended. This "Great Commission" means that the promise made to Abraham and the mission of Israel has come to fruition.

With You Always

Nearly every line of Matthew's final paragraph (Matt 28:16–20) connects to a major theme or idea expressed earlier in the Gospel. This is the perfect conclusion. The eleven remaining disciples travel to Galilee (see Matt 26:32) and meet Jesus on a mountain. The mountain continues to be an important setting in Matthew (Matt 4:8; 5:1; 8:1; 14:23; 15:29; 17:1, 9; 21:1; 24:3; 26:30; 27:33; 28:16). It reminds us of earlier stories like rejecting Satan's offer of the kingdoms of this world (Matt 4:8). Jesus now has all authority in heaven and on earth without giving worship/allegiance to Satan. God's plan worked. We're reminded of the Sermon on the Mount, where Jesus describes what His kingdom will be like. We're reminded of the Transfiguration, where Jesus shined in divine radiance (Matt 17:1–9).

When the disciples see Jesus on the mountain, "they worshiped him" (Matt 28:17). Jesus has been worshipped throughout Matthew (Matt 2:11–12; 8:2; 9:18; 14:33; 15:25; 18:26; 20:20; 28:9, 17), beginning with the Gentile wise men after His birth (Matt 2:11–12). While worship belongs only to God (Matt 4:10), it is appropriately received by the divine Son.

Not only does Jesus appear on the mountain and receive worship, but He also says things that only God can say. He claims to have "all authority in heaven and on earth" (Matt 28:18). No one other than God can have all authority on heaven and earth. Remember, God is a jealous God who does not allow any man or idol to be worshipped. Yet, Jesus shares all authority and is worshipped. Not only is Jesus worshipped as the divinely authoritative Son, but He is included with God in the baptismal description: "baptizing them in the name of the Father and of the Son and of the Holy Spirit" (Matt 28:19). That makes no sense if Jesus was a mere man or prophet.

Nearly every detail of this final paragraph points to the divinity of Jesus. It connects back to the very first "fulfilled" passage, which names Jesus "God with us" (Matt 1:23). That is why He appears on the mountain, is worshipped, has all authority in heaven and earth, and all are baptized into His name just like the Father and the Holy Spirit. Through the incarnation, Jesus has become "God with us," and Matthew ends with a promise spoken by Jesus, alluding back to Matthew 1:23, saying, "I am *with you* always, to the end of the age" (Matt 28:20).

The authority of Christ, which equals the authority of God, has been a topic of conversation throughout Matthew (Matt 7:29; 8:9; 9:6, 8; 10:1; 21:23, 24, 27, 28:18). It is based on this authority that Jesus is Lord over all the nations. As we have already discussed, this is the central storyline throughout the entire Bible, going back to Abraham. The question of how God will bless and unite the nations has been at the forefront of the Biblical narrative. The nations have always been opposed to God in the Bible: Egypt, Assyria, Babylon, Persia, Greece, Rome, and at times even Israel. That's what nations do. That is why they are the "beasts" of Daniel 7 and Revelation.

The nature of the beast does not change with the death and resurrection of Jesus. Those nations will reject His Lordship and govern themselves in ways that dishonor God and promote their own authority. The kingdoms of this earth are the rivals of God's kingdom. Worldly governments compete with the heavenly government of the Son of Man. However, sprinkled within the nations are faithful dissidents who will give their allegiance to Christ, live under His reign, love their enemies, and share Jesus's teachings with others. Jesus sends His disciples out to those nations to make disciples of the true King.

Disciples are made by "baptizing them in the name of the Father and of the Son and of the Holy Spirit" and by "teaching them to observe all that I have commanded you." Baptism reminds us of several earlier passages (Matt 3:1–2, 11, 13–17; 21:23–27). It is noteworthy that Jesus was declared God's Son at baptism. He also received the Spirit and "fulfilled righteousness." In imitation of Jesus, we undergo the same practice.

The Triune God was present at Jesus's baptism. The Son went under the water, the Spirit came from the heavens, and God spoke. At the end of Matthew, as this Trinitarian formula is introduced, we again see profound unity between God, Jesus, and the Holy Spirit. This united Godhead is present in our baptism as well.

By "teaching them to observe all that I have commanded you," followers are challenged to go back and read the teachings of Jesus again. Read and reread those five major speech sections. Let the teachings of Jesus live on in the life of the church. Let them live on within you. They are the material out of which discipleship is made. Do not neglect or forget the Sermon on the Mount. Engage in the life-long journey of living out Christ's strange and difficult call and remember that you are not alone in this, but that Jesus is with you always, even to the end of the age.

Reflection Questions

1. How does the Great Commission fulfill the call of Abraham in Genesis 12:1–4? How does the Great Commission fulfill the prophetic vision of Daniel 7:13–14 and Isaiah 2:2–4? How does the Great Commission fulfill the mission and ministry of Jesus? How does the Great Commission challenge the church today?
2. What does the resurrection mean for you? Does the resurrection give you hope? How does the resurrection relate to Matthew 16:18? How does the resurrection relate to Jesus having all authority in heaven and on earth? What does the resurrection mean about our true King and His kingdom?

BIBLIOGRAPHY

Bookout, Travis. *Cruciform Christ: 52 Reflections on the Gospel of Mark*. Florence, AL: Cypress, 2022.

Boring, Eugene M. *Matthew*. TNIBC. Nashville: Abingdon, 2015.

Dickson, John. *Bullies and Saints: An Honest Look at the Good and Evil of Christian History*. Grand Rapids: Zondervan, 2021.

Didache 9:5

France, R.T. *Matthew: An Introduction and Commentary* Vol. 1 in Tyndale New Testament Commentaries. Downers Grove, IL: IVP Academic, 1985.

Gallagher, Ed. *The Book of Exodus: Explorations in Christian Theology*. Florence, AL: Heritage Christian University Press, 2020.

———. *The Sermon on the Mount: Explorations in Christian Practice*. Florence, AL: Heritage Christian University Press, 2021.

Goldingay, John. *The First Testament: A New Translation*. Downers Grove, IL: IVP Academic, 2018.

Hays, Richard B. *Echoes of Scripture in the Gospels*. Waco: Baylor University Press, 2016.

Harris, Randy. *Living Jesus: Doing What Jesus Says in the Sermon on the Mount*. Abilene: Leafwood Publishers, 2012.

Hauerwas, Stanley and William Willimon. *Resident Aliens: Life in the Christian Colony*. Expanded 25th anniversary ed. Nashville: Abingdon Press, 2014.

Jerome. *Commentary on Matthew*. The Fathers of the Church. Translated by Thomas P. Scheck. Washington, DC: The Catholic University of America Press, 2008.

Keener, Craig. *The IVP Bible Background Commentary: New Testament*. 2nd ed. Downers Grove: IVP Academic, 2014.

McKnight, Scot. *Sermon on the Mount*. The Story of God Bible Commentary. Grand Rapids: Zondervan, 2013.

Nolland, John. *The Gospel of Matthew*. NIGTC. Grand Rapids: Eerdmans, 2005.

Pope, Alexander. "An Essay on Man." In *The Bedford Anthology of World Literature: The Eighteenth Century, 1650–1800*. Edited by Paul Davis, Gary Harrison, David M. Johnson, Patricia Clark Smith, and John F. Crawford. Boston: Bedford, 2003.

Shergill, Sukhwinder S., Paul M. Mays, Chris D. Frith, and Daniel M. Wolpert, "Two Eyes for an Eye: The Neuroscience of Force Escalation," *Science* 301 (5630): (July 22, 2003); 187.

Volf, Miroslav. *The End of Memory: Remembering Rightly in a Violent World*. Grand Rapids: Eerdmans, 2006.

Willard, Dallas. *The Divine Conspiracy: Rediscovering Our Hidden Life in God.* HarperCollins e-books, 1998.

Wright, N. T. *Matthew for Everyone* Part 1: Chapters 1–15. London: Westminster John Knox Press, 2004.

———. *Matthew for Everyone.* Part 2: Chapters 16–28. Louisville: Westminster John Knox Press, 2004.

SCRIPTURE INDEX

ALSO BY TRAVIS J. BOOKOUT

Cruciform Christ: 52 Reflections on the Gospel of Mark

King of Glory: 52 Reflections on the Gospel of John

ALSO BY CYPRESS PUBLICATIONS

Approaching Christian Scripture: Twenty Attempts at Biblical Interpretation by Ed Gallagher

Corrupt Communication: Myths that Target Church Leaders by Bill and Laura Bagents

Counseling for Church Leaders: A Practical Guide by Bill Bagents and Rosemary Snodgrass

Imperative: Studies from the Book of James by Ismael Berlanga

Lead Like the Lord: Lessons in Leadership from Jesus by W. Kirk Brothers

Rescue: God and Sin in the Old Testament by John Wakefield

Romans: A Practical Commentary by Brian Poe

The Book of Exodus: Explorations in Christian Theology by Ed Gallagher

The Gospel of Luke: Explorations in Christian Scripture by Ed Gallagher

The New Testament: A Study Guide by Coy D. Roper

The Old Testament: A Study Guide by Coy D. Roper

The Sermon on the Mount: Explorations in Christian Practice by Ed Gallagher

CYPRESS
PUBLICATIONS
An Imprint of Heritage Christian University Press

To see full catalog of Heritage Christian University Press and its imprint Cypress Publications, visit www.hcu.edu/publications

www.ingramcontent.com/pod-product-compliance
Lightning Source LLC
Chambersburg PA
CBHW020918140626
46545CB00015B/93

* 9 7 8 1 9 5 6 8 1 1 6 5 0 *